BBC

DOCTOR WHO

THE TWELFTH DOCTOR

VOL 2: FRACTURES

"Has every trademark of a classic, Moffat-written episode."
MIND OF THE GEEK

"The artwork by Brian Williamson is excellent!"
MY GEEKY GEEKY WAYS

"Fantastic!"
GEEK GIRL WORLD

"Nails the tone of the show."
COMIC BOOK

"The art is fantastic!"
WIRED

"I loved it!"
AIN'T IT COOL NEWS

"Highly recommended!"
COMIC OF THE DAY

"Exciting, fast-moving, funny and mysterious."
GEEK MOM

"Sublime. Makes you tick days off on your calendar until the next issue is out!"
WARPED FACTOR

"Good, old-fashioned scary *Who*!"
NEWSARAMA

"Feels like an episode of the series!"
HOW TO LOVE COMICS

"Very interesting and beautiful."
FANGIRL NATION

"The artwork is beautiful."
NERDLY

"Captures Capaldi's Doctor."
KABOOOOOM

"I'm strapped in for the ride!"
NEEDLESS ESSENTIALS

"Script and art work together effortlessly!"
POP CULTURE BANDIT

"Feels exactly like the best-written episodes from the eighth season!"
WHATCHA READING

"An excellent tale!"
TM STASH

"I thoroughly enjoyed this!"
PROJECT FANDOM

TITAN COMICS

EDITOR
Andrew James

ASSISTANT EDITOR
Kirsten Murray

COLLECTION DESIGNER
Rob Farmer

SENIOR EDITOR
Steve White

TITAN COMICS EDITORIAL
Lizzie Kaye, Tom Williams

PRODUCTION SUPERVISORS
Maria Pearson, Jackie Flook

PRODUCTION CONTROLLER
Obi Onuora

STUDIO MANAGER
Selina Juneja

SENIOR SALES MANAGER
Steve Tothill

SENIOR MARKETING & PRESS OFFICER
Owen Johnson

DIRECT SALES & MARKETING MANAGER
Ricky Claydon

COMMERCIAL MANAGER
Michelle Fairlamb

PUBLISHING MANAGER
Darryl Tothill

PUBLISHING DIRECTOR
Chris Teather

OPERATIONS DIRECTOR
Leigh Baulch

EXECUTIVE DIRECTOR
Vivian Cheung

PUBLISHER
Nick Landau

Special thanks to
Steven Moffat, Brian Minchin, Matt Nicholls, James Dudley, Georgie Britton, Edward Russell, Derek Ritchie, Scott Handcock, Kirsty Mullan, Kate Bush, Julia Nocciolino, Ed Casey, Marcus Wilson and Richard Cookson for their invaluable assistance.

BBC WORLDWIDE
DIRECTOR OF EDITORIAL GOVERNANCE
Nicolas Brett

DIRECTOR OF CONSUMERPRODUCTS AND PUBLISHING
Andrew Moultrie

HEAD OF UK PUBLISHING
Chris Kerwin

PUBLISHER
Mandy Thwaites

PUBLISHING CO-ORDINATOR
Eva Abramik

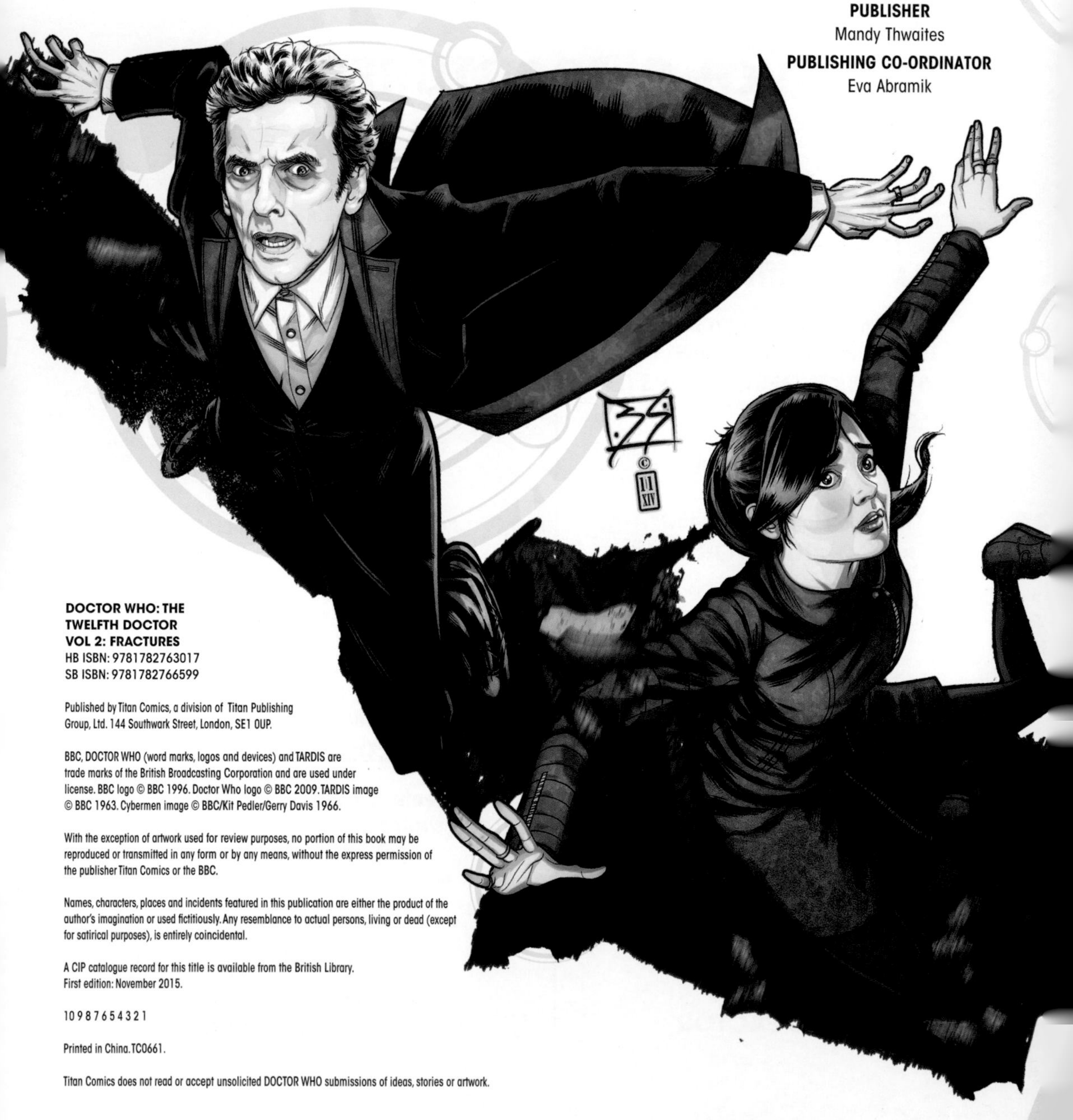

DOCTOR WHO: THE TWELFTH DOCTOR VOL 2: FRACTURES
HB ISBN: 9781782763017
SB ISBN: 9781782766599

Published by Titan Comics, a division of Titan Publishing Group, Ltd. 144 Southwark Street, London, SE1 0UP.

A CIP catalogue record for this title is available from the British Library.
First edition: November 2015.

10 9 8 7 6 5 4 3 2 1

Printed in China. TC0661.

BBC

DOCTOR WHO

THE TWELFTH DOCTOR

VOL 2: FRACTURES

WRITER: ROBBIE MORRISON

ARTISTS: BRIAN WILLIAMSON & MARIANO LACLAUSTRA

COLORIST: HI-FI

LETTERS: RICHARD STARKINGS AND COMICRAFT'S JIMMY BETANCOURT

www.titan-comics.com

BBC

DOCTOR WHO

THE TWELFTH DOCTOR

POLICE BOX
POLICE BOX

THE DOCTOR

An alien who walks like a man. Last of the Time Lords of Gallifrey. Never cruel or cowardly, he champions the oppressed across time and space. Forever traveling, the Doctor lives to see the universe anew through the eyes of his human companions!

THE TARDIS

'Time and Relative Dimension in Space'. Bigger on the inside, this unassuming blue box is your ticket to unforgettable adventure!
The Doctor likes to think he's in control, but more often than not, the TARDIS takes him where and when he needs to be...

CLARA OSWALD

Clara Oswald has stuck with the Doctor through thick and thin, witnessing all manner of strange, wonderful and terrifying things in his company!

Now a teacher at Coal Hill School, she juggles her 'real life' on Earth with her secret adventures aboard the TARDIS!

PREVIOUSLY...

In Mumbai, India, 2315, the Doctor and Clara defeated the Family Scindia and put paid to the resurrection of the 'goddess' Kali – though not before Kali attempted to resurrect in Clara's body!

Having ensured the safety of the future, and brought Clara back to herself, the Doctor and Clara returned to the present... But Coal Hill School and its environs can be just as deadly as any alien planet or far future, as the pair will soon find out!

When you've finished reading the collection, please email your thoughts to doctorwhocomic@titanemail.com

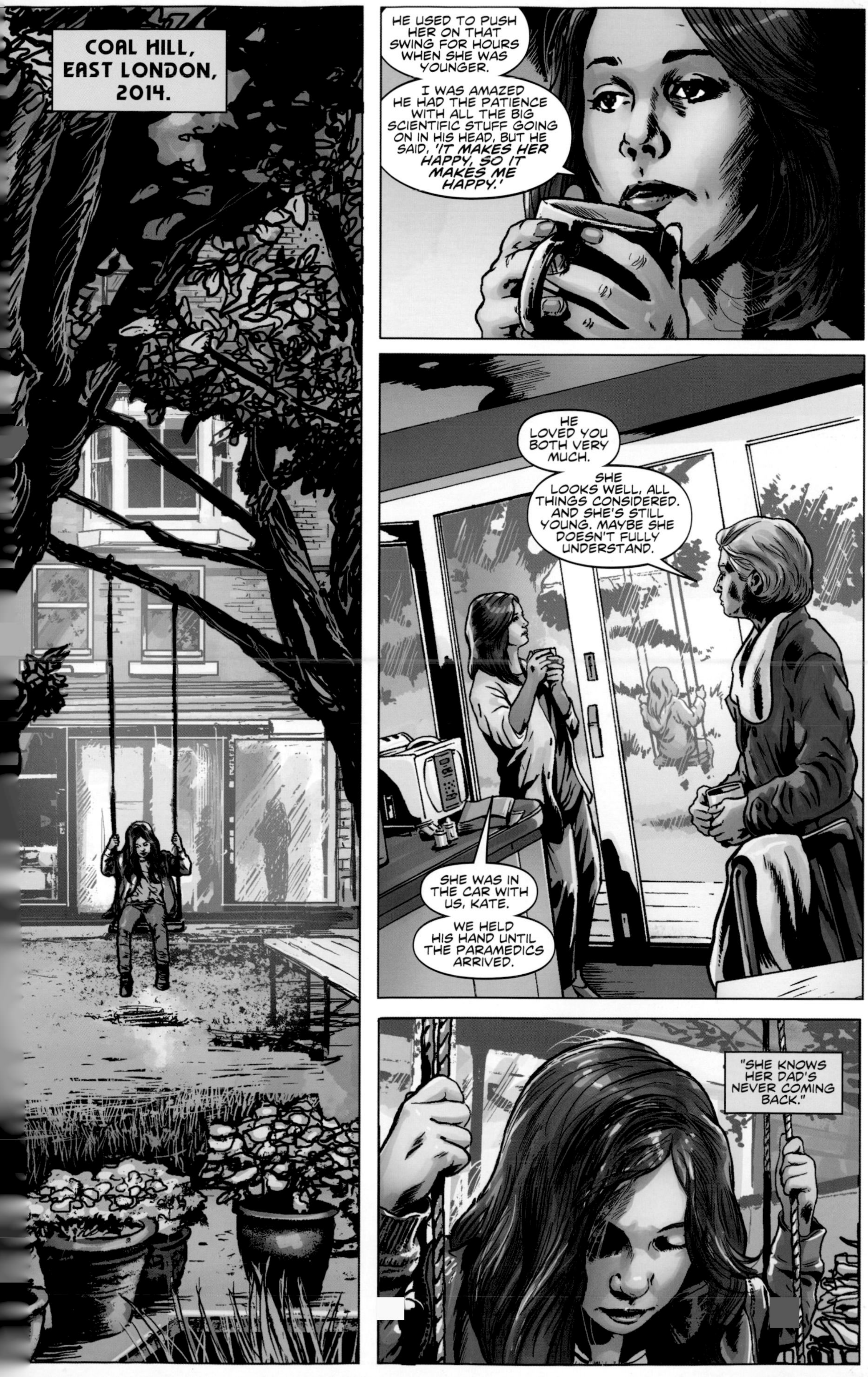
COAL HILL, EAST LONDON, 2014.
HE USED TO PUSH HER ON THAT SWING FOR HOURS WHEN SHE WAS YOUNGER.
I WAS AMAZED HE HAD THE PATIENCE WITH ALL THE BIG SCIENTIFIC STUFF GOING ON IN HIS HEAD, BUT HE SAID, *'IT MAKES HER HAPPY, SO IT MAKES ME HAPPY.'*
HE LOVED YOU BOTH VERY MUCH.
SHE LOOKS WELL, ALL THINGS CONSIDERED. AND SHE'S STILL YOUNG. MAYBE SHE DOESN'T FULLY UNDERSTAND.
SHE WAS IN THE CAR WITH US, KATE.
WE HELD HIS HAND UNTIL THE PARAMEDICS ARRIVED.
"SHE KNOWS HER DAD'S NEVER COMING BACK."

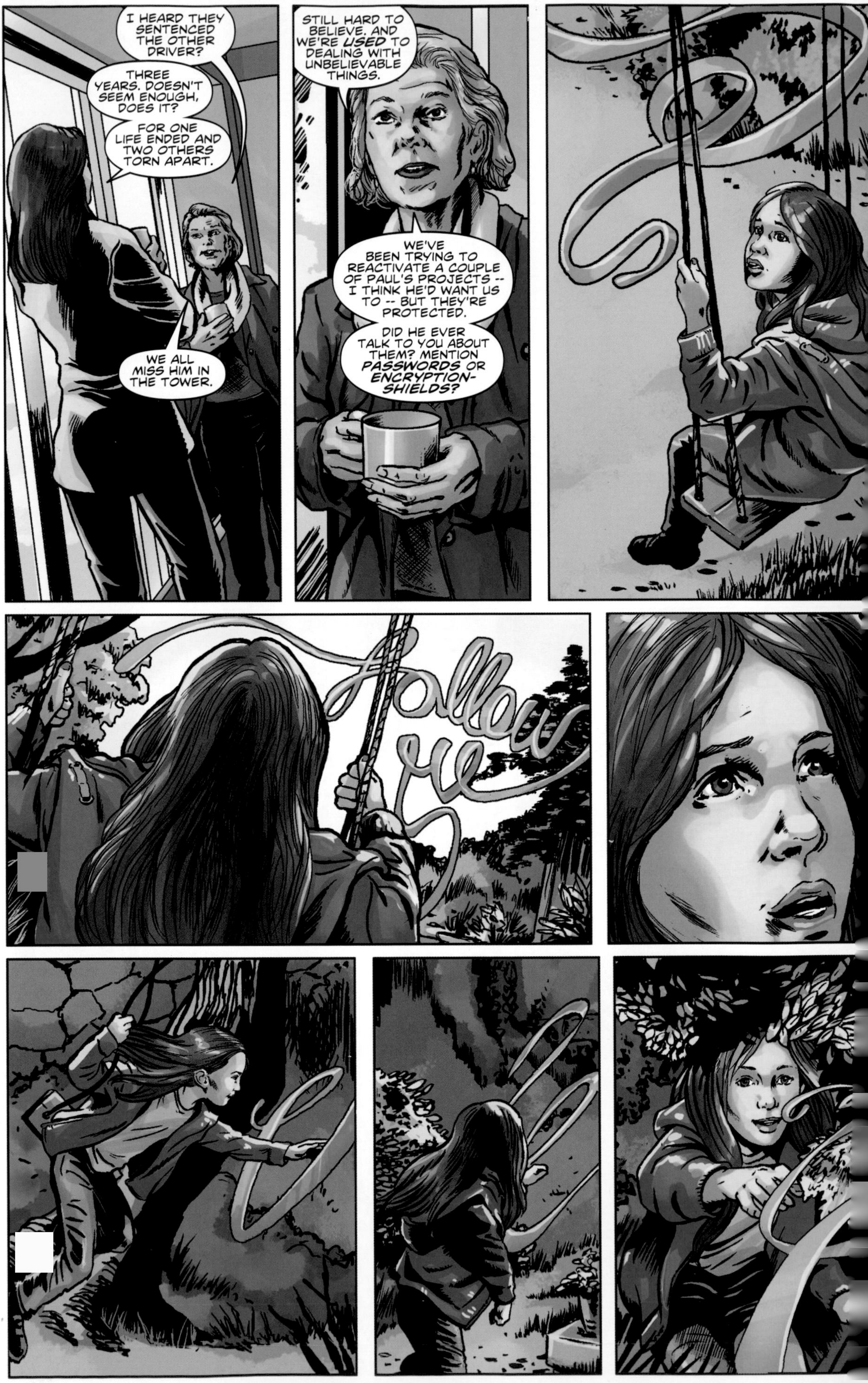
I HEARD THEY SENTENCED THE OTHER DRIVER?
THREE YEARS. DOESN'T SEEM ENOUGH, DOES IT?
FOR ONE LIFE ENDED AND TWO OTHERS TORN APART.
WE ALL MISS HIM IN THE TOWER.
STILL HARD TO BELIEVE. AND WE'RE *USED* TO DEALING WITH UNBELIEVABLE THINGS.
WE'VE BEEN TRYING TO REACTIVATE A COUPLE OF PAUL'S PROJECTS -- I THINK HE'D WANT US TO -- BUT THEY'RE PROTECTED.
DID HE EVER TALK TO YOU ABOUT THEM? MENTION *PASSWORDS* OR *ENCRYPTION-SHIELDS?*
Follow me

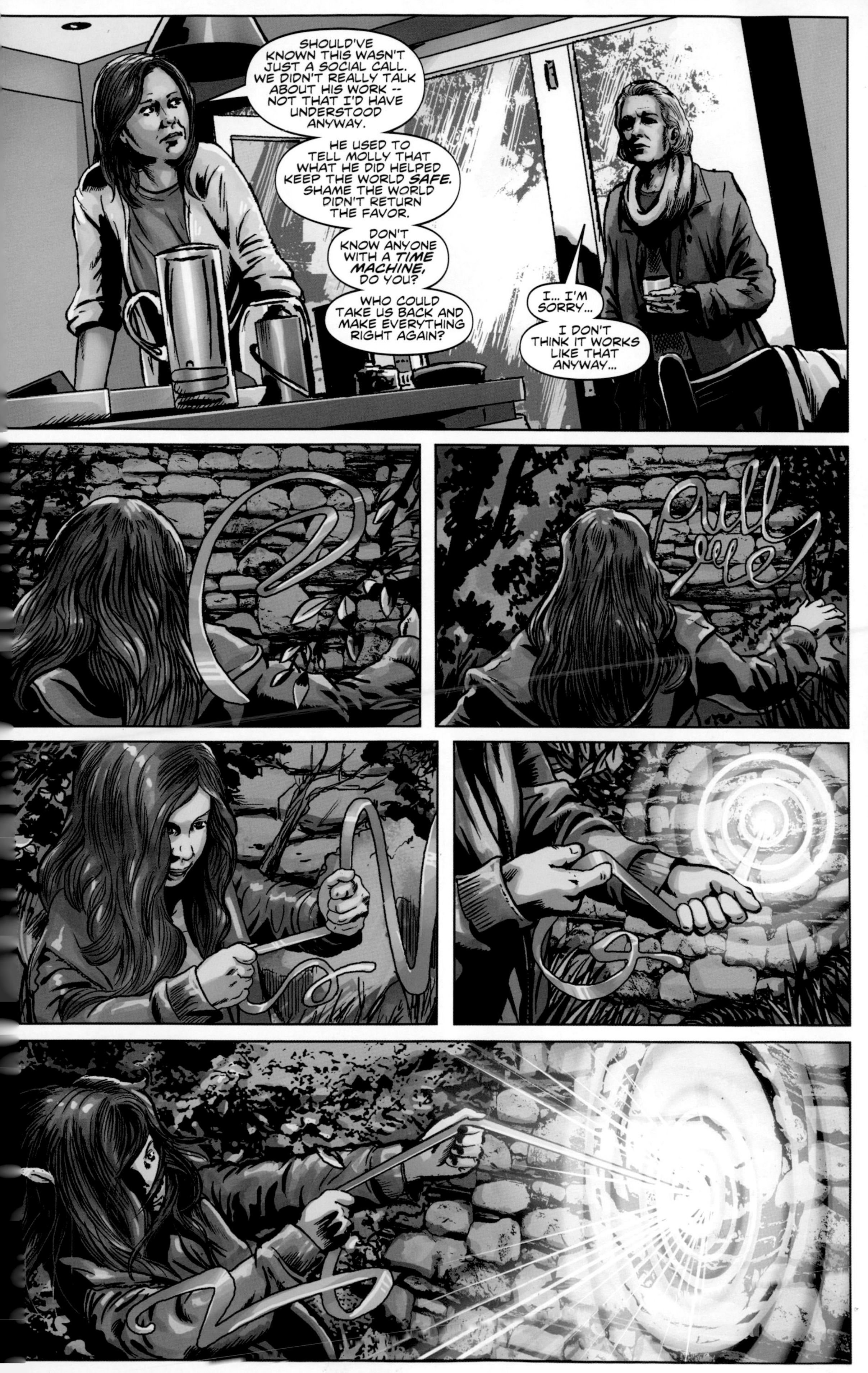
SHOULD'VE KNOWN THIS WASN'T JUST A SOCIAL CALL. WE DIDN'T REALLY TALK ABOUT HIS WORK -- NOT THAT I'D HAVE UNDERSTOOD ANYWAY.
HE USED TO TELL MOLLY THAT WHAT HE DID HELPED KEEP THE WORLD *SAFE.* SHAME THE WORLD DIDN'T RETURN THE FAVOR.
DON'T KNOW ANYONE WITH A *TIME MACHINE,* DO YOU?
WHO COULD TAKE US BACK AND MAKE EVERYTHING RIGHT AGAIN?
I... I'M SORRY...
I DON'T THINK IT WORKS LIKE THAT ANYWAY...
pull me

D-DAD?
BUT, YOU... YOU'RE...

I KNOW MOLLY! KNOW

BUT I'VE CC BACK

I'VE COM BACK BECAU OF YOU

FRACTURES

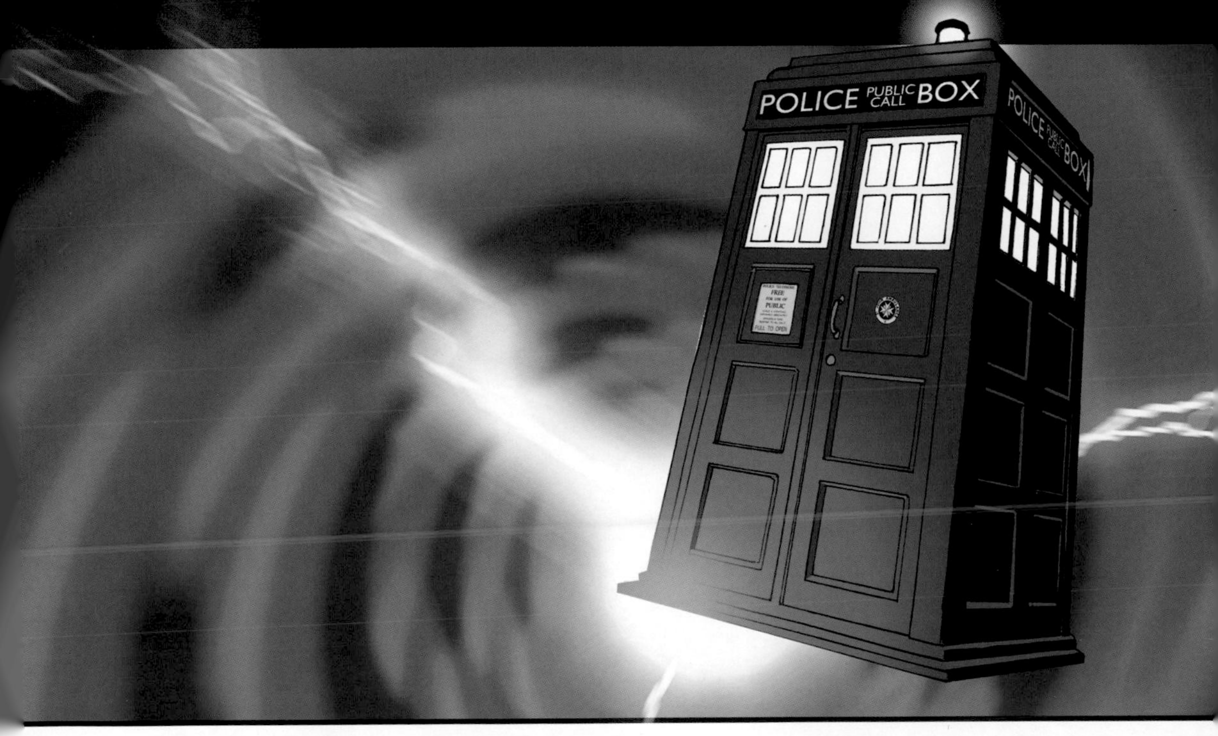
POLICE PUBLIC CALL BOX
PULL TO OPEN

WRITER
ROBBIE MORRISON

ARTIST
BRIAN WILLIAMSON

COLORIST
HI-FI

LETTERER
RICHARD STARKINGS AND COMICRAFT'S JIMMY BETANCOURT

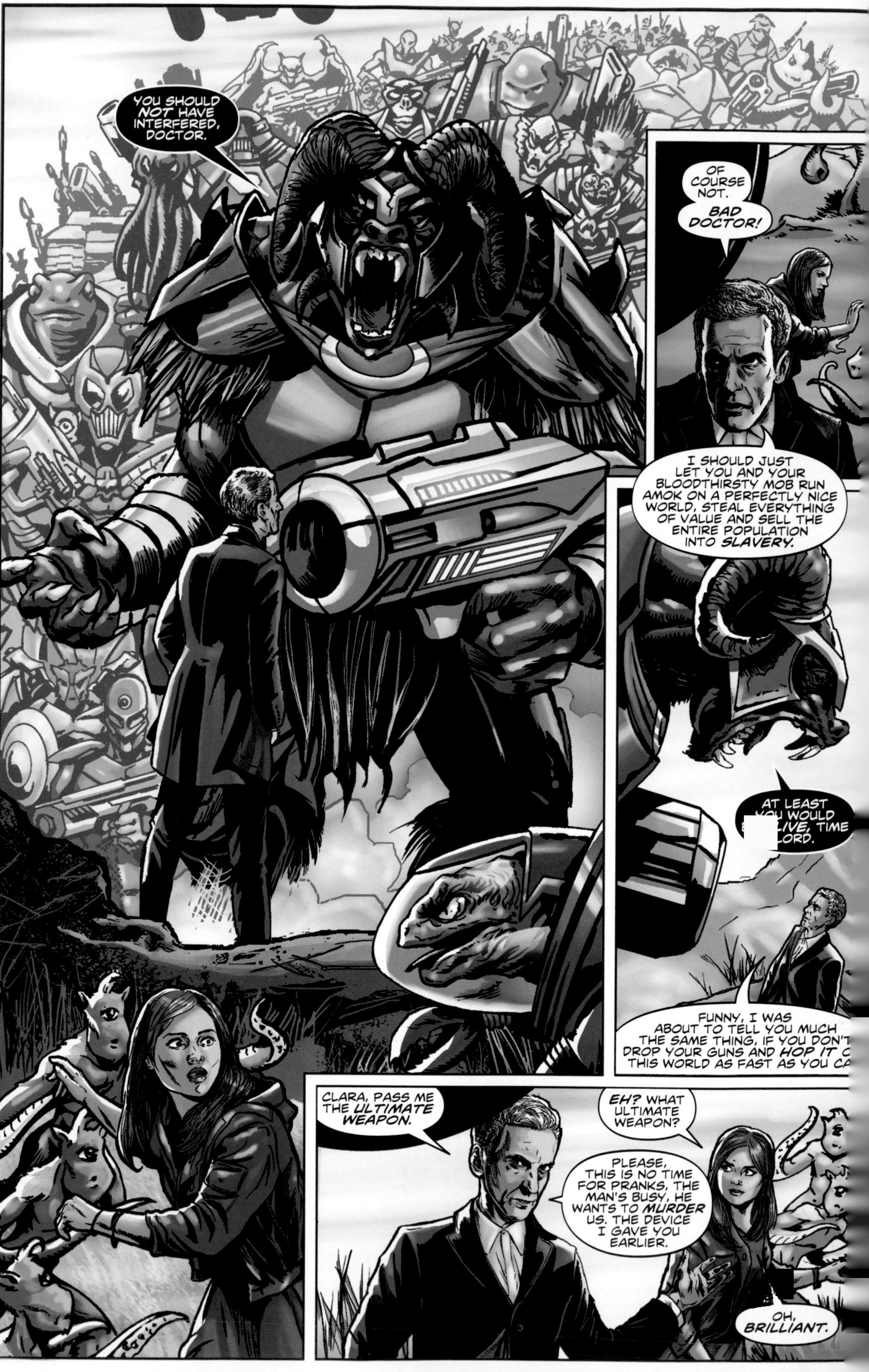
YOU SHOULD NOT HAVE INTERFERED, DOCTOR.
OF COURSE NOT. BAD DOCTOR!
I SHOULD JUST LET YOU AND YOUR BLOODTHIRSTY MOB RUN AMOK ON A PERFECTLY NICE WORLD, STEAL EVERYTHING OF VALUE AND SELL THE ENTIRE POPULATION INTO SLAVERY.
AT LEAST YOU WOULD LIVE, TIME LORD.
FUNNY, I WAS ABOUT TO TELL YOU MUCH THE SAME THING, IF YOU DON'T DROP YOUR GUNS AND HOP IT THIS WORLD AS FAST AS YOU
CLARA, PASS ME THE ULTIMATE WEAPON.
EH? WHAT ULTIMATE WEAPON?
PLEASE, THIS IS NO TIME FOR PRANKS, THE MAN'S BUSY, HE WANTS TO MURDER US. THE DEVICE I GAVE YOU EARLIER.
OH, BRILLIANT.

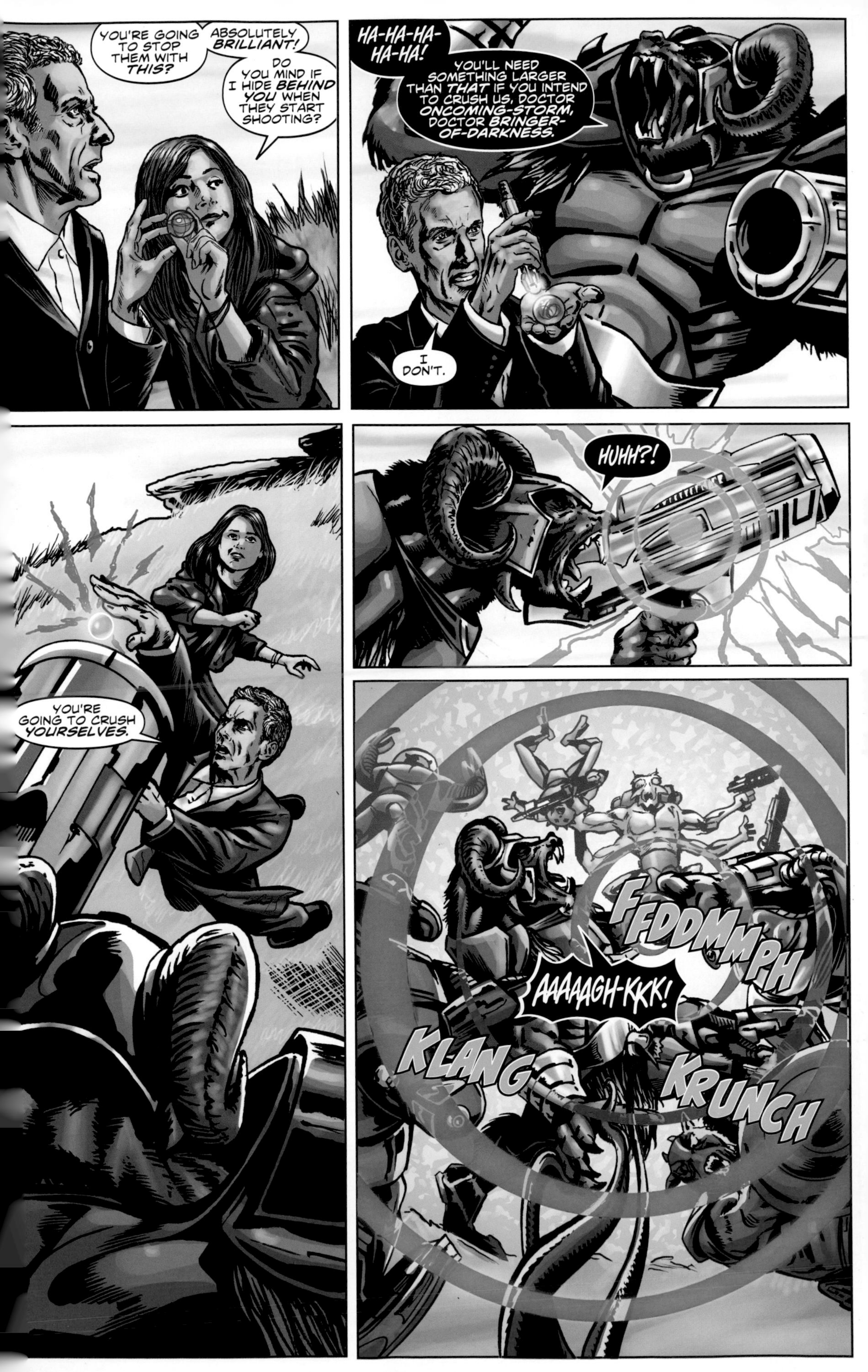
YOU'RE GOING TO STOP THEM WITH THIS?
ABSOLUTELY BRILLIANT!
DO YOU MIND IF I HIDE BEHIND YOU WHEN THEY START SHOOTING?
HA-HA-HA-HA-HA!
YOU'LL NEED SOMETHING LARGER THAN THAT IF YOU INTEND TO CRUSH US, DOCTOR ONCOMING-STORM, DOCTOR BRINGER-OF-DARKNESS.
I DON'T.
YOU'RE GOING TO CRUSH YOURSELVES.
HUHH?!
FFDDMMPH
AAAAAGH-KKK!
KLANG
KRUNCH

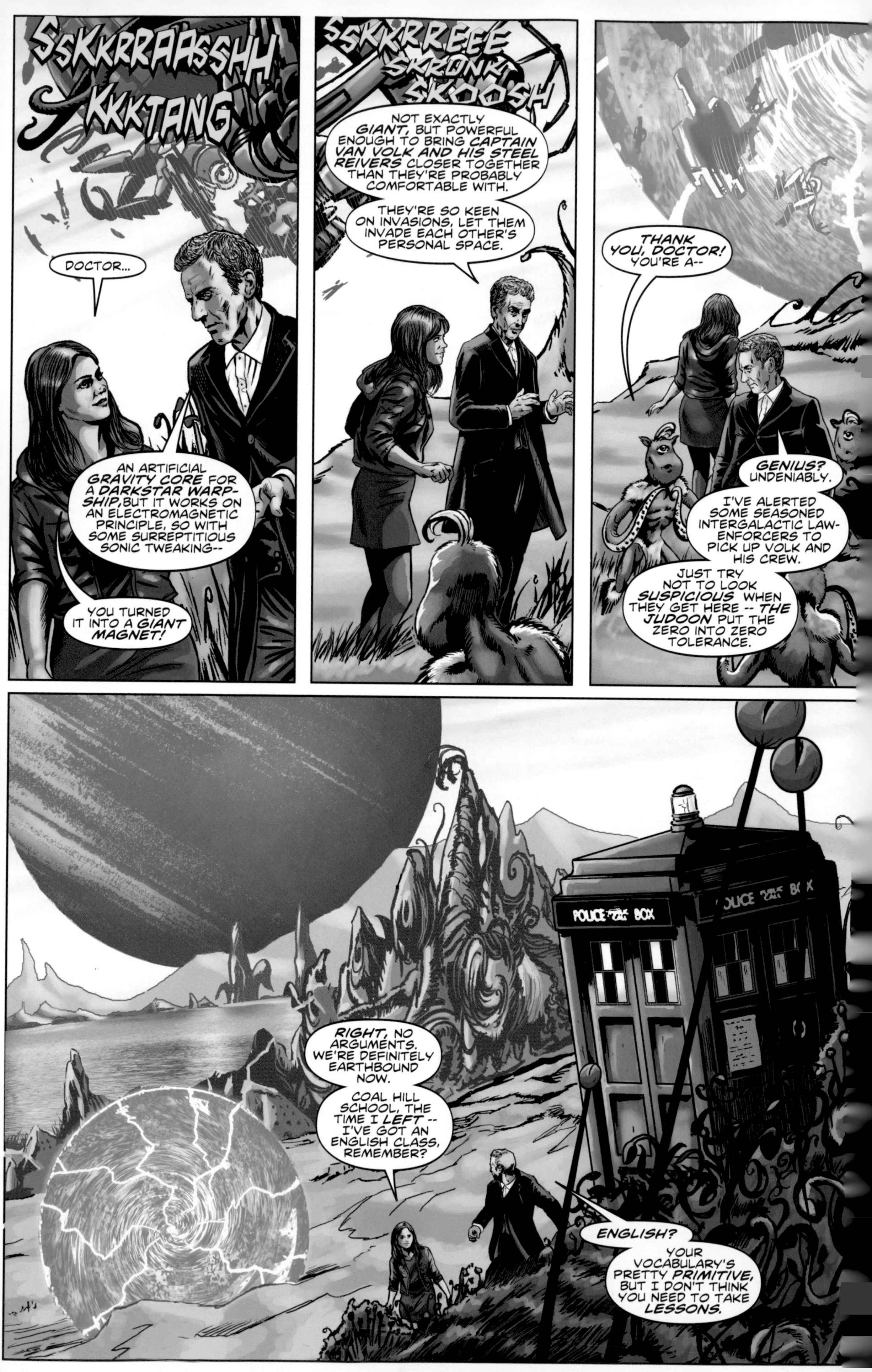
SSKKRRAASSHH KKKTANG
DOCTOR...
AN ARTIFICIAL GRAVITY CORE FOR A DARKSTAR WARP-SHIP, BUT IT WORKS ON AN ELECTROMAGNETIC PRINCIPLE, SO WITH SOME SURREPTITIOUS SONIC TWEAKING--
YOU TURNED IT INTO A GIANT MAGNET!
SSKKRREEE SKRONK! SKOOSH
NOT EXACTLY GIANT, BUT POWERFUL ENOUGH TO BRING CAPTAIN VAN VOLK AND HIS STEEL REIVERS CLOSER TOGETHER THAN THEY'RE PROBABLY COMFORTABLE WITH.
THEY'RE SO KEEN ON INVASIONS, LET THEM INVADE EACH OTHER'S PERSONAL SPACE.
THANK YOU, DOCTOR! YOU'RE A--
GENIUS? UNDENIABLY.
I'VE ALERTED SOME SEASONED INTERGALACTIC LAW-ENFORCERS TO PICK UP VOLK AND HIS CREW.
JUST TRY NOT TO LOOK SUSPICIOUS WHEN THEY GET HERE -- THE JUDOON PUT THE ZERO INTO ZERO TOLERANCE.
RIGHT, NO ARGUMENTS. WE'RE DEFINITELY EARTHBOUND NOW.
COAL HILL SCHOOL, THE TIME I LEFT -- I'VE GOT AN ENGLISH CLASS, REMEMBER?
ENGLISH?
YOUR VOCABULARY'S PRETTY PRIMITIVE, BUT I DON'T THINK YOU NEED TO TAKE LESSONS.

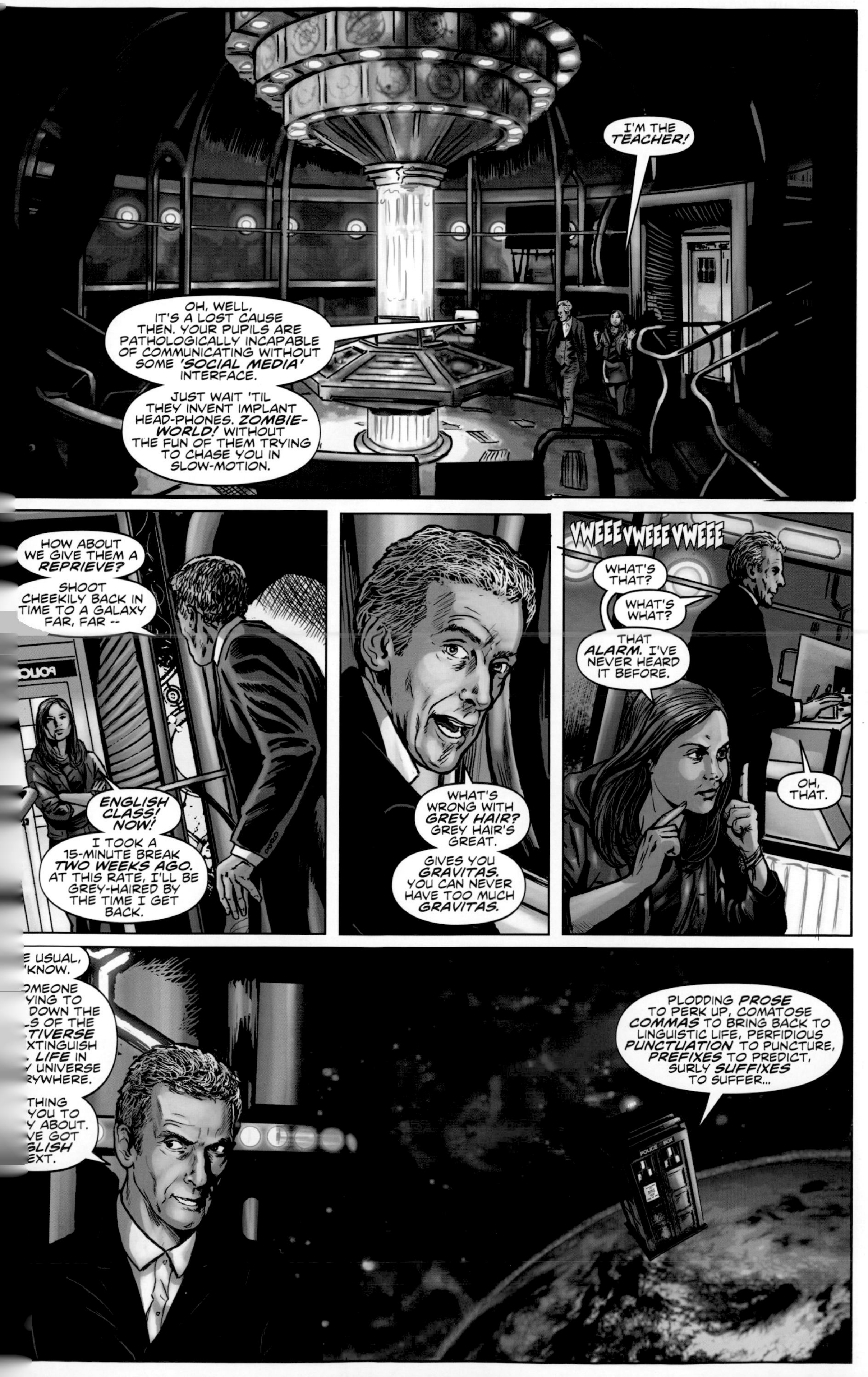
I'M THE TEACHER!
OH, WELL, IT'S A LOST CAUSE THEN. YOUR PUPILS ARE PATHOLOGICALLY INCAPABLE OF COMMUNICATING WITHOUT SOME 'SOCIAL MEDIA' INTERFACE.
JUST WAIT 'TIL THEY INVENT IMPLANT HEAD-PHONES. ZOMBIE-WORLD! WITHOUT THE FUN OF THEM TRYING TO CHASE YOU IN SLOW-MOTION.
HOW ABOUT WE GIVE THEM A REPRIEVE?
SHOOT CHEEKILY BACK IN TIME TO A GALAXY FAR, FAR --
ENGLISH CLASS! NOW!
I TOOK A 15-MINUTE BREAK TWO WEEKS AGO. AT THIS RATE, I'LL BE GREY-HAIRED BY THE TIME I GET BACK.
WHAT'S WRONG WITH GREY HAIR? GREY HAIR'S GREAT.
GIVES YOU GRAVITAS. YOU CAN NEVER HAVE TOO MUCH GRAVITAS.
VWEEE VWEEE VWEEE
WHAT'S THAT?
WHAT'S WHAT?
THAT ALARM. I'VE NEVER HEARD IT BEFORE.
OH, THAT.
E USUAL, 'KNOW.
OMEONE YING TO DOWN THE LS OF THE TIVERSE XTINGUISH LIFE IN Y UNIVERSE RYWHERE.
THING YOU TO Y ABOUT. VE GOT GLISH EXT.
PLODDING PROSE TO PERK UP, COMATOSE COMMAS TO BRING BACK TO LINGUISTIC LIFE, PERFIDIOUS PUNCTUATION TO PUNCTURE, PREFIXES TO PREDICT, SURLY SUFFIXES TO SUFFER...
POLICE BOX

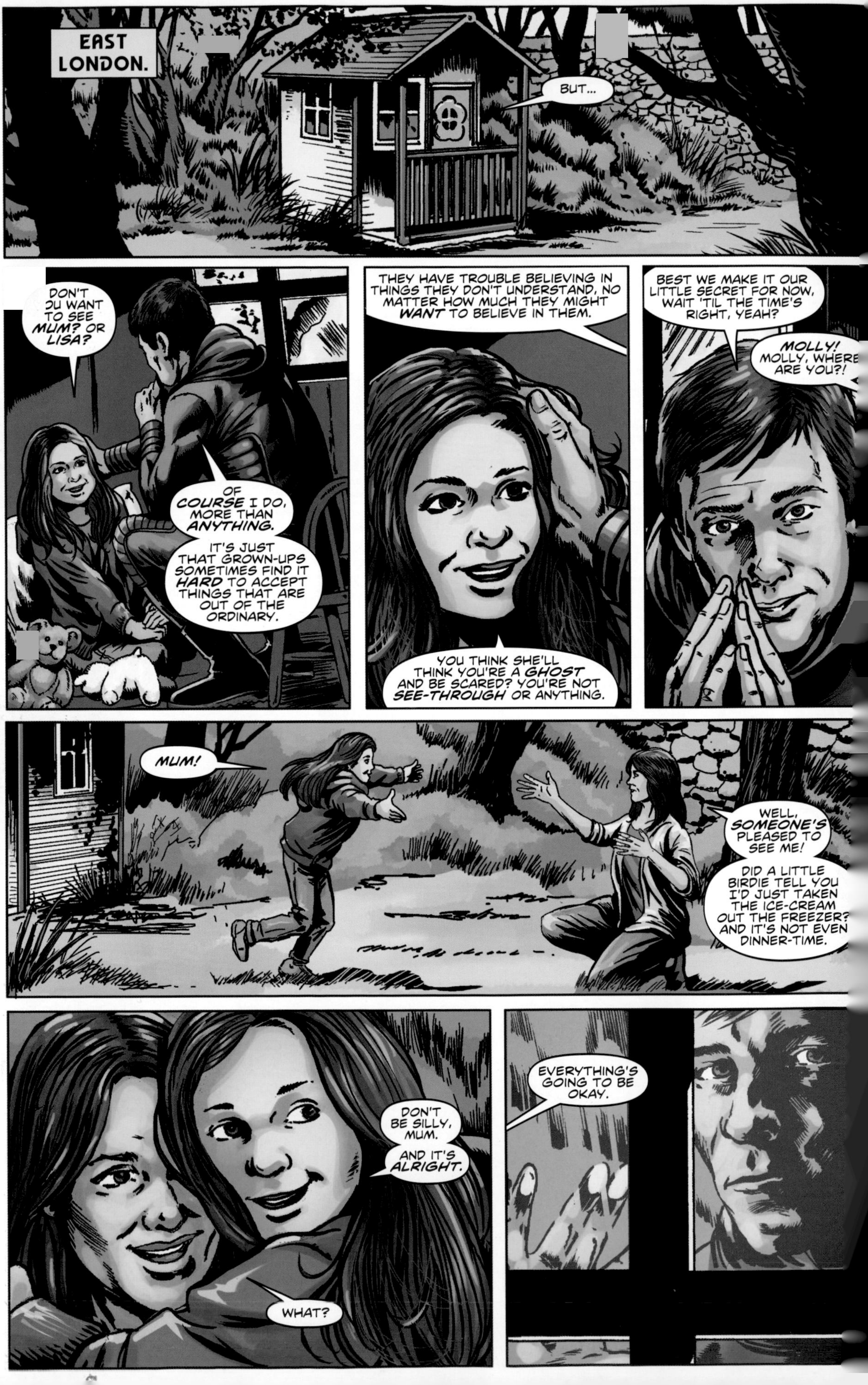
EAST LONDON.
BUT...
DON'T YOU WANT TO SEE MUM? OR LISA?
OF COURSE I DO, MORE THAN ANYTHING.
IT'S JUST THAT GROWN-UPS SOMETIMES FIND IT HARD TO ACCEPT THINGS THAT ARE OUT OF THE ORDINARY.
THEY HAVE TROUBLE BELIEVING IN THINGS THEY DON'T UNDERSTAND, NO MATTER HOW MUCH THEY MIGHT WANT TO BELIEVE IN THEM.
YOU THINK SHE'LL THINK YOU'RE A GHOST AND BE SCARED? YOU'RE NOT SEE-THROUGH OR ANYTHING.
BEST WE MAKE IT OUR LITTLE SECRET FOR NOW, WAIT 'TIL THE TIME'S RIGHT, YEAH?
MOLLY! MOLLY, WHERE ARE YOU?!
MUM!
WELL, SOMEONE'S PLEASED TO SEE ME!
DID A LITTLE BIRDIE TELL YOU I'D JUST TAKEN THE ICE-CREAM OUT THE FREEZER? AND IT'S NOT EVEN DINNER-TIME.
DON'T BE SILLY, MUM.
AND IT'S ALRIGHT.
WHAT?
EVERYTHING'S GOING TO BE OKAY.

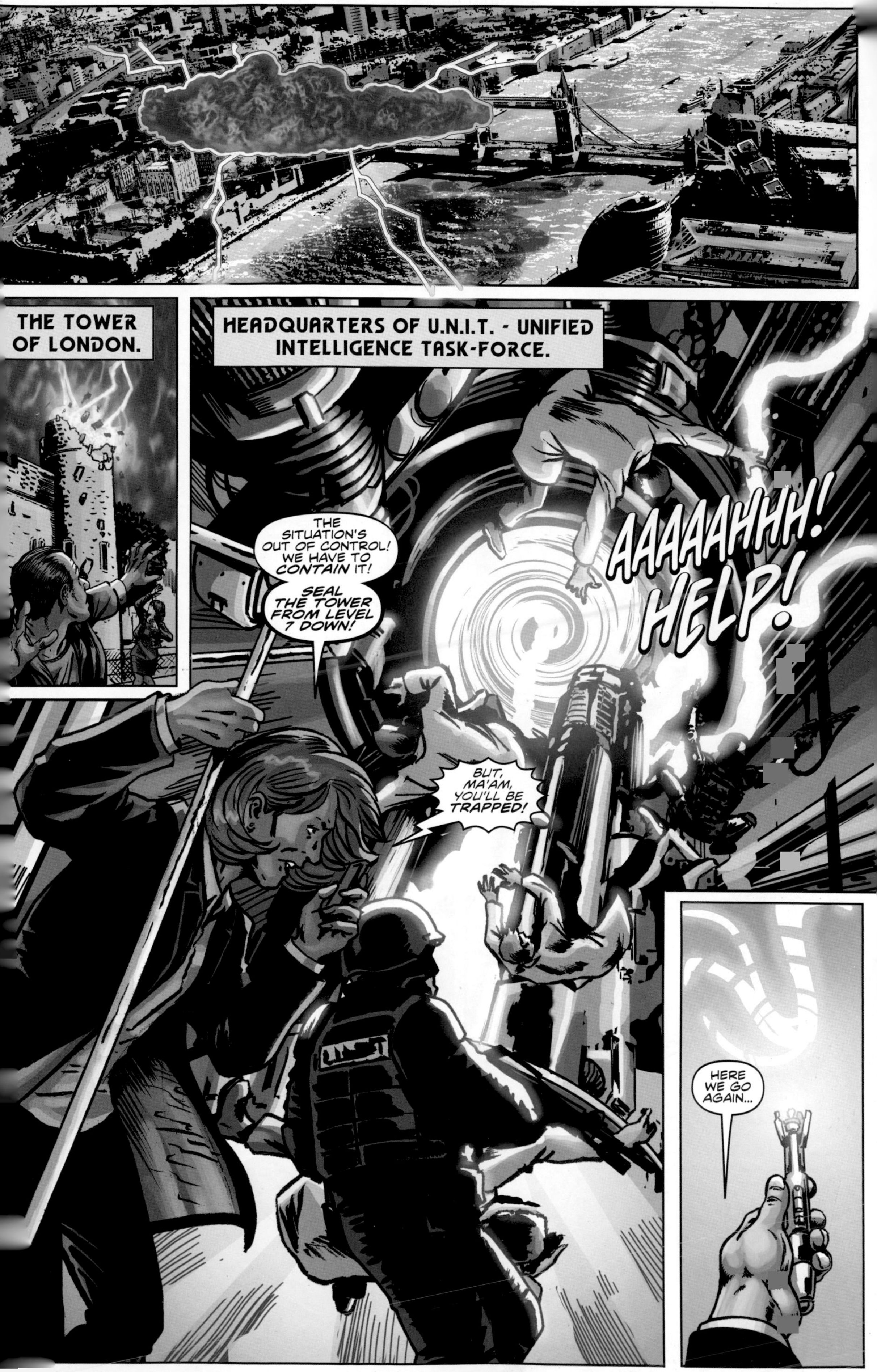
THE TOWER OF LONDON.
HEADQUARTERS OF U.N.I.T. - UNIFIED INTELLIGENCE TASK-FORCE.
THE SITUATION'S OUT OF CONTROL! WE HAVE TO CONTAIN IT!
SEAL THE TOWER FROM LEVEL 7 DOWN!
AAAAAHHH! HELP!
BUT, MA'AM, YOU'LL BE TRAPPED!
HERE WE GO AGAIN...

RETURN TO THE PLANET OF THE PUDDING-HEADS! WHAT'S THE POINT OF ME *SAVING* YOU IF ALL YOU DO IS GET YOURSELF INTO *MORE* TROUBLE?

AH, DOCTOR, *THERE* YOU ARE. WE WERE--

-- TRYING TO BRING ABOUT THE EARLY EXTINCTION OF THE HUMAN RACE?

ARE THESE ALIEN MENACES YOU KEEP STIRRING UP JUST AN ELABORATE WAY TO GET MY *ATTENTION*?

I'M *OLD* ENOUGH TO BE YOUR GREAT-GREAT-GREAT-GREAT-*GREAT* GRANDFATHER, YOU KNOW. *TIMES TEN.*

THAT'S NOTHING COMPARED TO THE SIZE OF YOUR *EGO*.

NOW, NOW, CHILDREN, PLAY *NICE*. DOCTOR, WHAT IS THAT THING?

SOMETHING MANKIND SHOULDN'T BE TINKERING WITH *AGAIN* FOR ANOTHER 500 YEARS. WAS CANARY WHARF NOT *ENOUGH* OF A WARNING?

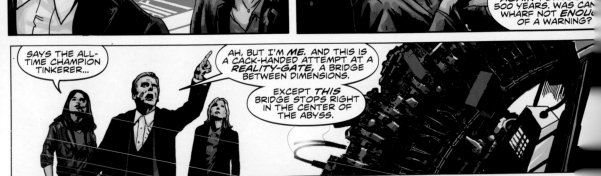

SAYS THE ALL-TIME CHAMPION TINKERER...

AH, BUT I'M *ME*. AND THIS IS A CACK-HANDED ATTEMPT AT A *REALITY-GATE*, A BRIDGE BETWEEN DIMENSIONS.

EXCEPT *THIS* BRIDGE STOPS RIGHT IN THE CENTER OF THE ABYSS.

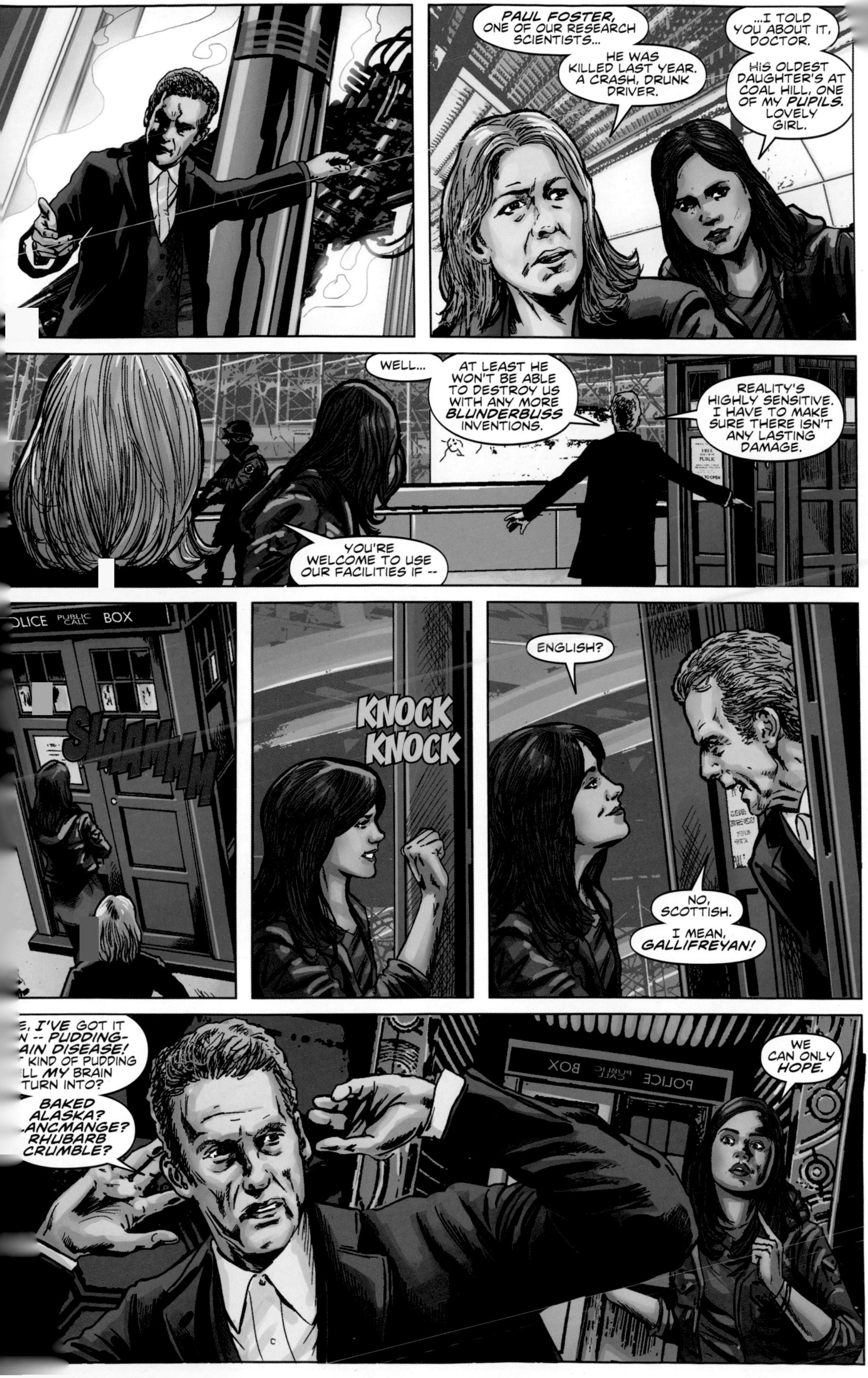
PAUL FOSTER, ONE OF OUR RESEARCH SCIENTISTS...
HE WAS KILLED LAST YEAR. A CRASH, DRUNK DRIVER.
...I TOLD YOU ABOUT IT, DOCTOR.
HIS OLDEST DAUGHTER'S AT COAL HILL, ONE OF MY PUPILS. LOVELY GIRL.
WELL...
AT LEAST HE WON'T BE ABLE TO DESTROY US WITH ANY MORE BLUNDERBUSS INVENTIONS.
REALITY'S HIGHLY SENSITIVE. I HAVE TO MAKE SURE THERE ISN'T ANY LASTING DAMAGE.
YOU'RE WELCOME TO USE OUR FACILITIES IF --
POLICE PUBLIC CALL BOX
SLAMMM
KNOCK KNOCK
ENGLISH?
NO, SCOTTISH. I MEAN, GALLIFREYAN!
E, I'VE GOT IT N -- PUDDING- AIN DISEASE! T KIND OF PUDDING LL MY BRAIN TURN INTO?
BAKED ALASKA? ANCMANGE? RHUBARB CRUMBLE?
WE CAN ONLY HOPE.

THE STEWARTS MADE AN OFFER ON 49 HINCHCLIFFE ROAD, YEAH?

TELL 'EM THE VENDOR'S RECEIVED A *HIGHER* OFFER.

I DIDN'T KNOW THERE WAS ANY OTHER INTEREST.

KEEP UP, *MELANIE.* THERE ISN'T, BUT I FIGURE WE CAN PUSH 'EM HIGHER. IS *DAVE* THERE?

JUST GOT IN.

TELL HIM HE'S *SACKED.*

WHAT?

IF YOU DON'T HIT YOUR TARGETS IN MY OFFICE, YOU BECOME *MY* TARGET.

BUT... HIS WIFE'S BEEN ILL.

THEN HE SHOULD SELL *HARDER.* MAKE MORE MONEY. GET HER PRIVATE HEALTH CARE.

DAMN IT. NO CHANGE.

WYN IRR

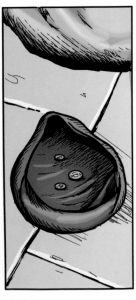

DARRYL?

DARRYL, ARE YOU STILL THERE?

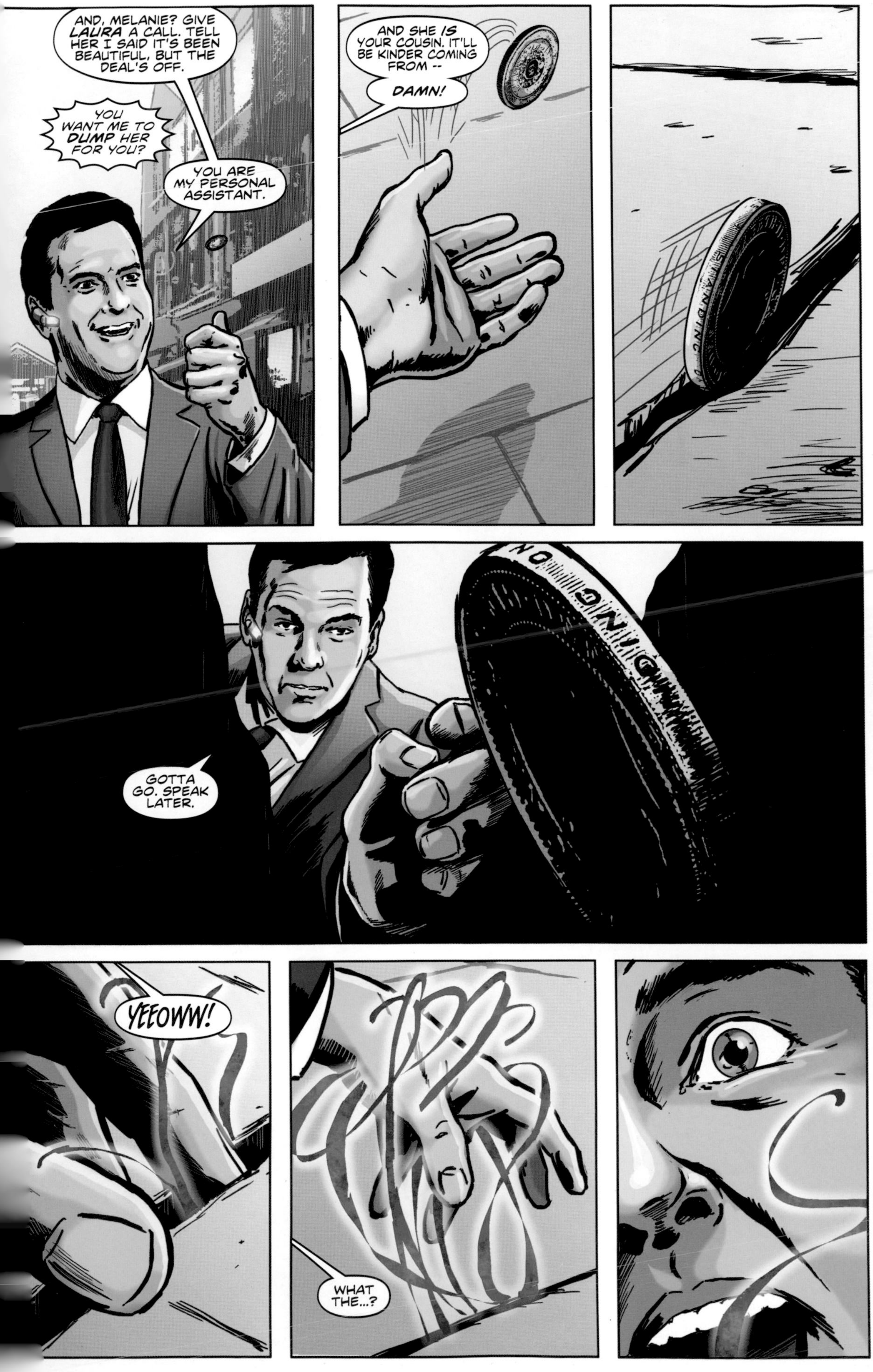

AND, MELANIE? GIVE LAURA A CALL. TELL HER I SAID IT'S BEEN BEAUTIFUL, BUT THE DEAL'S OFF.
YOU WANT ME TO DUMP HER FOR YOU?
YOU ARE MY PERSONAL ASSISTANT.
AND SHE IS YOUR COUSIN. IT'LL BE KINDER COMING FROM --
DAMN!
GOTTA GO. SPEAK LATER.
YEEOWW!
WHAT THE...?

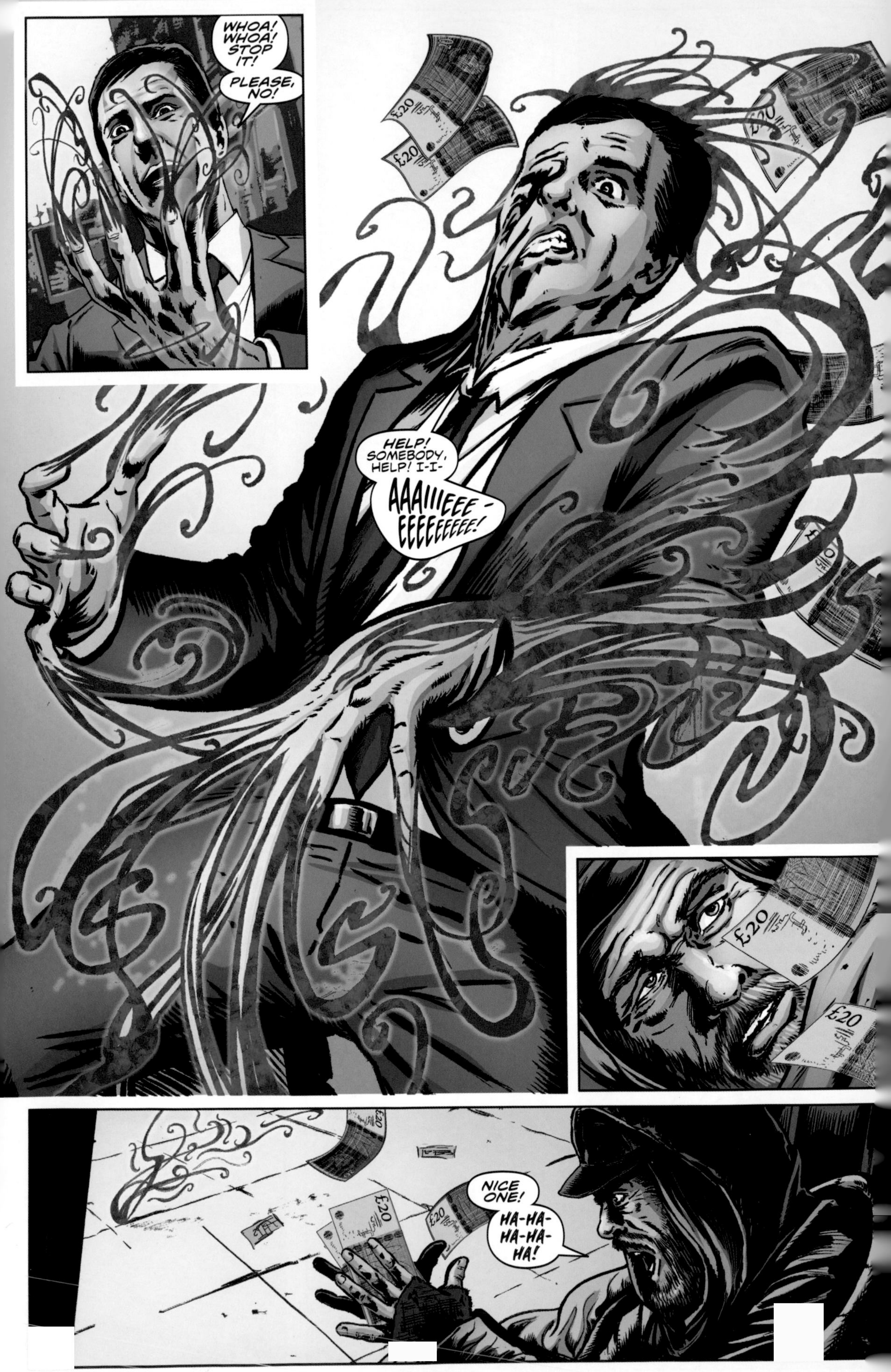
WHOA! WHOA! STOP IT!
PLEASE, NO!
HELP! SOMEBODY, HELP! I-I-
AAAIIIEEE-EEEEEEEEE!
NICE ONE!
HA-HA-HA-HA-HA!

COAL HILL
SECONDARY SCHOOL

RRRRRRRRRRR!

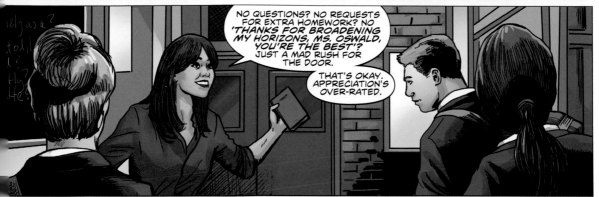

NO QUESTIONS? NO REQUESTS FOR EXTRA HOMEWORK? NO 'THANKS FOR BROADENING MY HORIZONS, MS. OSWALD, YOU'RE THE BEST'? JUST A MAD RUSH FOR THE DOOR.

THAT'S OKAY. APPRECIATION'S OVER-RATED.

'THANKS, MISS OSWALD, YOU'RE THE BEST.'

THAT'S MORE LIKE IT. HOW ARE YOU, LISA?

ALRIGHT, I GUESS, MISS.

SOMETIMES IT DOESN'T SEEM *REAL.* AND SOMETIMES IT'S SO REAL IT JUST TAKES OVER EVERYTHING.

MOLLY, MY LITTLE SISTER? SHE STILL DREAMS ABOUT *DAD,* THE *CRASH.* WAKES UP CRYING. MUM KEPT HER OFF SCHOOL TODAY.

'M SO SORRY, LISA. CAN'T IMAGINE WHAT IT FEELS LIKE...

...TO LOSE SOMEONE SO CLOSE TO YOU LIKE THAT.

BUT I'M HERE OR YOU, *WHATEVER* OU NEED, *WHENEVER* YOU NEED IT.

THANKS, MISS.

DOES IT EVER *STOP,* DO YOU THINK? WILL IT STOP HURTING ONE DAY?

OH, LISA... YOU'LL *NEVER* FORGET HIM, BUT IT WILL GET BETTER. I *PROMISE...*

SOMEDAY YOU'LL ONLY THINK OF ALL THE *GOOD* THINGS YOU CAN REMEMBER ABOUT HIM.

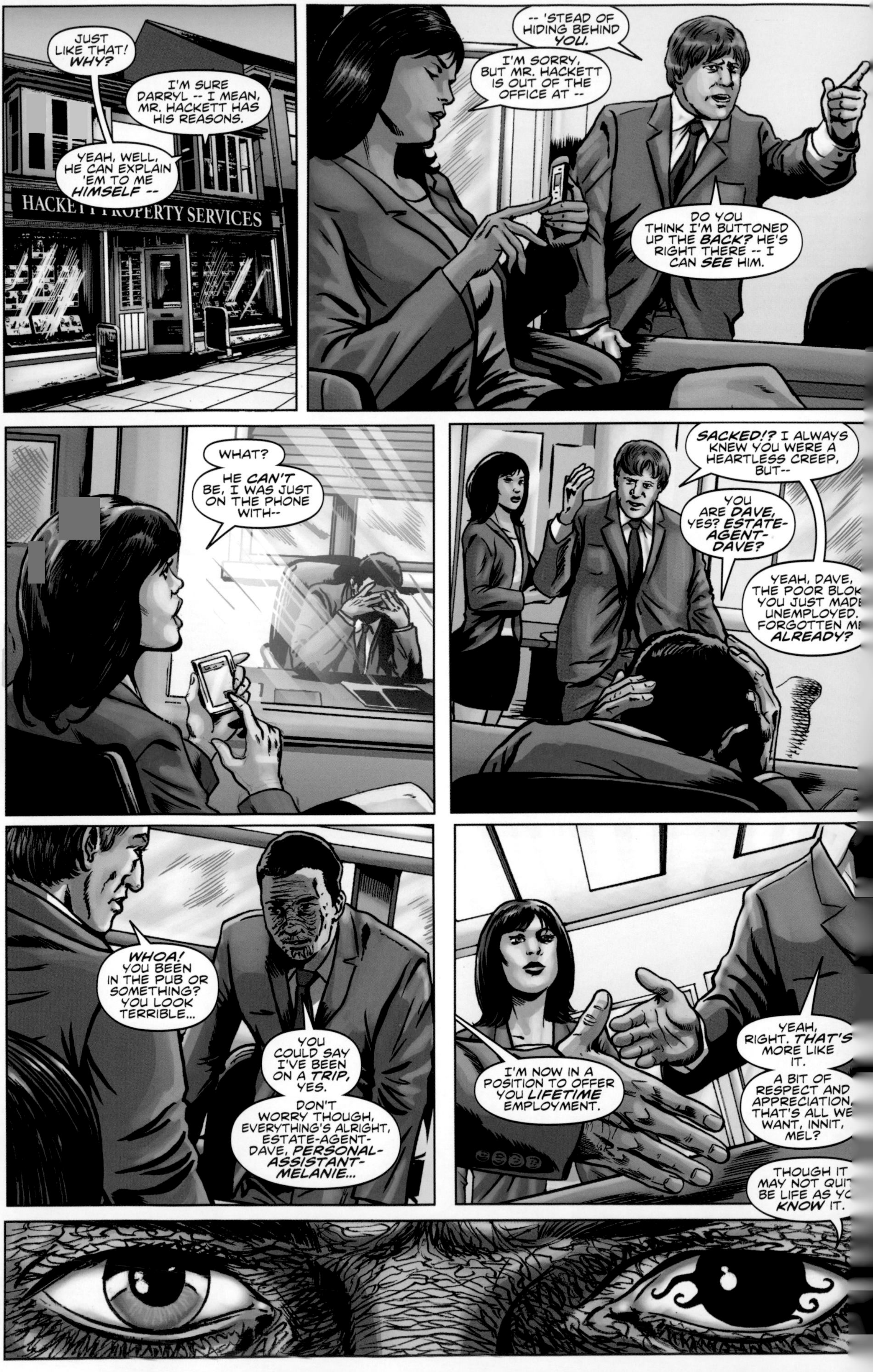
JUST LIKE THAT! WHY?
I'M SURE DARRYL -- I MEAN, MR. HACKETT HAS HIS REASONS.
YEAH, WELL, HE CAN EXPLAIN 'EM TO ME HIMSELF --
HACKETT PROPERTY SERVICES
-- 'STEAD OF HIDING BEHIND YOU.
I'M SORRY, BUT MR. HACKETT IS OUT OF THE OFFICE AT --
DO YOU THINK I'M BUTTONED UP THE BACK? HE'S RIGHT THERE -- I CAN SEE HIM.
WHAT?
HE CAN'T BE, I WAS JUST ON THE PHONE WITH--
SACKED!? I ALWAYS KNEW YOU WERE A HEARTLESS CREEP, BUT--
YOU ARE DAVE, YES? ESTATE-AGENT-DAVE?
YEAH, DAVE, THE POOR BLOK YOU JUST MADE UNEMPLOYED. FORGOTTEN ME ALREADY?
WHOA! YOU BEEN IN THE PUB OR SOMETHING? YOU LOOK TERRIBLE...
YOU COULD SAY I'VE BEEN ON A TRIP, YES.
DON'T WORRY THOUGH, EVERYTHING'S ALRIGHT, ESTATE-AGENT-DAVE, PERSONAL-ASSISTANT-MELANIE...
I'M NOW IN A POSITION TO OFFER YOU LIFETIME EMPLOYMENT.
YEAH, RIGHT. THAT'S MORE LIKE IT.
A BIT OF RESPECT AND APPRECIATION, THAT'S ALL WE WANT, INNIT, MEL?
THOUGH IT MAY NOT QUIT BE LIFE AS YO KNOW IT.

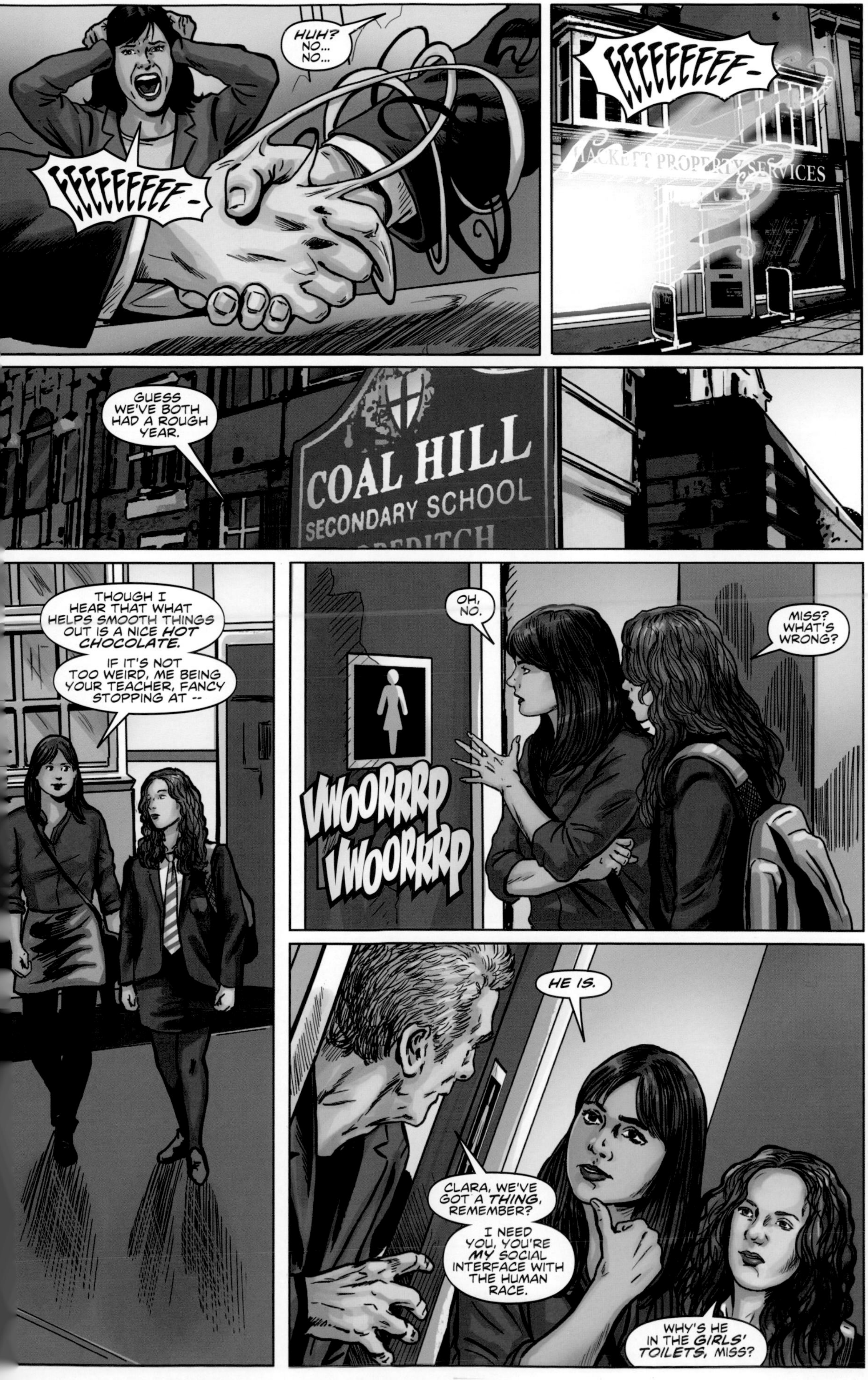

HUH? NO... NO...
EEEEEEEEE-
EEEEEEEEE-
HACKETT PROPERTY SERVICES
GUESS WE'VE BOTH HAD A ROUGH YEAR.
COAL HILL SECONDARY SCHOOL
THOUGH I HEAR THAT WHAT HELPS SMOOTH THINGS OUT IS A NICE *HOT CHOCOLATE.*
IF IT'S NOT TOO WEIRD, ME BEING YOUR TEACHER, FANCY STOPPING AT --
OH, NO.
MISS? WHAT'S WRONG?
VWOORRRP VWOORRRP
HE IS.
CLARA, WE'VE GOT A *THING,* REMEMBER?
I NEED YOU, YOU'RE *MY* SOCIAL INTERFACE WITH THE HUMAN RACE.
WHY'S HE IN THE *GIRLS' TOILETS,* MISS?

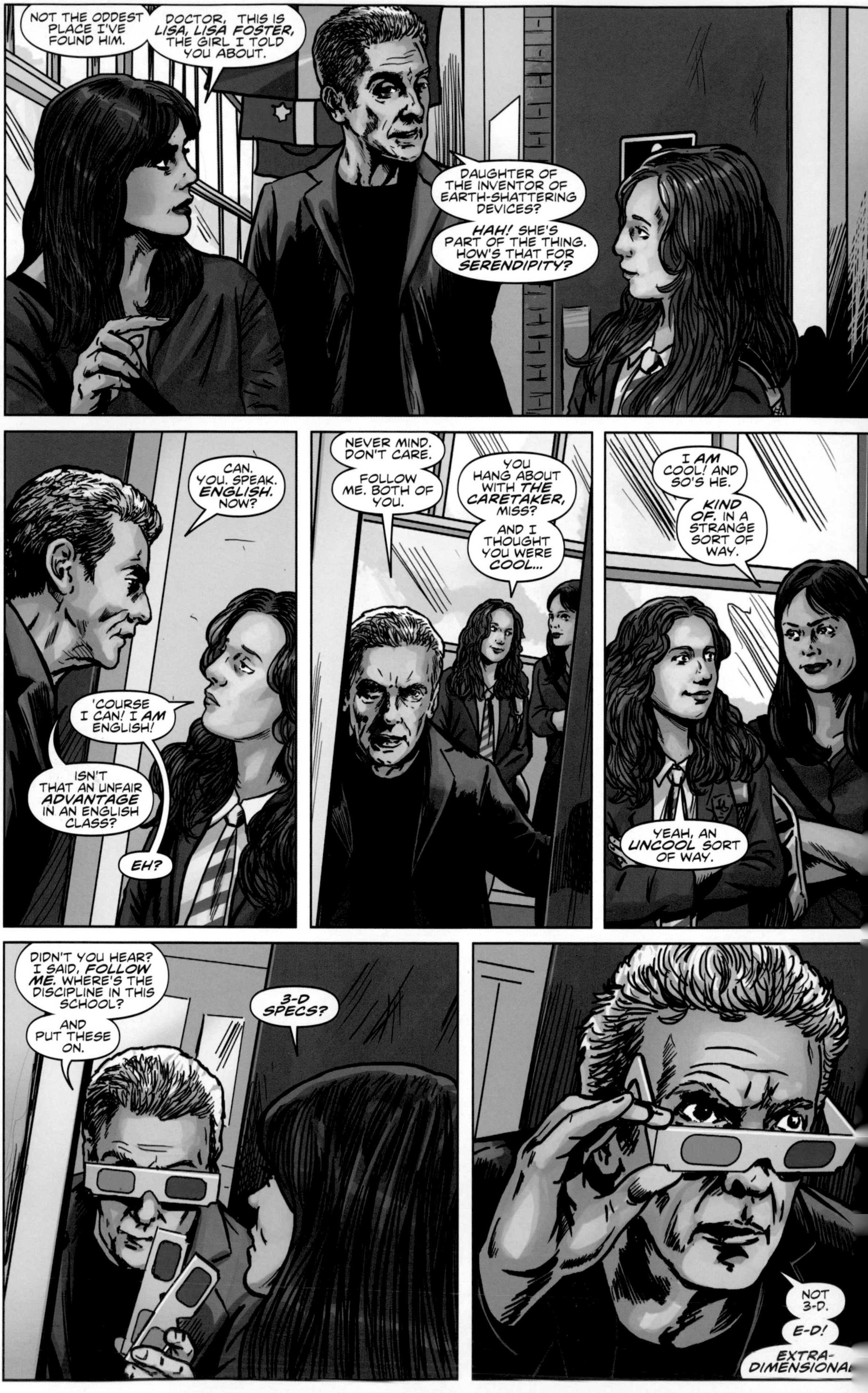
NOT THE ODDEST PLACE I'VE FOUND HIM.
DOCTOR, THIS IS LISA, LISA FOSTER, THE GIRL I TOLD YOU ABOUT.
DAUGHTER OF THE INVENTOR OF EARTH-SHATTERING DEVICES?
HAH! SHE'S PART OF THE THING. HOW'S THAT FOR SERENDIPITY?
CAN. YOU. SPEAK. ENGLISH. NOW?
'COURSE I CAN! I AM ENGLISH!
ISN'T THAT AN UNFAIR ADVANTAGE IN AN ENGLISH CLASS?
EH?
NEVER MIND. DON'T CARE.
FOLLOW ME. BOTH OF YOU.
YOU HANG ABOUT WITH THE CARETAKER, MISS?
AND I THOUGHT YOU WERE COOL...
I AM COOL! AND SO'S HE.
KIND OF. IN A STRANGE SORT OF WAY.
YEAH, AN UNCOOL SORT OF WAY.
DIDN'T YOU HEAR? I SAID, FOLLOW ME. WHERE'S THE DISCIPLINE IN THIS SCHOOL?
AND PUT THESE ON.
3-D SPECS?
NOT 3-D.
E-D!
EXTRA-DIMENSIONA

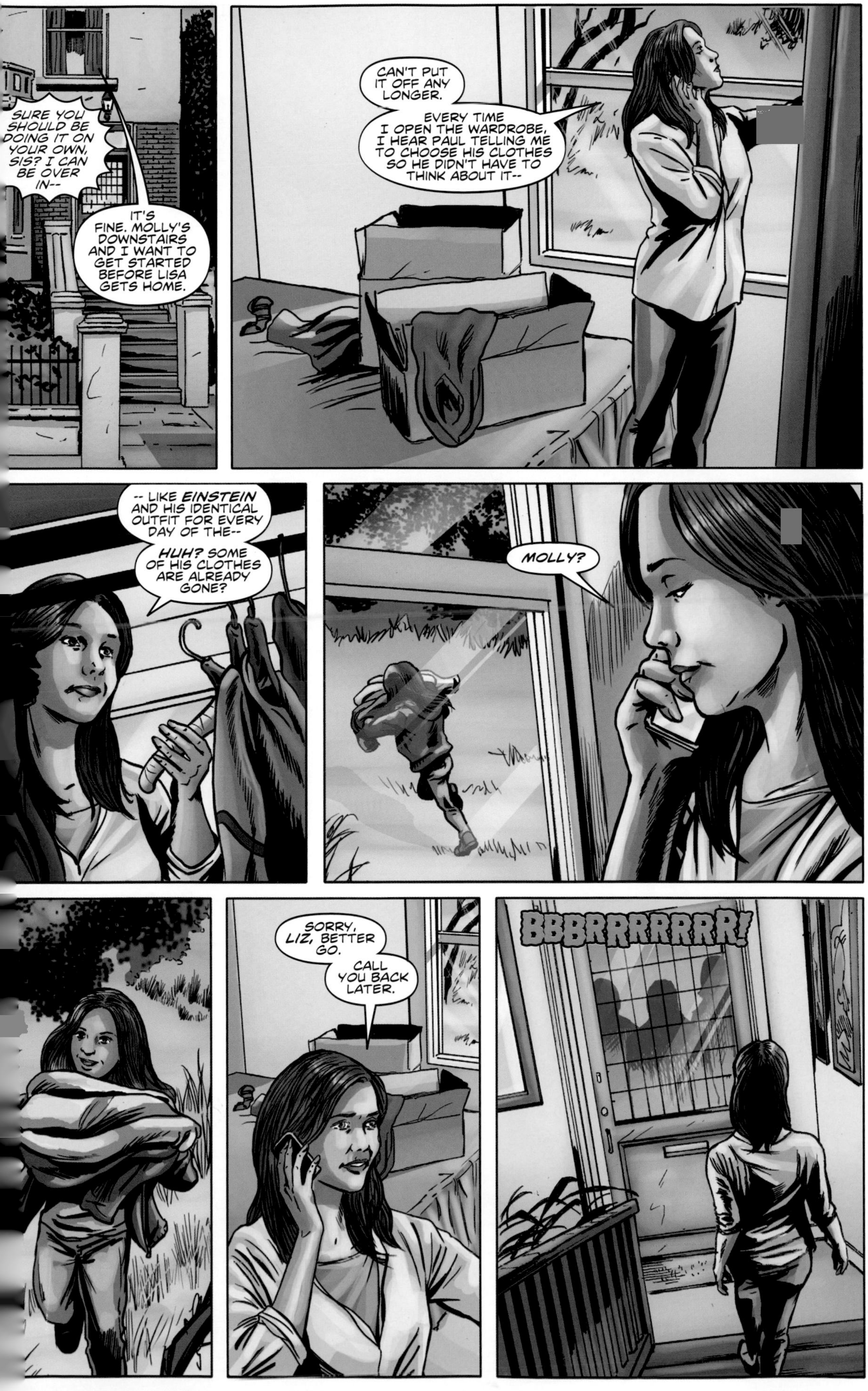
SURE YOU SHOULD BE DOING IT ON YOUR OWN, SIS? I CAN BE OVER IN--
IT'S FINE. MOLLY'S DOWNSTAIRS AND I WANT TO GET STARTED BEFORE LISA GETS HOME.
CAN'T PUT IT OFF ANY LONGER.
EVERY TIME I OPEN THE WARDROBE, I HEAR PAUL TELLING ME TO CHOOSE HIS CLOTHES SO HE DIDN'T HAVE TO THINK ABOUT IT--
-- LIKE EINSTEIN AND HIS IDENTICAL OUTFIT FOR EVERY DAY OF THE--
HUH? SOME OF HIS CLOTHES ARE ALREADY GONE?
MOLLY?
SORRY, LIZ, BETTER GO.
CALL YOU BACK LATER.
BBBRRRRRRRR!

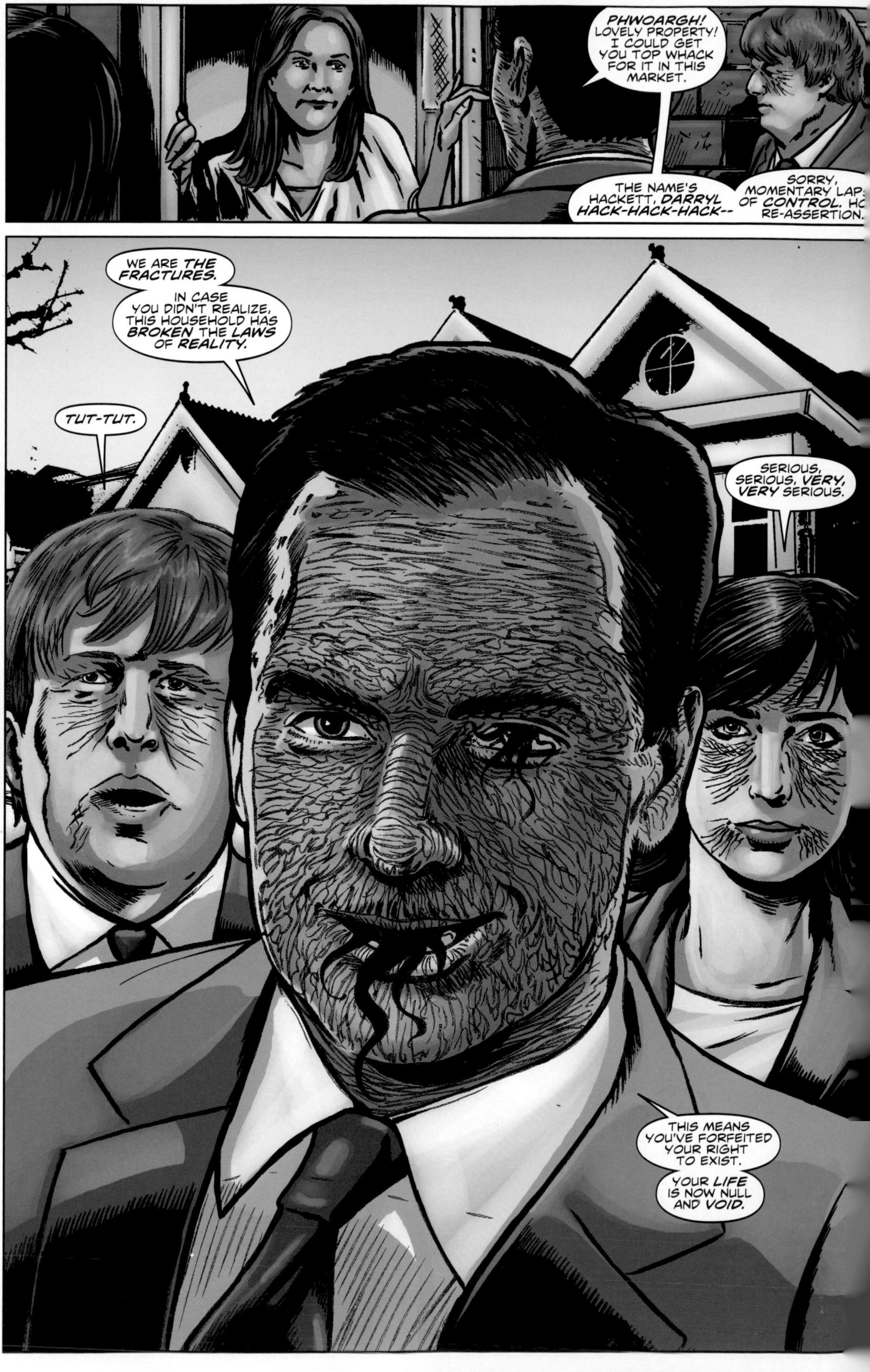
PHWOARGH! LOVELY PROPERTY! I COULD GET YOU TOP WHACK FOR IT IN THIS MARKET.
THE NAME'S HACKETT, DARRYL HACK-HACK-HACK--
SORRY, MOMENTARY LAP OF CONTROL. H RE-ASSERTION.
WE ARE THE FRACTURES.
IN CASE YOU DIDN'T REALIZE, THIS HOUSEHOLD HAS BROKEN THE LAWS OF REALITY.
TUT-TUT.
SERIOUS, SERIOUS, VERY, VERY SERIOUS.
THIS MEANS YOU'VE FORFEITED YOUR RIGHT TO EXIST.
YOUR LIFE IS NOW NULL AND VOID.

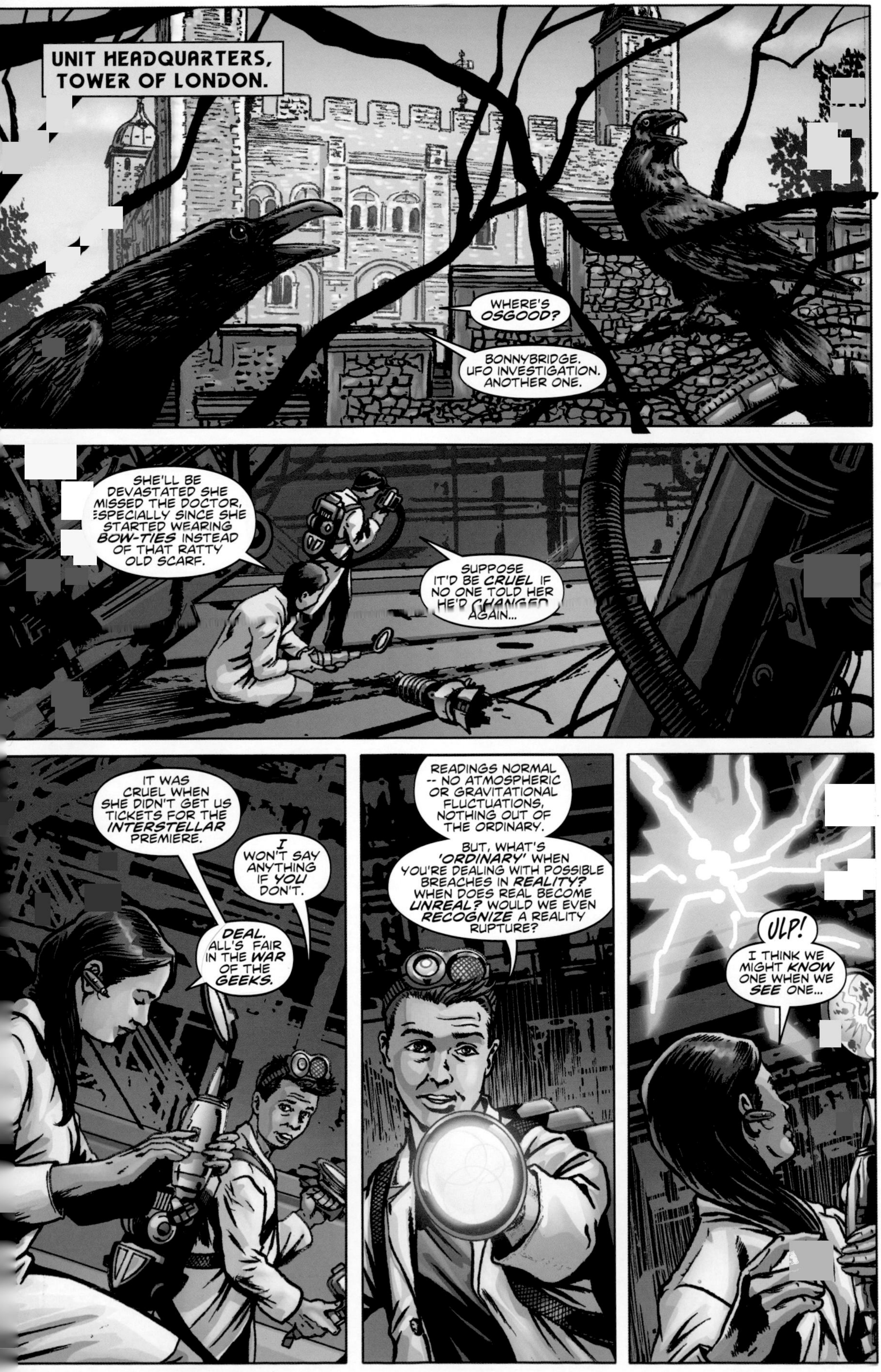
UNIT HEADQUARTERS, TOWER OF LONDON.
WHERE'S OSGOOD?
BONNYBRIDGE. UFO INVESTIGATION. ANOTHER ONE.
SHE'LL BE DEVASTATED SHE MISSED THE DOCTOR, ESPECIALLY SINCE SHE STARTED WEARING BOW-TIES INSTEAD OF THAT RATTY OLD SCARF.
SUPPOSE IT'D BE CRUEL IF NO ONE TOLD HER HE'D CHANGED AGAIN...
IT WAS CRUEL WHEN SHE DIDN'T GET US TICKETS FOR THE INTERSTELLAR PREMIERE.
I WON'T SAY ANYTHING IF YOU DON'T.
DEAL. ALL'S FAIR IN THE WAR OF THE GEEKS.
READINGS NORMAL -- NO ATMOSPHERIC OR GRAVITATIONAL FLUCTUATIONS, NOTHING OUT OF THE ORDINARY.
BUT, WHAT'S 'ORDINARY' WHEN YOU'RE DEALING WITH POSSIBLE BREACHES IN REALITY? WHEN DOES REAL BECOME UNREAL? WOULD WE EVEN RECOGNIZE A REALITY RUPTURE?
ULP!
I THINK WE MIGHT KNOW ONE WHEN WE SEE ONE...

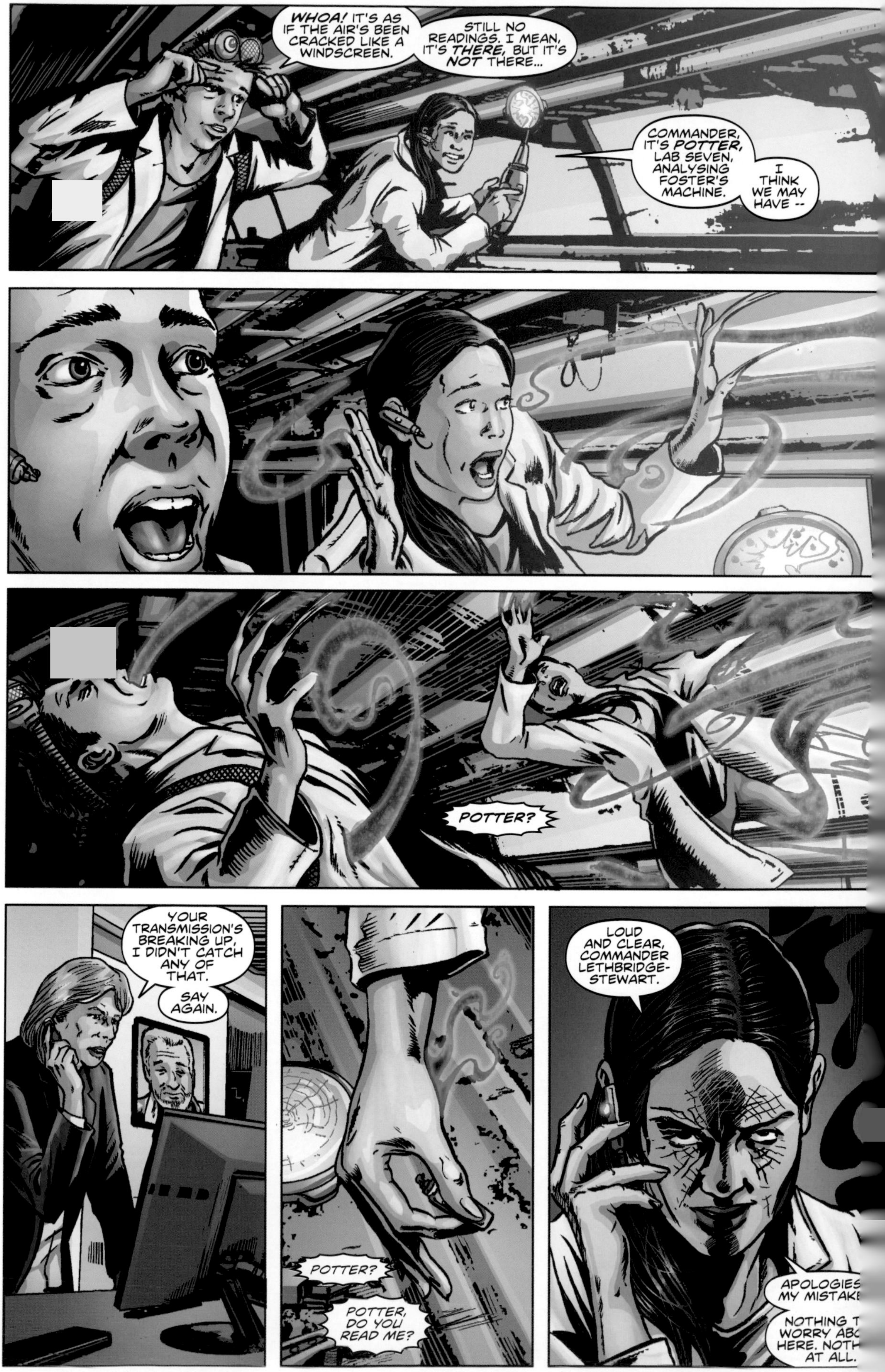
WHOA! IT'S AS IF THE AIR'S BEEN CRACKED LIKE A WINDSCREEN.
STILL NO READINGS. I MEAN, IT'S THERE, BUT IT'S NOT THERE...
COMMANDER, IT'S POTTER, LAB SEVEN, ANALYSING FOSTER'S MACHINE.
I THINK WE MAY HAVE --
POTTER?
YOUR TRANSMISSION'S BREAKING UP, I DIDN'T CATCH ANY OF THAT.
SAY AGAIN.
POTTER?
POTTER, DO YOU READ ME?
LOUD AND CLEAR, COMMANDER LETHBRIDGE-STEWART.
APOLOGIES MY MISTAKE
NOTHING T WORRY ABO HERE. NOTH AT ALL.

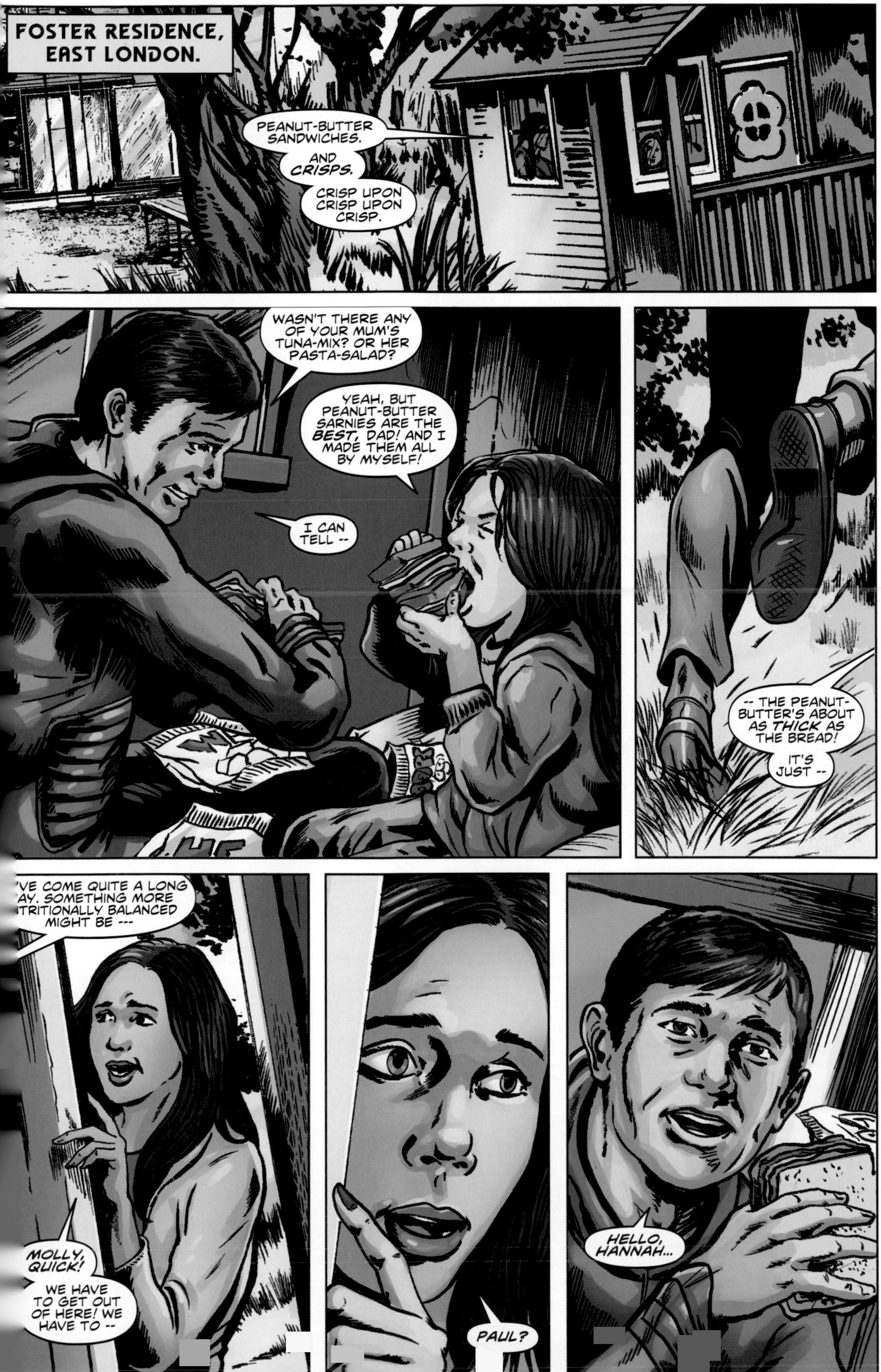
FOSTER RESIDENCE, EAST LONDON.
PEANUT-BUTTER SANDWICHES.
AND *CRISPS.*
CRISP UPON CRISP UPON CRISP.
WASN'T THERE ANY OF YOUR MUM'S TUNA-MIX? OR HER PASTA-SALAD?
YEAH, BUT PEANUT-BUTTER SARNIES ARE THE *BEST,* DAD! AND I MADE THEM ALL BY MYSELF!
I CAN TELL --
-- THE PEANUT-BUTTER'S ABOUT AS *THICK* AS THE BREAD!
IT'S JUST --
'VE COME QUITE A LONG AY. SOMETHING MORE TRITIONALLY BALANCED MIGHT BE ---
MOLLY, QUICK!
WE HAVE TO GET OUT OF HERE! WE HAVE TO --
PAUL?
HELLO, HANNAH...

NO... NO, IT CAN'T BE... GET AWAY FROM HIM, MOLLY!

IT'S ALRIGHT, MUM! DON'T BE SCARED, HE'S NOT A GHOST OR ANYTHING LIKE THAT.

IT'S DAD! HE'S COME BACK TO US...

SHE'S RIGHT, HANNAH, IT'S ME. IT'S PAUL. I'M THE SAME. I'M HERE.

YOU... YOU DON'T KNOW HOW GOOD IT IS TO SEE YOU AGAIN...

DON'T... DON'T TOUCH ME!

YOU'RE DEAD. HE'S DEAD. PAUL, MY HUSBAND, IS DEAD.

WE WATCHED HIM DIE, TRAPPED IN THE CAR. I LEANED FORWARD TO KISS HIM AND WHEN I LEANED BACK, HE WAS GONE.

I KNOW! I KNOW HOW YOU FEEL, PLEASE BELIEVE ME.

WHERE I'M FROM, IT WASN'T ME THAT WAS KILLED, IT WAS YOU.

AND MOLLY. AND LISA. I WATCHED YOU DIE. ALL OF YOU.

STOP IT! YOU'RE CRAZY! SOME KIND OF IMPOSTER OR... I DON'T KNOW!

YOU'RE WHY THOSE THINGS ARE HERE, THE THINGS AT THE DOOR...

EH? WHAT THINGS?

STAY BACK, I'M WARNING YOU! I'M CALLING THE POLICE, SO YOU AND YOUR FRIENDS IN THERE BETTER START--

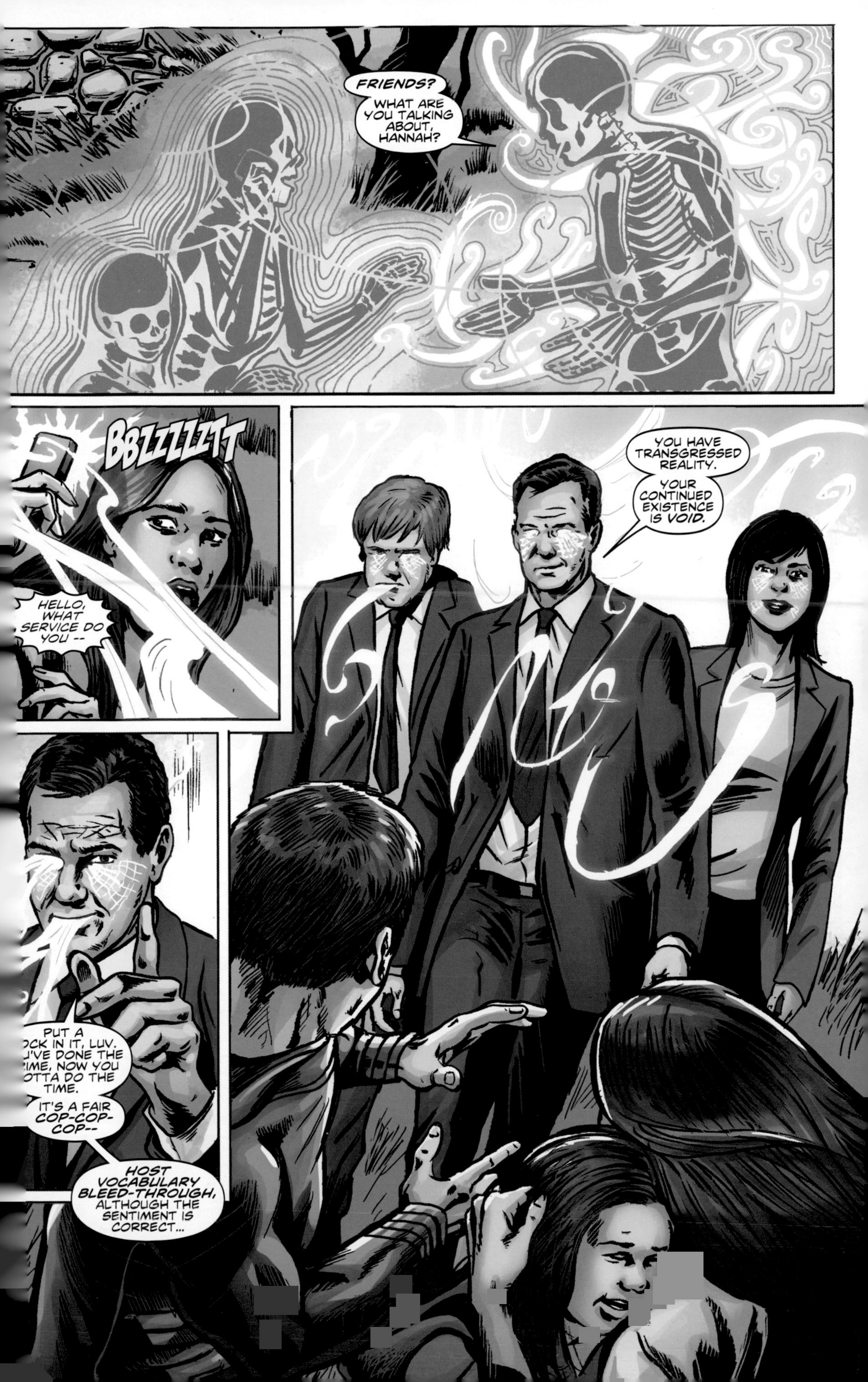
FRIENDS?
WHAT ARE YOU TALKING ABOUT, HANNAH?
BBZZZZZTT
HELLO, WHAT SERVICE DO YOU --
YOU HAVE TRANSGRESSED REALITY.
YOUR CONTINUED EXISTENCE IS VOID.
PUT A OCK IN IT, LUV. U'VE DONE THE IME, NOW YOU OTTA DO THE TIME.
IT'S A FAIR COP-COP-COP--
HOST VOCABULARY BLEED-THROUGH, ALTHOUGH THE SENTIMENT IS CORRECT...

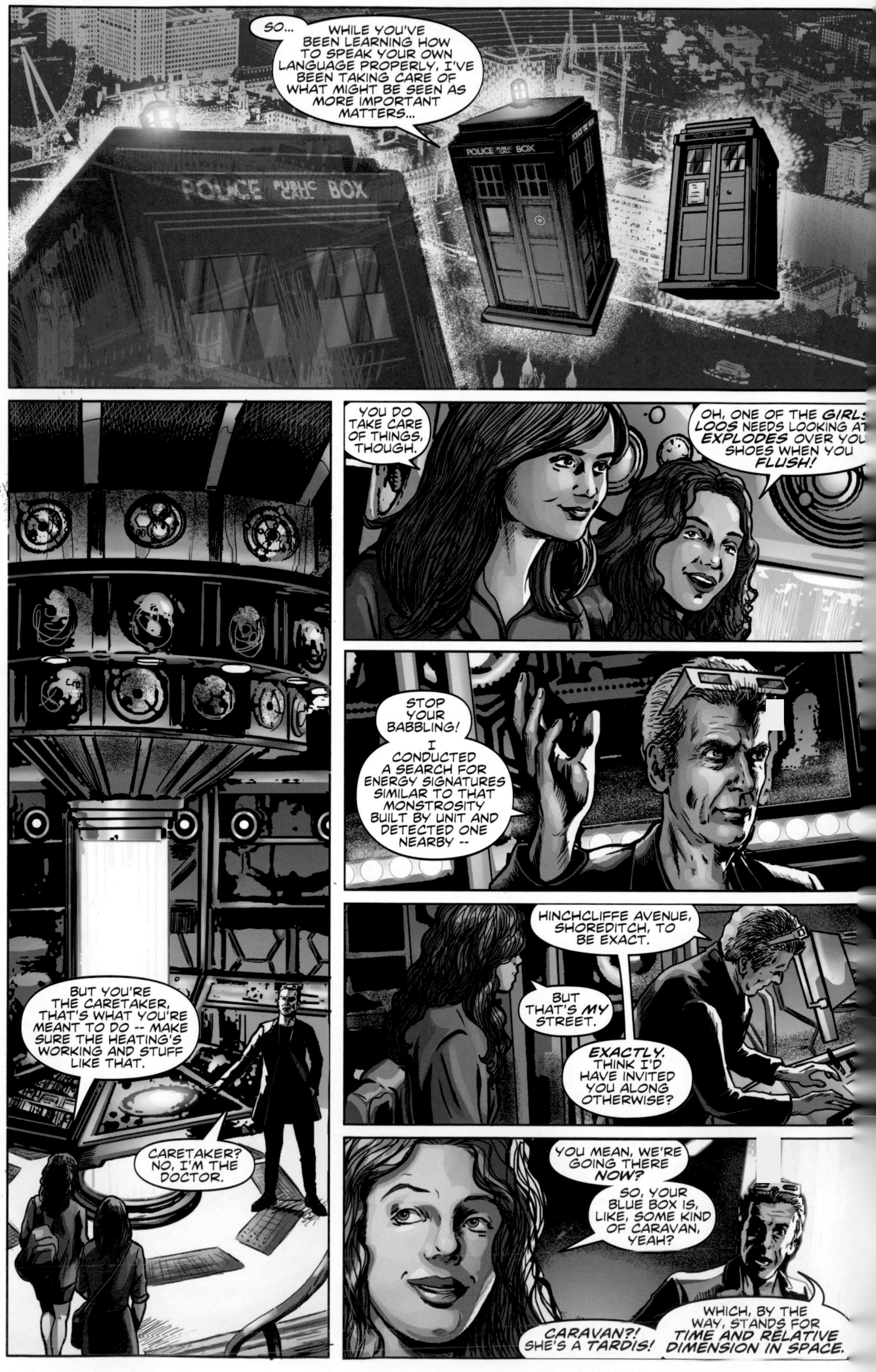

POLICE PUBLIC CALL BOX
SO... WHILE YOU'VE BEEN LEARNING HOW TO SPEAK YOUR OWN LANGUAGE PROPERLY, I'VE BEEN TAKING CARE OF WHAT MIGHT BE SEEN AS MORE IMPORTANT MATTERS...
POLICE PUBLIC CALL BOX
BUT YOU'RE THE CARETAKER, THAT'S WHAT YOU'RE MEANT TO DO -- MAKE SURE THE HEATING'S WORKING AND STUFF LIKE THAT.
CARETAKER? NO, I'M THE DOCTOR.
YOU DO TAKE CARE OF THINGS, THOUGH.
OH, ONE OF THE GIRLS LOOS NEEDS LOOKING AT EXPLODES OVER YOU SHOES WHEN YOU FLUSH!
STOP YOUR BABBLING! I CONDUCTED A SEARCH FOR ENERGY SIGNATURES SIMILAR TO THAT MONSTROSITY BUILT BY UNIT AND DETECTED ONE NEARBY --
HINCHCLIFFE AVENUE, SHOREDITCH, TO BE EXACT.
BUT THAT'S MY STREET.
EXACTLY. THINK I'D HAVE INVITED YOU ALONG OTHERWISE?
YOU MEAN, WE'RE GOING THERE NOW?
SO, YOUR BLUE BOX IS, LIKE, SOME KIND OF CARAVAN, YEAH?
CARAVAN?! SHE'S A TARDIS!
WHICH, BY THE WAY, STANDS FOR TIME AND RELATIVE DIMENSION IN SPACE.

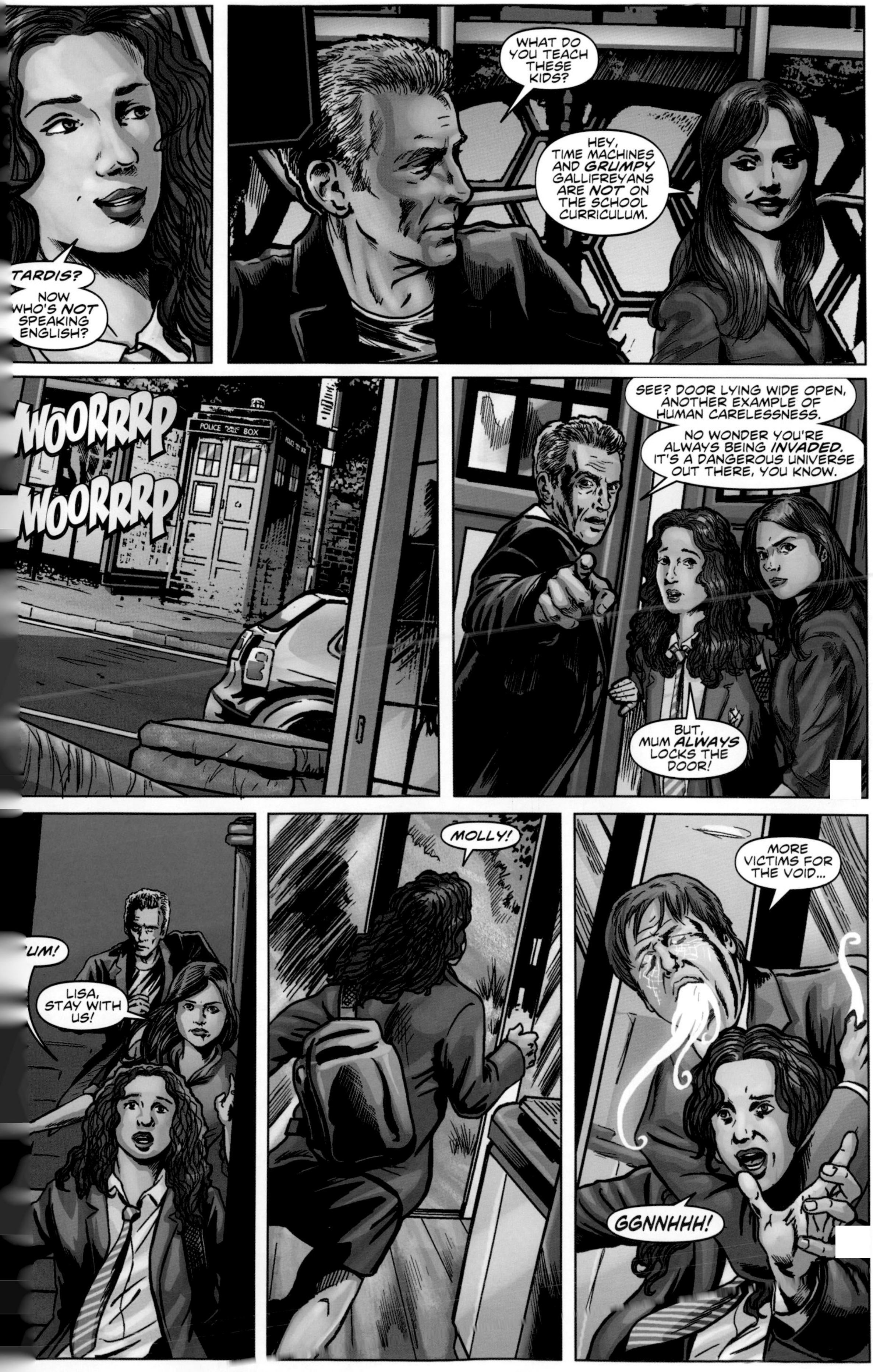
TARDIS?
NOW WHO'S NOT SPEAKING ENGLISH?
WHAT DO YOU TEACH THESE KIDS?
HEY, TIME MACHINES AND GRUMPY GALLIFREYANS ARE NOT ON THE SCHOOL CURRICULUM.
WOORRRP
WOORRRP
POLICE BOX
SEE? DOOR LYING WIDE OPEN, ANOTHER EXAMPLE OF HUMAN CARELESSNESS.
NO WONDER YOU'RE ALWAYS BEING INVADED. IT'S A DANGEROUS UNIVERSE OUT THERE, YOU KNOW.
BUT, MUM ALWAYS LOCKS THE DOOR!
UM!
LISA, STAY WITH US!
MOLLY!
MORE VICTIMS FOR THE VOID...
GGNNHHH!

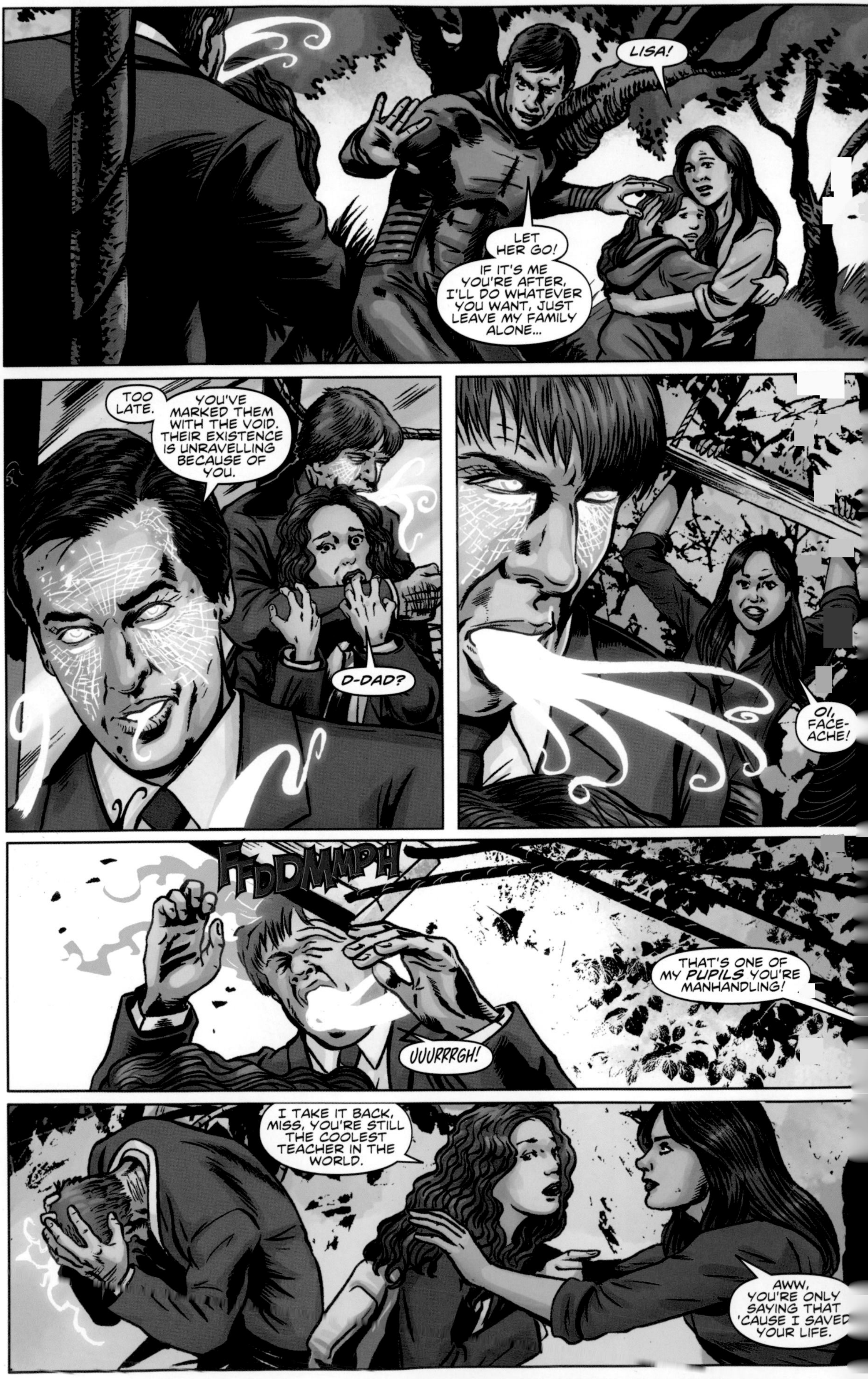
LISA!
LET HER GO! IF IT'S ME YOU'RE AFTER, I'LL DO WHATEVER YOU WANT, JUST LEAVE MY FAMILY ALONE...
TOO LATE.
YOU'VE MARKED THEM WITH THE VOID. THEIR EXISTENCE IS UNRAVELLING BECAUSE OF YOU.
D-DAD?
OI, FACE-ACHE!
FFDDMMPH
THAT'S ONE OF MY PUPILS YOU'RE MANHANDLING!
UUURRRGH!
I TAKE IT BACK, MISS, YOU'RE STILL THE COOLEST TEACHER IN THE WORLD.
AWW, YOU'RE ONLY SAYING THAT 'CAUSE I SAVED YOUR LIFE.

FOOLISH. RESISTANCE IS --

-- MY SPECIALITY. I'M THE DOCTOR. THIS WORLD IS UNDER MY PROTECTION. GO BACK TO YOUR OWN REALITY -- WHILE YOU STILL CAN.

WE HAVE NO REALITY.

WE ARE *THE FRACTURES,* BORN OF UNREALITY, FORGED IN CHAOS.

WE SOAR THE VOID BETWEEN UNIVERSES --

-- HUNTING, DEVOURING, DESTROYING THOSE WHO BREAK THE BARRIERS OR SLIP THROUGH THE CRACKS OF THEIR REALITIES.

WE ARE THE MOST NECESSARY OF EVILS.

WITHOUT US, CHAOS WOULD *SEEP* INTO YOUR WORLDS. WHY DO YOU STAND *AGAINST* US?

MAYBE I'M JUST A REBEL AT HEART.

OR MAYBE I JUST DON'T LIKE YOUR FACES.

HAVE NOT YET SEEN OUR *TRUE* FACES...

SSHHLLLOUURRRKKK

NICE ONE, DOCTOR!

AS IF IT WASN'T *CREEPY* ENOUGH WHEN THEY LOOKED LIKE EVIL ESTATE AGENTS...

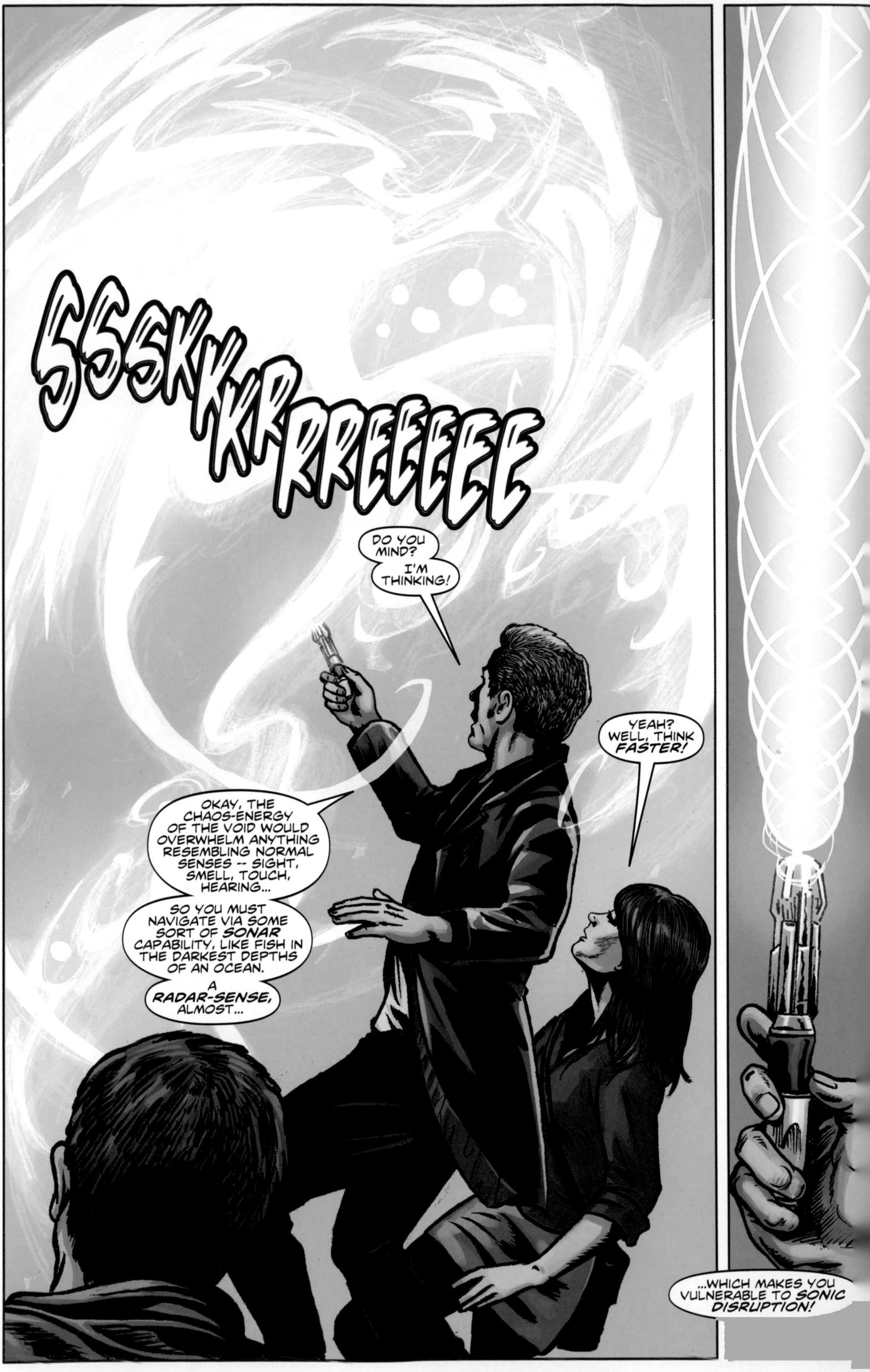
SSSKKRRREEEEE
DO YOU MIND? I'M THINKING!
YEAH? WELL, THINK FASTER!
OKAY, THE CHAOS-ENERGY OF THE VOID WOULD OVERWHELM ANYTHING RESEMBLING NORMAL SENSES -- SIGHT, SMELL, TOUCH, HEARING...
SO YOU MUST NAVIGATE VIA SOME SORT OF SONAR CAPABILITY, LIKE FISH IN THE DARKEST DEPTHS OF AN OCEAN.
A RADAR-SENSE, ALMOST...
...WHICH MAKES YOU VULNERABLE TO SONIC DISRUPTION!

DAD? MUM, WHAT'S...?

STAY AWAY FROM HIM, LISA! HE'S *NOT* YOUR FATHER, WHATEVER HE TRIES TO SAY.

HANNAH, PLEASE!

I MAY NOT BE THE PAUL FOSTER OF *THIS* WORLD, BUT I'M STILL *ME*, STILL THE MAN YOU KNEW.

WHAT *ARE* THOSE THINGS, DOCTOR?

A SPECIES I'VE NEVER ENCOUNTERED BEFORE -- CREATURES FROM *BETWEEN* REALITIES.

FASCINATING, EH?

SSSKKRRREEEE!

NOT THE WORD THAT SPRINGS TO MY MIND!

Fenn St **6**
Hob's End
Cool Hill

HONK HONK
HONK HONK

... AND THEY OSCILLATE IN SHAPE AND COLOR! WONDER WHAT THE SIGNIFIC--

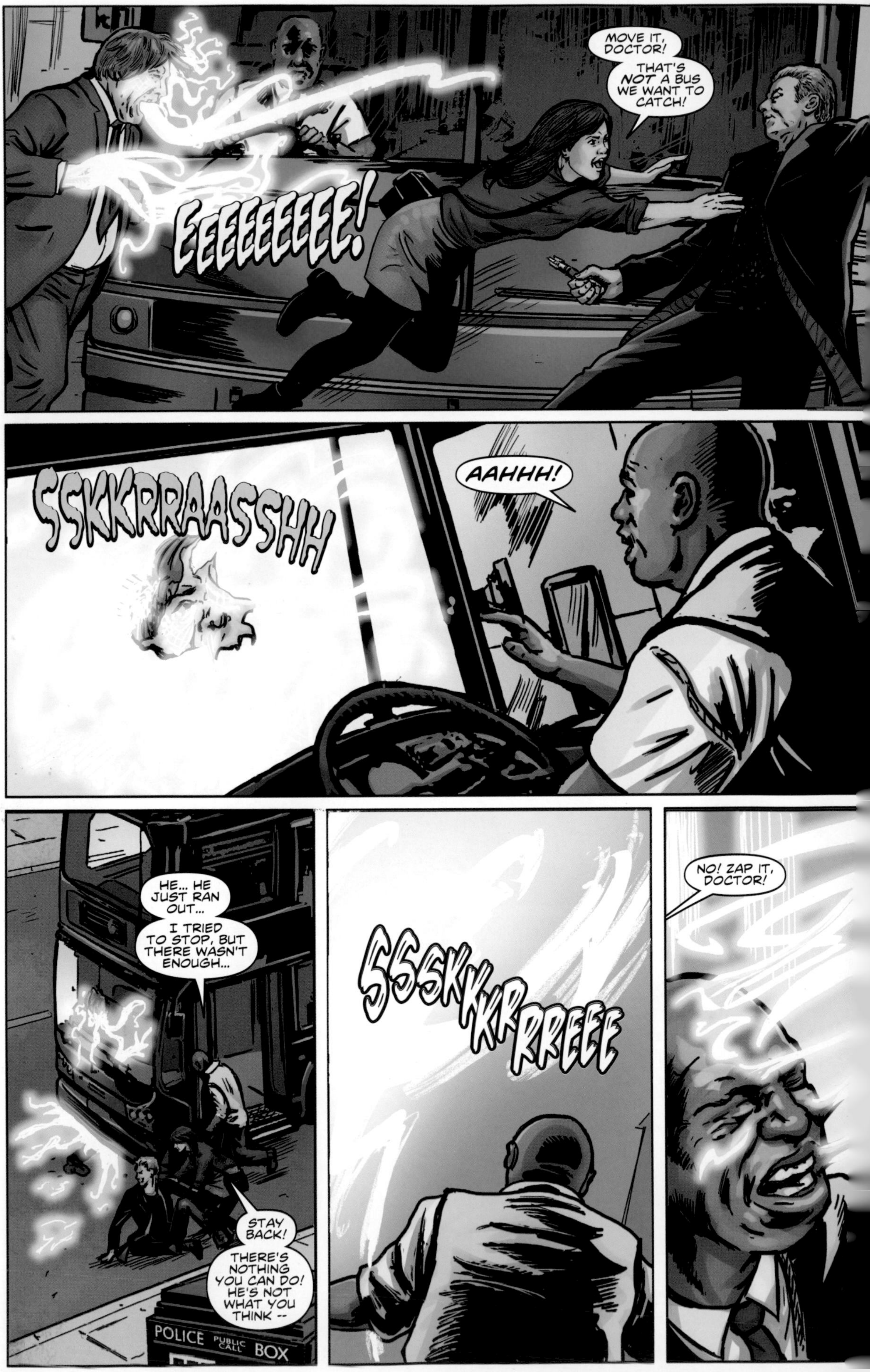
MOVE IT, DOCTOR!
THAT'S NOT A BUS WE WANT TO CATCH!
EEEEEEEEE!
SSKKRRAASSHH
AAHHH!
HE... HE JUST RAN OUT...
I TRIED TO STOP, BUT THERE WASN'T ENOUGH...
STAY BACK!
THERE'S NOTHING YOU CAN DO! HE'S NOT WHAT YOU THINK --
POLICE PUBLIC CALL BOX
SSSKKKRRREEE
NO! ZAP IT, DOCTOR!

SSSKKKRREEEE

NO TIME, WE HAVE TO GO.

...ALWAYS SHIFTING THEIR FORM...

TO THE TARDIS!

STEP LIVELY PLEASE, DANGEROUS ALIEN PREDATOR APPROACHING.

IS THERE ANY OTHER KIND?

VWOORRRP

VWOORRRP

VWOORRRP

VWOORRRP

POLICE BOX

POLICE TELEPHONE
FREE
FOR USE OF
PUBLIC
ADVICE & ASSISTANCE
OBTAINABLE IMMEDIATELY
OFFICERS & CARS
RESPOND TO ALL CALLS

THIS IS YOUR FLAT, MISS? IT'S TEENY-TINY.

HEY, YOU TRY SURVIVING IN LONDON ON A SECOND-YEAR TEACHER'S WAGES.

AND IT DOESN'T HELP THAT THERE'S A 1960s POLICE-BOX PARKED IN THE MIDDLE OF THE LIVING-ROOM.

I SHOULD CHARGE YOU RENT.

I SHOULD CHARGE YOU TAXI-FARE.

WHAT'S *WRONG* WITH YOU PEOPLE?

A MAN WAS JUST *KILLED!* MY DEAD HUSBAND IS SUDDENLY WALKING AROUND LARGER-THAN-LIFE! WE'RE BEING CHASED BY ALIEN-*THINGS* THAT EXPLODE OUT OF ESTATE AGENTS!

AND YOU'RE LAUGHING AND *JOKING!*

IT'S HIM, MUM! IT'S *DAD!* I KNOW IT IS!

IT *CAN'T* BE, MOLLY...

HANNAH, LISA, PLEASE? REMEMBER THAT CHRISTMAS, WHEN WE --

BABBLE-BABBLE-BABBLE--

SHUSH!

MRS. FOSTER, I REALIZE YOU'RE HAVING AN EVENTFUL DAY, BUT HYSTERICS AND HISTRIONICS WILL GET *YOU* NOWHERE AND GIVE *ME* A SORE HEAD.

PUT SIMPLY: *YES,* THIS MAN *IS* YOUR HUSBAND.

BUT, AT THE SAME TIME: NO, HE *ISN'T.*

HE'S YOUR... *ALTERNATE* HUSBAND.

DEAD SIMPLE, DOCTOR.

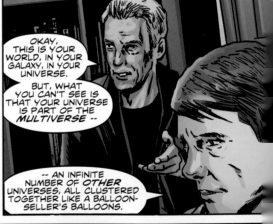

OKAY, THIS IS YOUR WORLD, IN YOUR GALAXY, IN YOUR UNIVERSE.

BUT, WHAT YOU CAN'T SEE IS THAT YOUR UNIVERSE IS PART OF THE *MULTIVERSE* --

-- AN INFINITE NUMBER OF *OTHER* UNIVERSES, ALL CLUSTERED TOGETHER LIKE A BALLOON-SELLER'S BALLOONS.

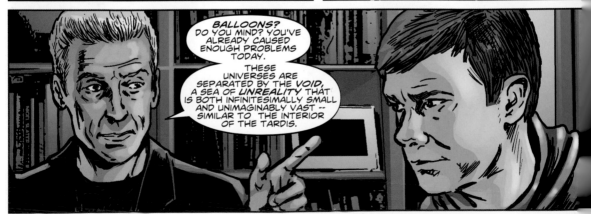

BALLOONS? DO YOU MIND? YOU'VE ALREADY CAUSED ENOUGH PROBLEMS TODAY.

THESE UNIVERSES ARE SEPARATED BY THE *VOID,* A SEA OF *UNREALITY* THAT IS BOTH INFINITESIMALLY SMALL AND UNIMAGINABLY VAST -- SIMILAR TO THE INTERIOR OF THE TARDIS.

LOOK, A SINGLE STRAND OF HAIR.

AOWW.

IMAGINE IT'S YOUR WORLD, YOUR UNIVERSE, EVERYTHING YOU KNOW AND ARE FAMILIAR WITH...

IF I *PING* IT, YOU SEE A BLUR OF MOVEMENT, THE IMAGE OF THAT SINGLE HAIR MULTIPLIED TENFOLD, A *HUNDREDFOLD*, EACH ONE OCCUPYING A SLIGHTLY DIFFERENT SPACE AND TIME.

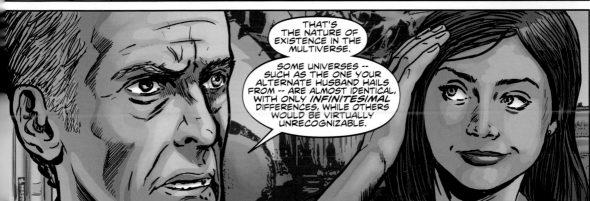

THAT'S THE NATURE OF EXISTENCE IN THE MULTIVERSE.

SOME UNIVERSES -- SUCH AS THE ONE YOUR ALTERNATE HUSBAND HAILS FROM -- ARE ALMOST IDENTICAL, WITH ONLY *INFINITESIMAL* DIFFERENCES, WHILE OTHERS WOULD BE VIRTUALLY UNRECOGNIZABLE.

"FOR EXAMPLE, THERE MIGHT BE ANOTHER EARTH WHERE DINOSAURS DIDN'T SUFFER AN EXTINCTION EVENT...

"-- AND, AFTER MILLENNIA OF EVOLUTION, ARE SITTING IN *GENTLESAURS' CLUBS*, SMOKING CIGARS, DRINKING PORT AND SAYING, 'TOP OF THE MORNING TO YOU, REX, OLD BOY.'"

THE DOCTOR'S RIGHT, HANNAH, THERE *ARE* DIFFERENCES. I WON'T DENY IT. YOU KNOW WHAT THEY ARE?

ON MY WORLD, A FATHER LOST HIS FAMILY, HIS WIFE AND DAUGHTERS. ON THIS WORLD, THAT FAMILY LOST A FATHER, A HUSBAND.

EVERYTHING *ELSE* IS THE SAME.

HERE WAS A CRASH. THE HER DRIVER WAS DRUNK, EXTING AS HE DROVE. I WAS THROWN CLEAR --

NO...

-- BUT YOU... *MY* HANNAH, *MY* LISA, *MY* MOLLY WERE TRAPPED IN THE WRECKAGE...

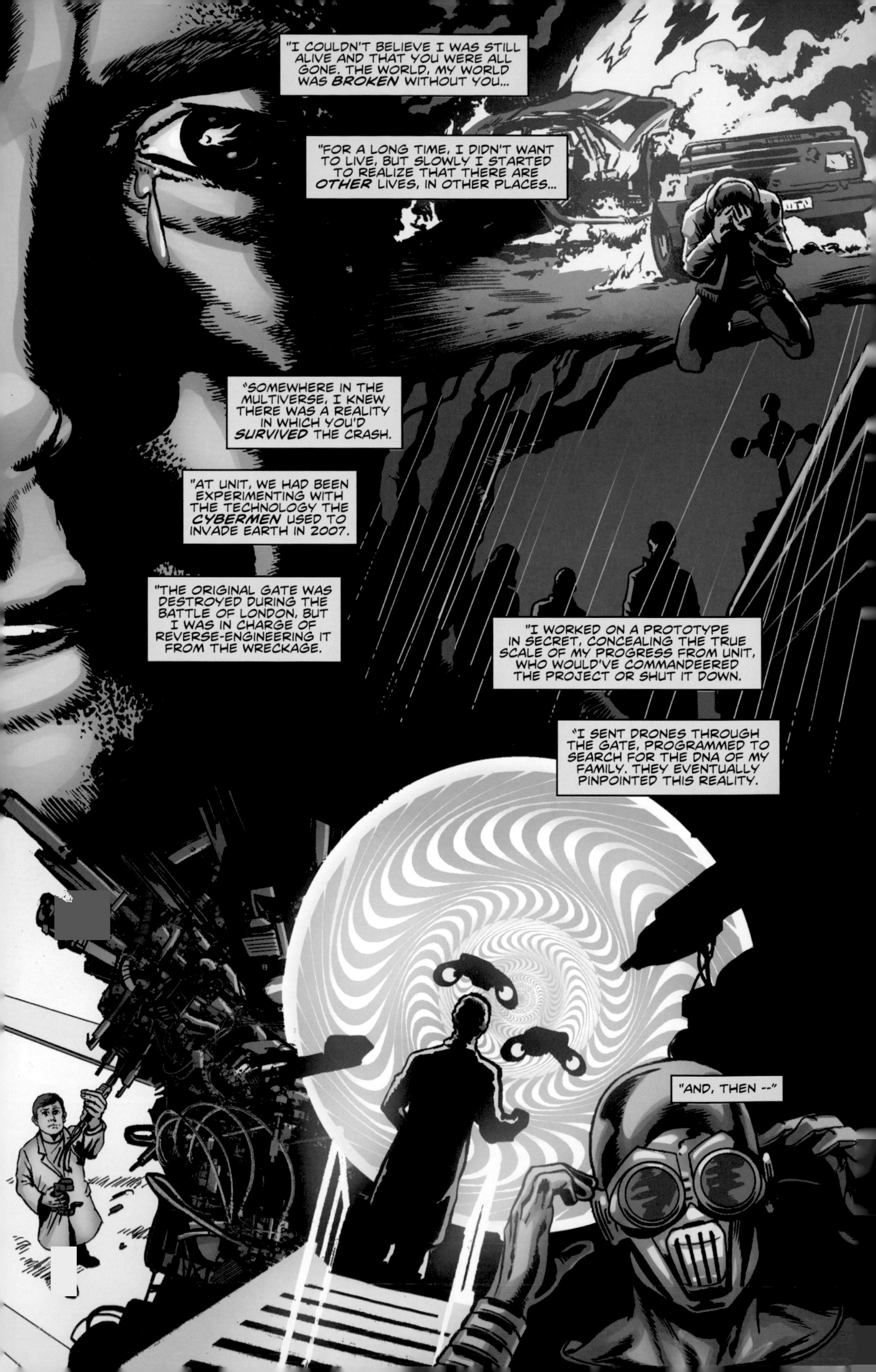
"I COULDN'T BELIEVE I WAS STILL ALIVE AND THAT YOU WERE ALL GONE. THE WORLD, MY WORLD WAS BROKEN WITHOUT YOU...
"FOR A LONG TIME, I DIDN'T WANT TO LIVE, BUT SLOWLY I STARTED TO REALIZE THAT THERE ARE OTHER LIVES, IN OTHER PLACES...
"SOMEWHERE IN THE MULTIVERSE, I KNEW THERE WAS A REALITY IN WHICH YOU'D SURVIVED THE CRASH.
"AT UNIT, WE HAD BEEN EXPERIMENTING WITH THE TECHNOLOGY THE CYBERMEN USED TO INVADE EARTH IN 2007.
"THE ORIGINAL GATE WAS DESTROYED DURING THE BATTLE OF LONDON, BUT I WAS IN CHARGE OF REVERSE-ENGINEERING IT FROM THE WRECKAGE.
"I WORKED ON A PROTOTYPE IN SECRET, CONCEALING THE TRUE SCALE OF MY PROGRESS FROM UNIT, WHO WOULD'VE COMMANDEERED THE PROJECT OR SHUT IT DOWN.
"I SENT DRONES THROUGH THE GATE, PROGRAMMED TO SEARCH FOR THE DNA OF MY FAMILY. THEY EVENTUALLY PINPOINTED THIS REALITY.
"AND, THEN --"

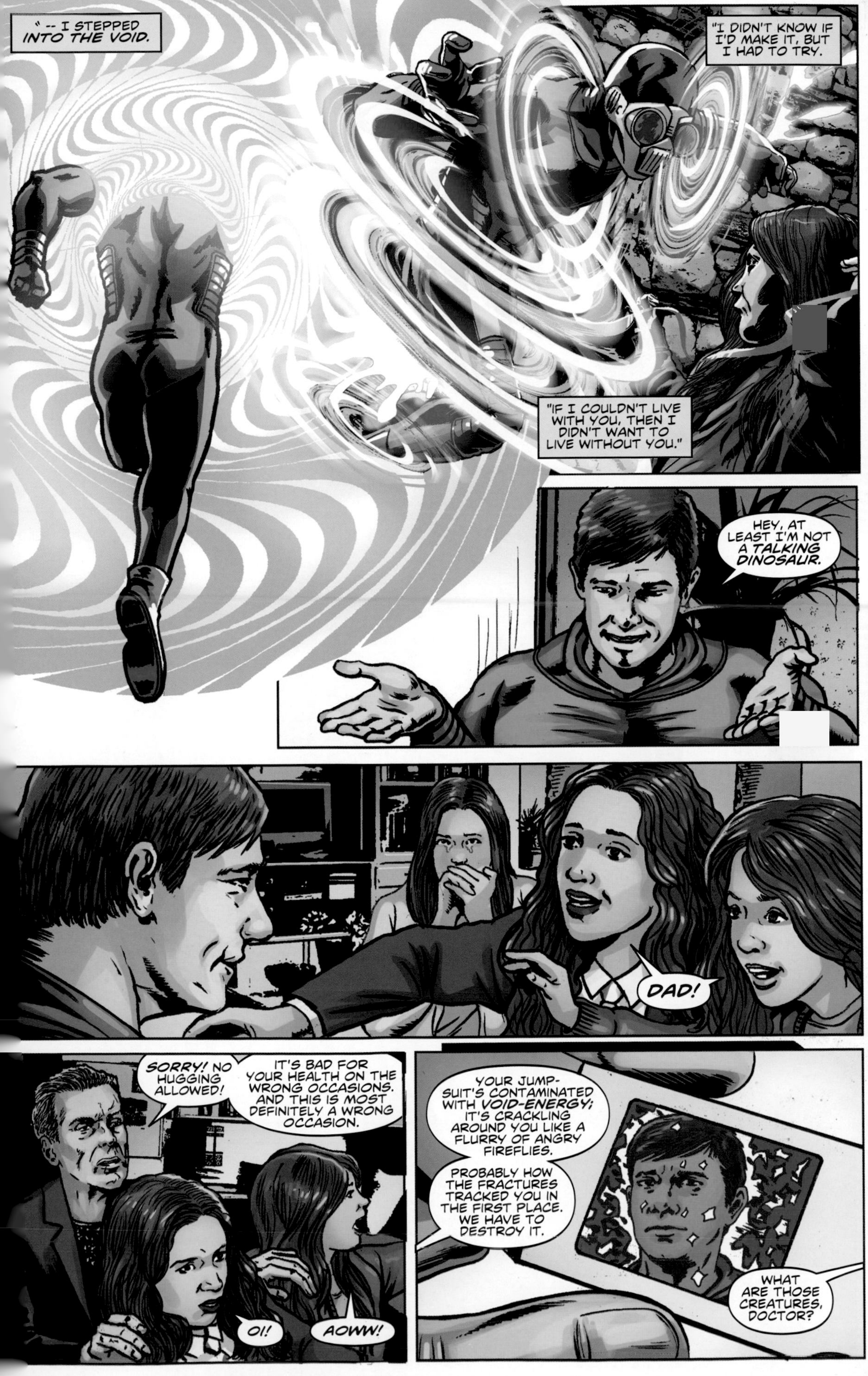
"-- I STEPPED INTO THE VOID.
"I DIDN'T KNOW IF I'D MAKE IT, BUT I HAD TO TRY.
"IF I COULDN'T LIVE WITH YOU, THEN I DIDN'T WANT TO LIVE WITHOUT YOU."
HEY, AT LEAST I'M NOT A TALKING DINOSAUR.
DAD!
SORRY! NO HUGGING ALLOWED!
IT'S BAD FOR YOUR HEALTH ON THE WRONG OCCASIONS. AND THIS IS MOST DEFINITELY A WRONG OCCASION.
OI!
AOWW!
YOUR JUMP-SUIT'S CONTAMINATED WITH VOID-ENERGY; IT'S CRACKLING AROUND YOU LIKE A FLURRY OF ANGRY FIREFLIES.
PROBABLY HOW THE FRACTURES TRACKED YOU IN THE FIRST PLACE. WE HAVE TO DESTROY IT.
WHAT ARE THOSE CREATURES, DOCTOR?

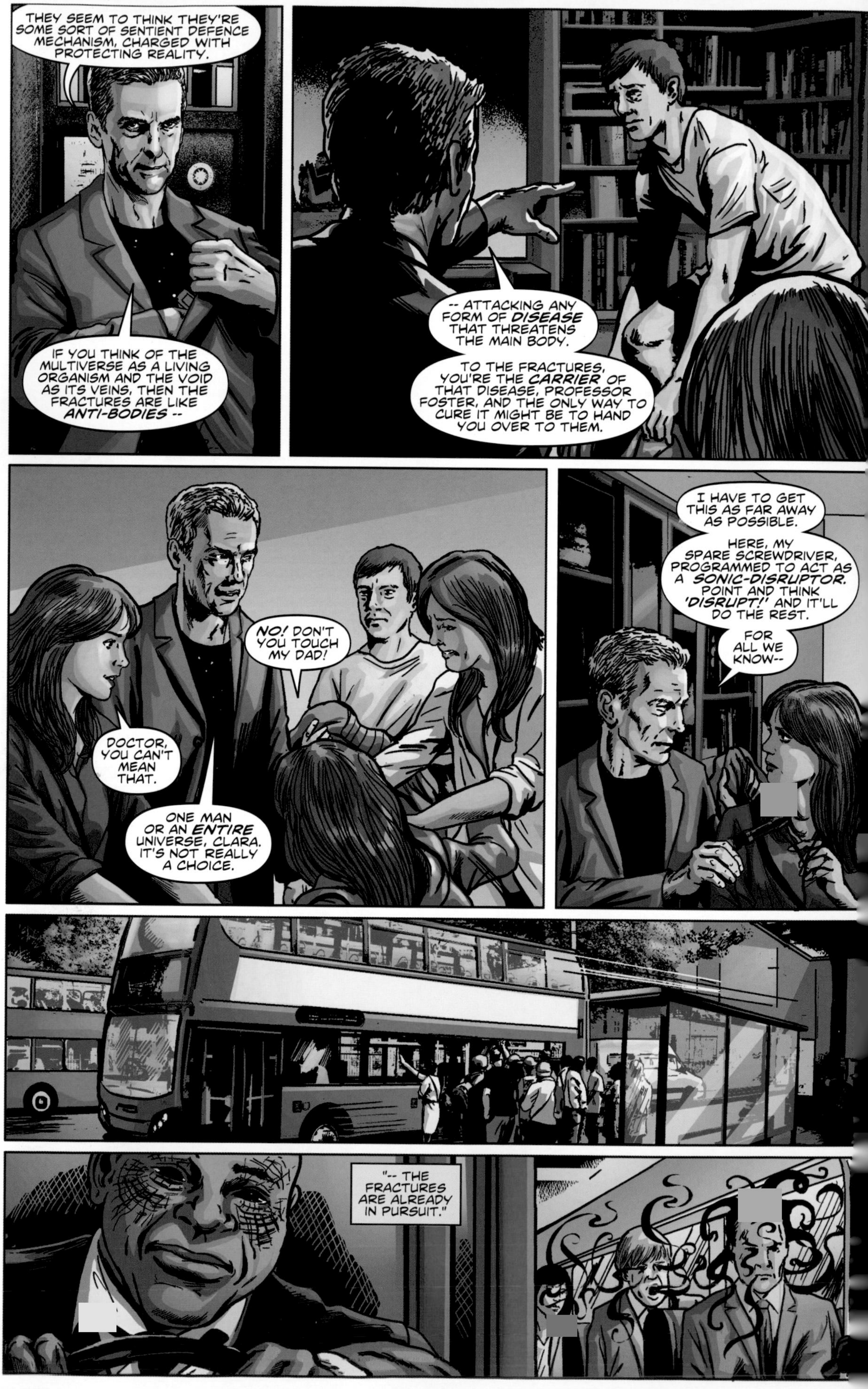
THEY SEEM TO THINK THEY'RE SOME SORT OF SENTIENT DEFENCE MECHANISM, CHARGED WITH PROTECTING REALITY.
IF YOU THINK OF THE MULTIVERSE AS A LIVING ORGANISM AND THE VOID AS ITS VEINS, THEN THE FRACTURES ARE LIKE ANTI-BODIES --
-- ATTACKING ANY FORM OF DISEASE THAT THREATENS THE MAIN BODY.
TO THE FRACTURES, YOU'RE THE CARRIER OF THAT DISEASE, PROFESSOR FOSTER, AND THE ONLY WAY TO CURE IT MIGHT BE TO HAND YOU OVER TO THEM.
NO! DON'T YOU TOUCH MY DAD!
DOCTOR, YOU CAN'T MEAN THAT.
ONE MAN OR AN ENTIRE UNIVERSE, CLARA. IT'S NOT REALLY A CHOICE.
I HAVE TO GET THIS AS FAR AWAY AS POSSIBLE.
HERE, MY SPARE SCREWDRIVER, PROGRAMMED TO ACT AS A SONIC-DISRUPTOR. POINT AND THINK 'DISRUPT!' AND IT'LL DO THE REST.
FOR ALL WE KNOW--
"-- THE FRACTURES ARE ALREADY IN PURSUIT."

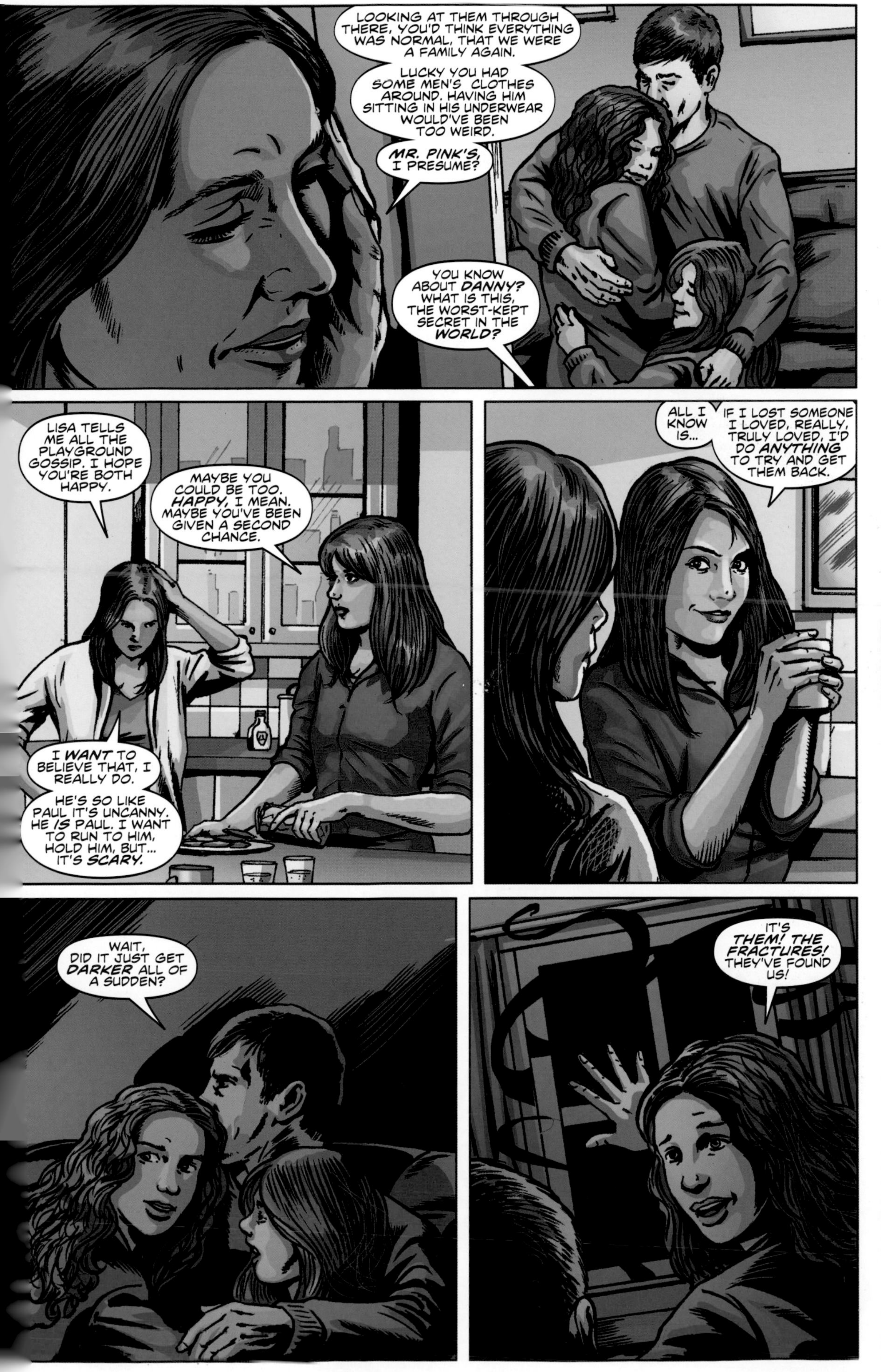
LOOKING AT THEM THROUGH THERE, YOU'D THINK EVERYTHING WAS NORMAL, THAT WE WERE A FAMILY AGAIN.
LUCKY YOU HAD SOME MEN'S CLOTHES AROUND. HAVING HIM SITTING IN HIS UNDERWEAR WOULD'VE BEEN TOO WEIRD.
MR. PINK'S, I PRESUME?
YOU KNOW ABOUT DANNY? WHAT IS THIS, THE WORST-KEPT SECRET IN THE WORLD?
LISA TELLS ME ALL THE PLAYGROUND GOSSIP. I HOPE YOU'RE BOTH HAPPY.
MAYBE YOU COULD BE TOO. HAPPY, I MEAN. MAYBE YOU'VE BEEN GIVEN A SECOND CHANCE.
I WANT TO BELIEVE THAT, I REALLY DO.
HE'S SO LIKE PAUL IT'S UNCANNY. HE IS PAUL. I WANT TO RUN TO HIM, HOLD HIM, BUT... IT'S SCARY.
ALL I KNOW IS...
IF I LOST SOMEONE I LOVED, REALLY, TRULY LOVED, I'D DO ANYTHING TO TRY AND GET THEM BACK.
WAIT, DID IT JUST GET DARKER ALL OF A SUDDEN?
IT'S THEM! THE FRACTURES! THEY'VE FOUND US!

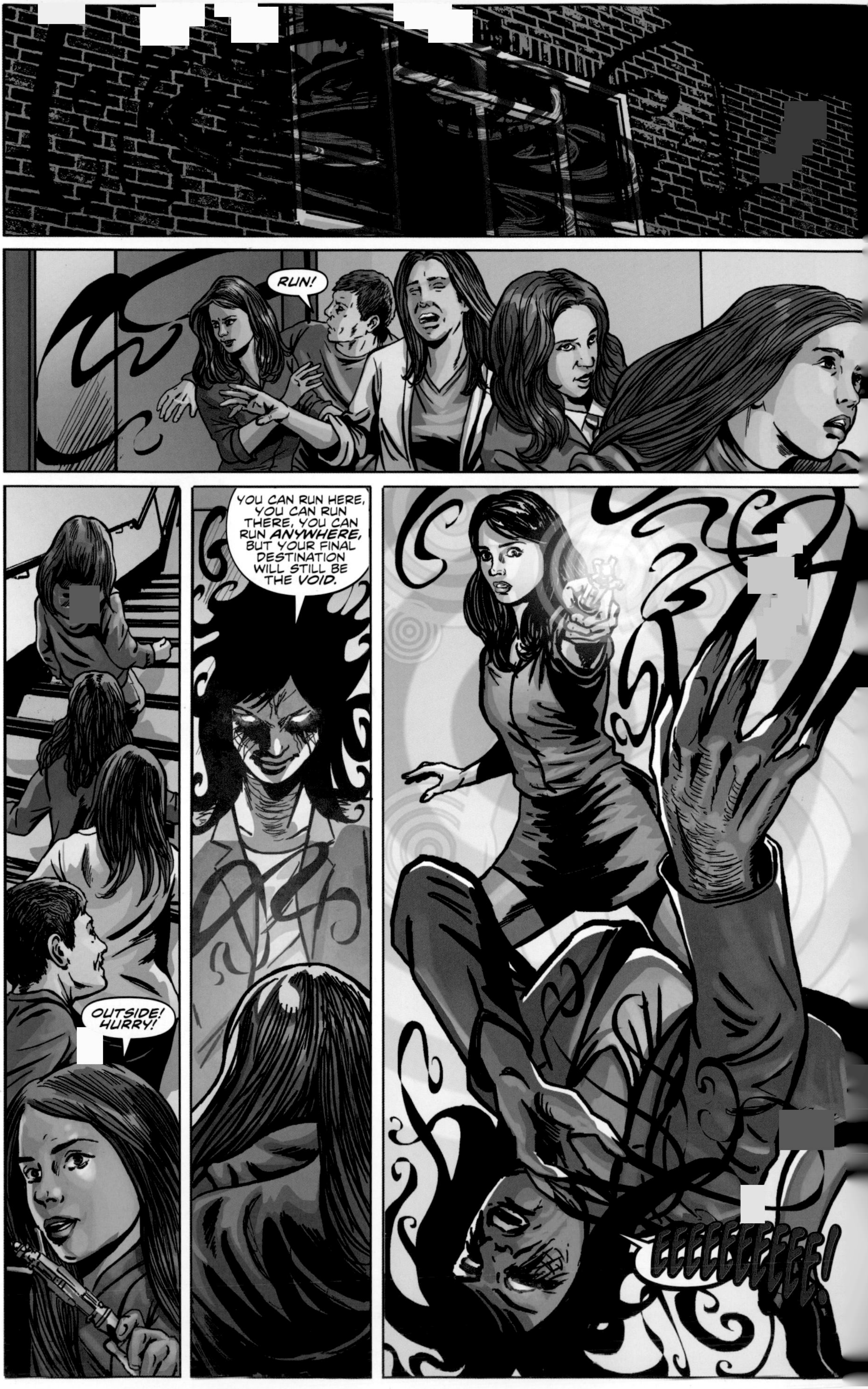
RUN!
YOU CAN RUN HERE, YOU CAN RUN THERE, YOU CAN RUN ANYWHERE, BUT YOUR FINAL DESTINATION WILL STILL BE THE VOID.
OUTSIDE! HURRY!
EEEEEEEEEEEE!

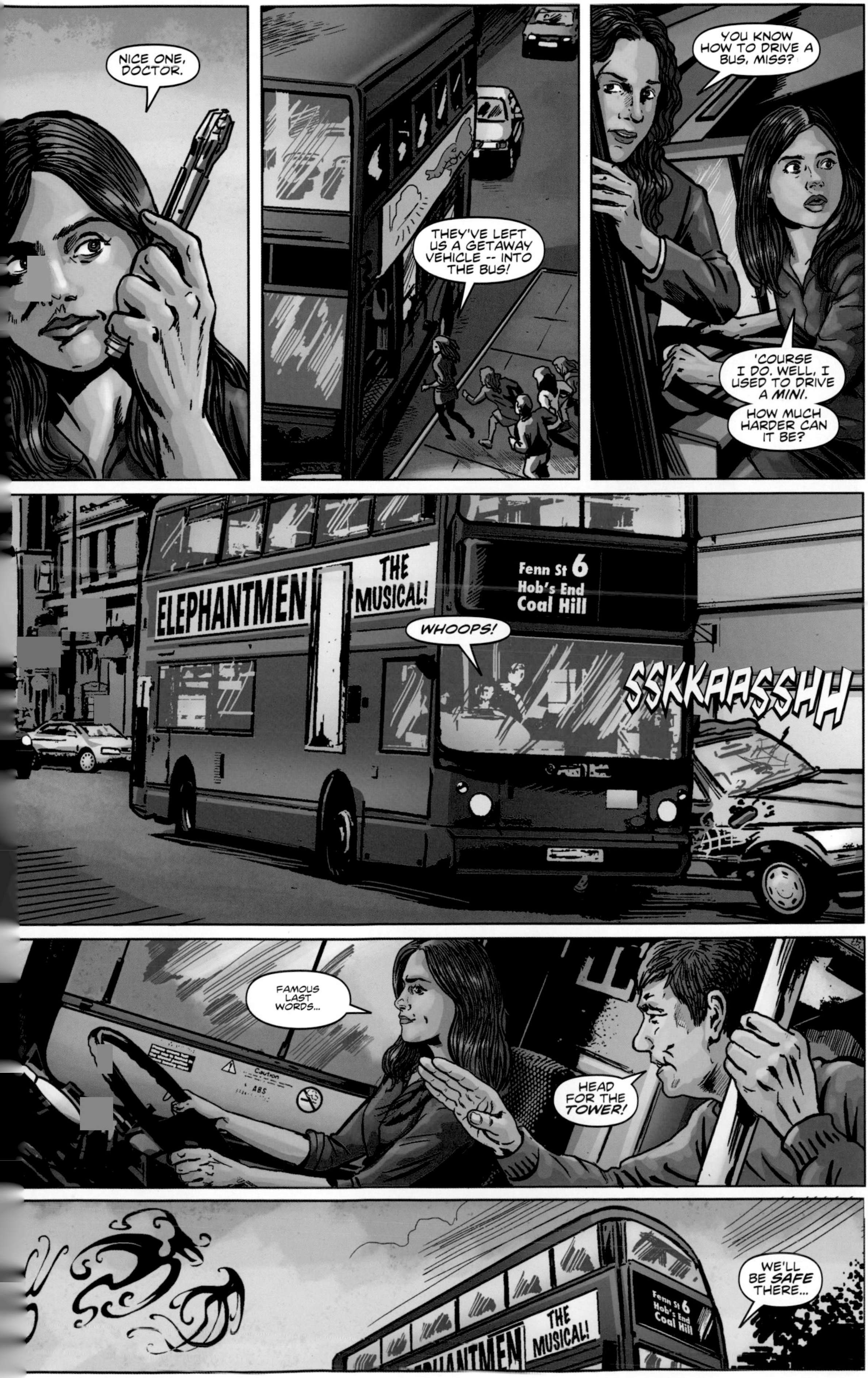
NICE ONE, DOCTOR.
THEY'VE LEFT US A GETAWAY VEHICLE -- INTO THE BUS!
YOU KNOW HOW TO DRIVE A BUS, MISS?
'COURSE I DO. WELL, I USED TO DRIVE A *MINI*.
HOW MUCH HARDER CAN IT BE?
ELEPHANTMEN THE MUSICAL!
Fenn St 6
Hob's End
Coal Hill
WHOOPS!
SSKKAASSHH
FAMOUS LAST WORDS...
Caution
ABS
HEAD FOR THE *TOWER!*
WE'LL BE *SAFE* THERE...

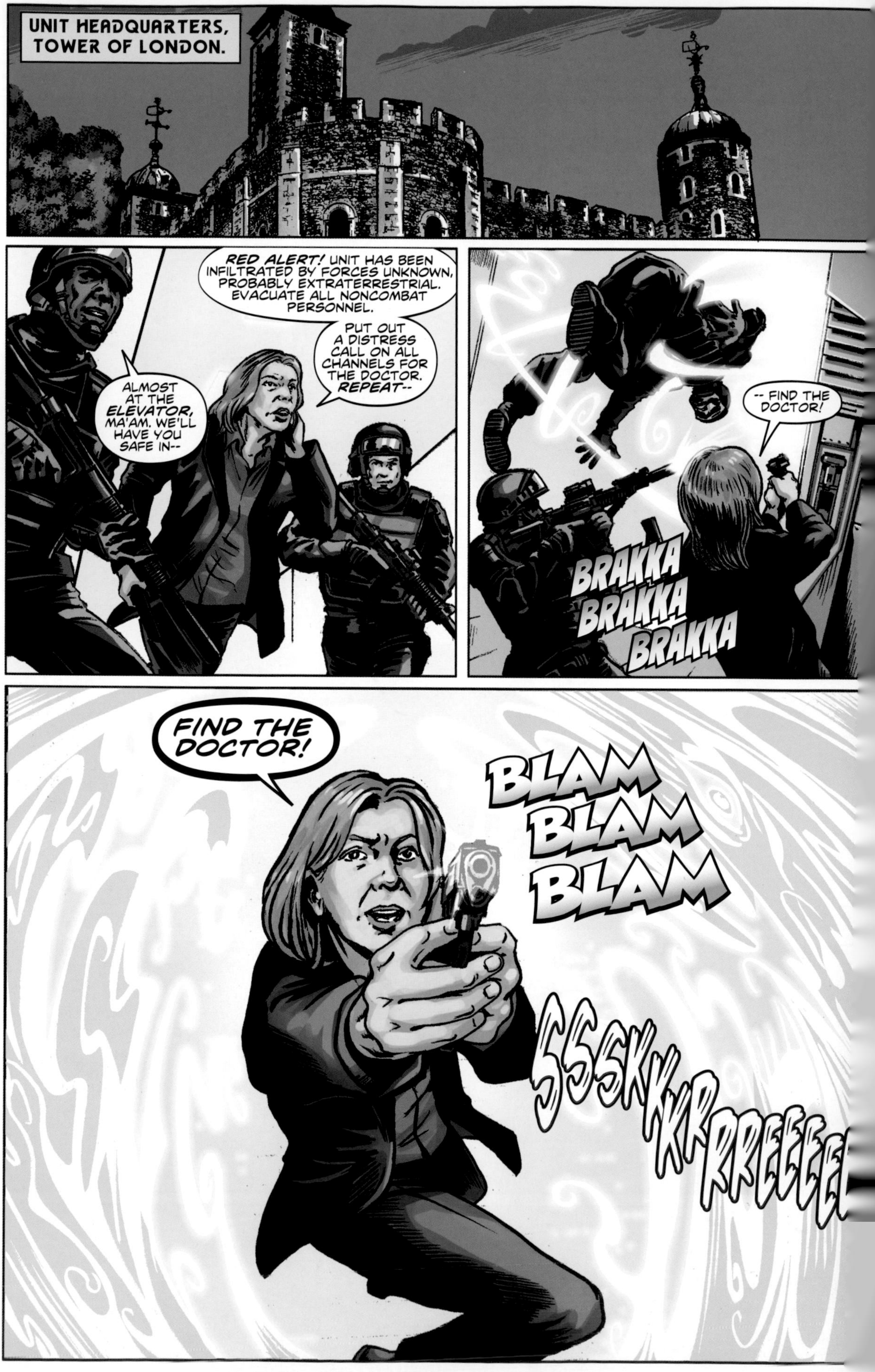
UNIT HEADQUARTERS, TOWER OF LONDON.
RED ALERT! UNIT HAS BEEN INFILTRATED BY FORCES UNKNOWN, PROBABLY EXTRATERRESTRIAL. EVACUATE ALL NONCOMBAT PERSONNEL.
PUT OUT A DISTRESS CALL ON ALL CHANNELS FOR THE DOCTOR. REPEAT--
ALMOST AT THE ELEVATOR, MA'AM. WE'LL HAVE YOU SAFE IN--
-- FIND THE DOCTOR!
BRAKKA
BRAKKA
BRAKKA
FIND THE DOCTOR!
BLAM
BLAM
BLAM
SSSKKRRREEEE

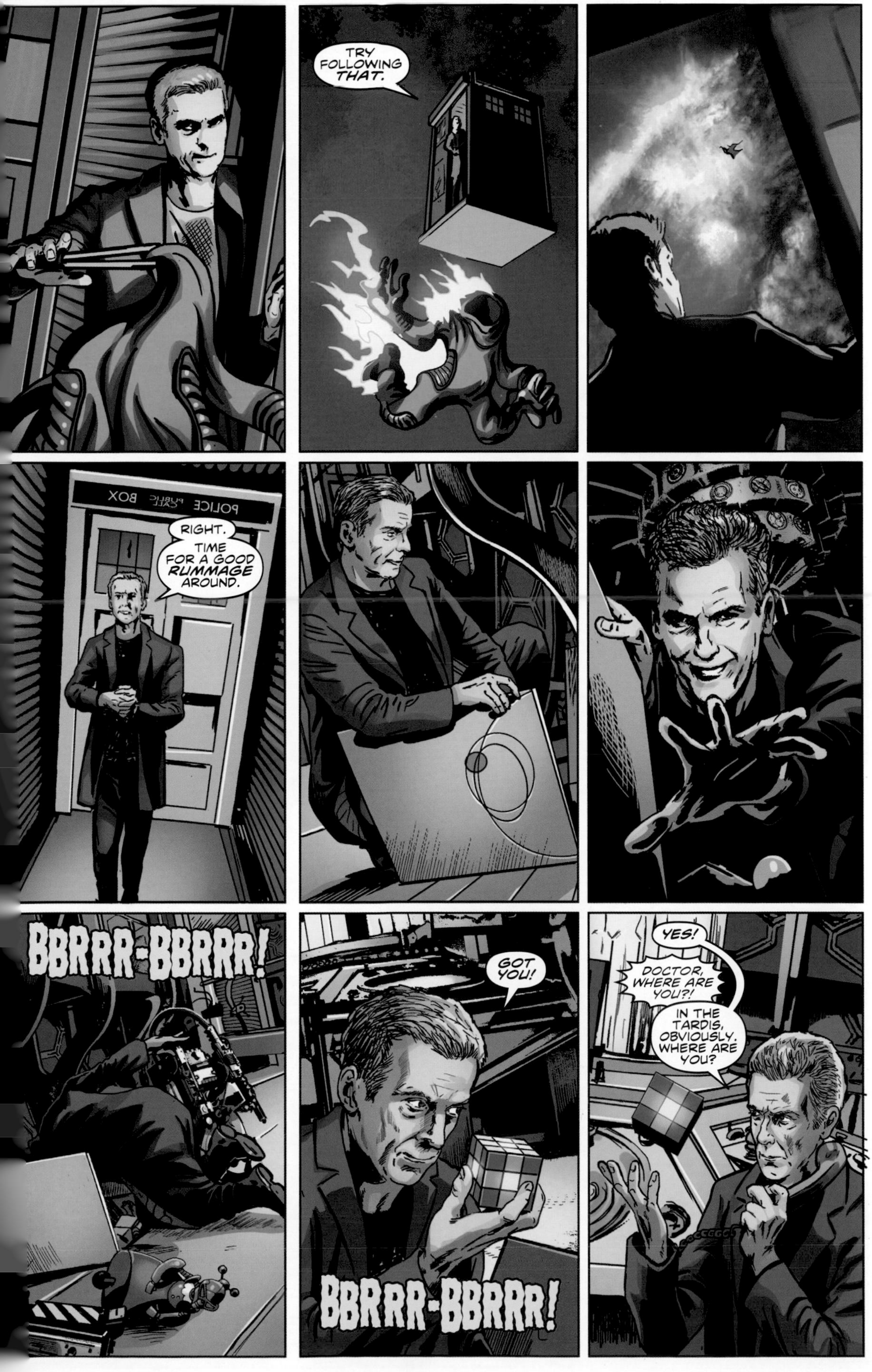
TRY FOLLOWING THAT.
POLICE PUBLIC CALL BOX
RIGHT.
TIME FOR A GOOD RUMMAGE AROUND.
BBRRR-BBRRR!
GOT YOU!
BBRRR-BBRRR!
YES!
DOCTOR, WHERE ARE YOU?!
IN THE TARDIS, OBVIOUSLY. WHERE ARE YOU?

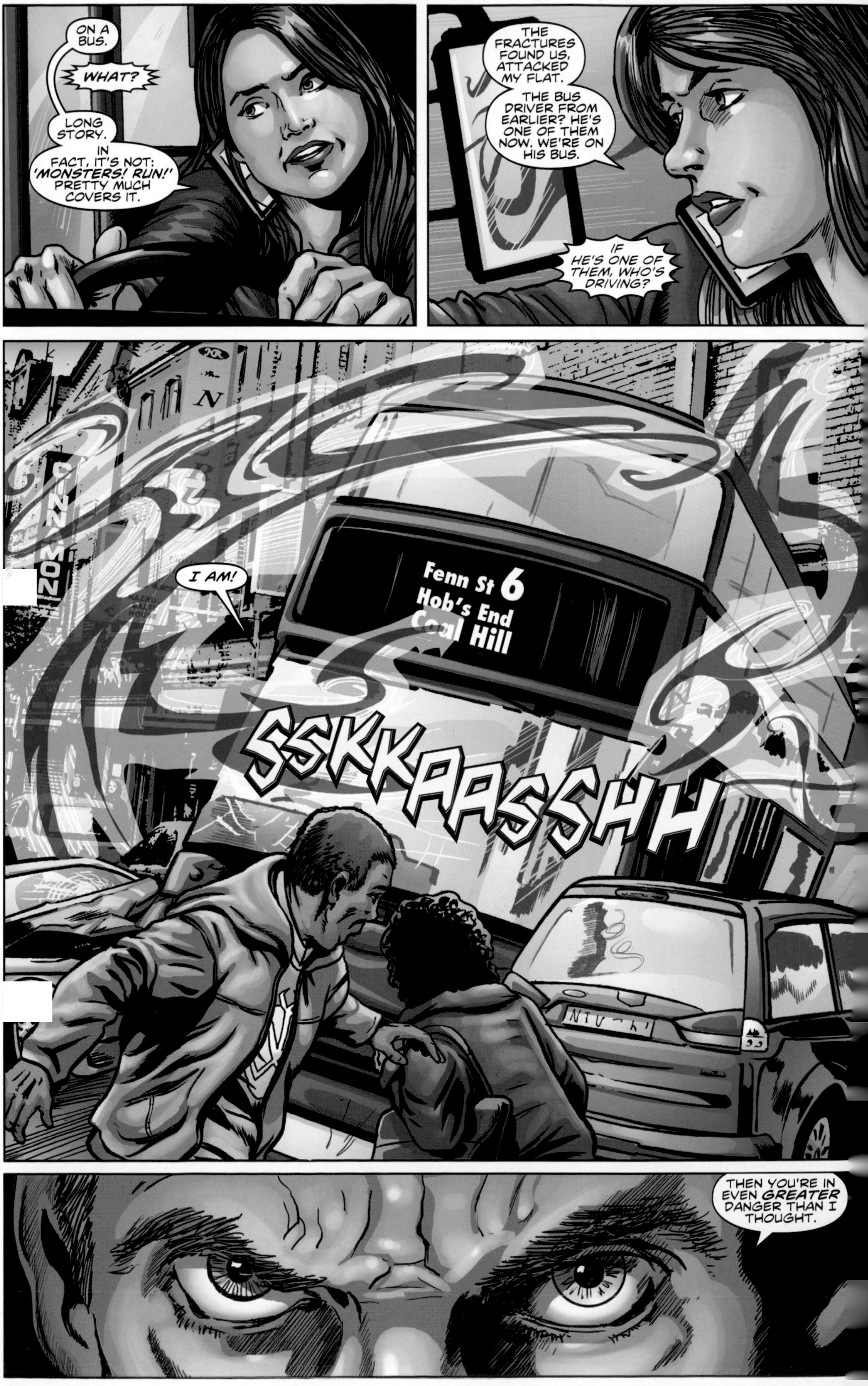
ON A BUS.
WHAT?
LONG STORY.
IN FACT, IT'S NOT: 'MONSTERS! RUN!' PRETTY MUCH COVERS IT.
THE FRACTURES FOUND US, ATTACKED MY FLAT.
THE BUS DRIVER FROM EARLIER? HE'S ONE OF THEM NOW. WE'RE ON HIS BUS.
IF HE'S ONE OF THEM, WHO'S DRIVING?
CINNAMON
Fenn St 6
Hob's End
Coal Hill
I AM!
SSKKAASSHH
THEN YOU'RE IN EVEN GREATER DANGER THAN I THOUGHT.

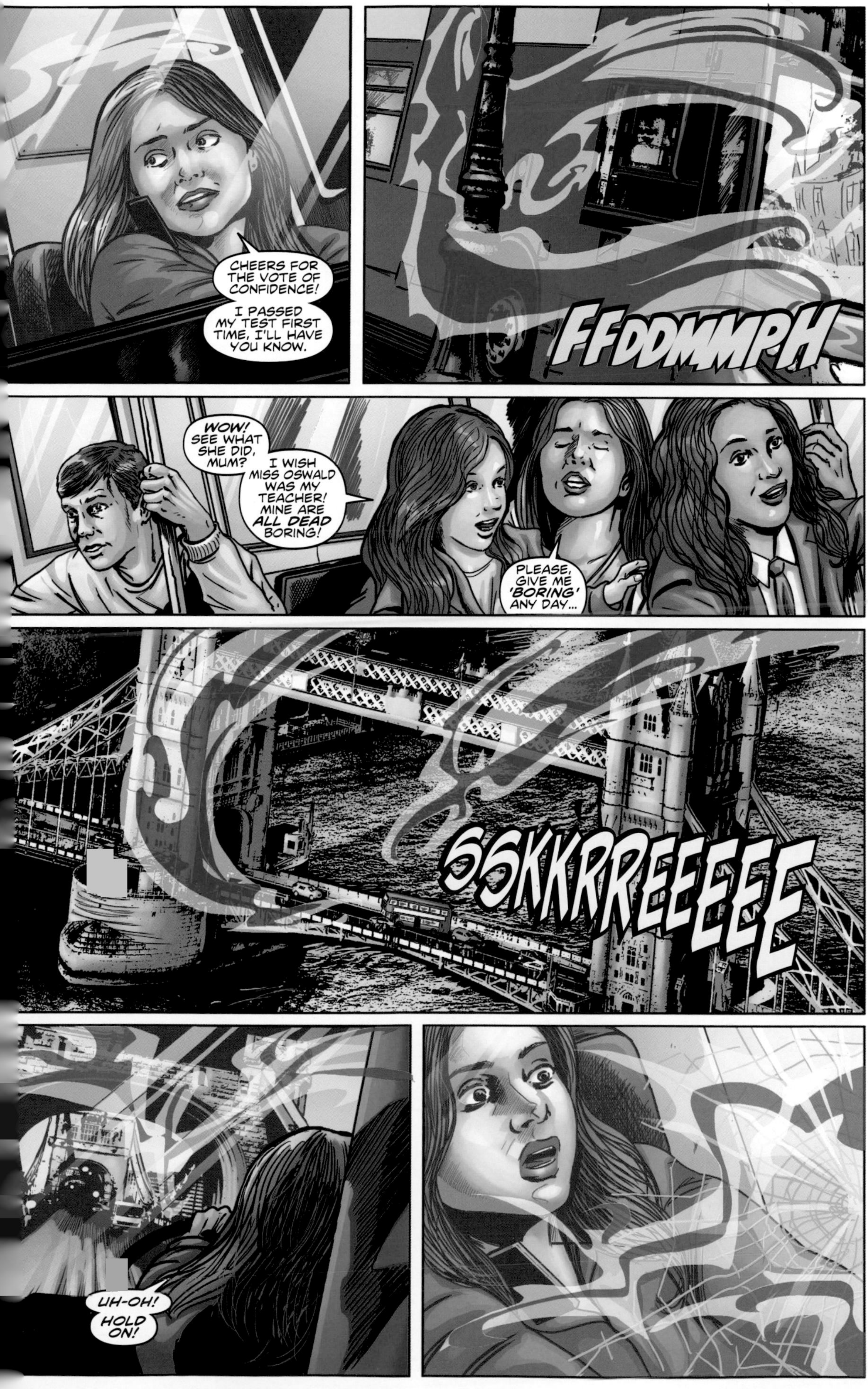
CHEERS FOR THE VOTE OF CONFIDENCE!
I PASSED MY TEST FIRST TIME, I'LL HAVE YOU KNOW.
FFDDMMMPH
WOW! SEE WHAT SHE DID, MUM?
I WISH MISS OSWALD WAS MY TEACHER! MINE ARE ALL DEAD BORING!
PLEASE, GIVE ME 'BORING' ANY DAY...
SSKKRREEEEEE
UH-OH! HOLD ON!

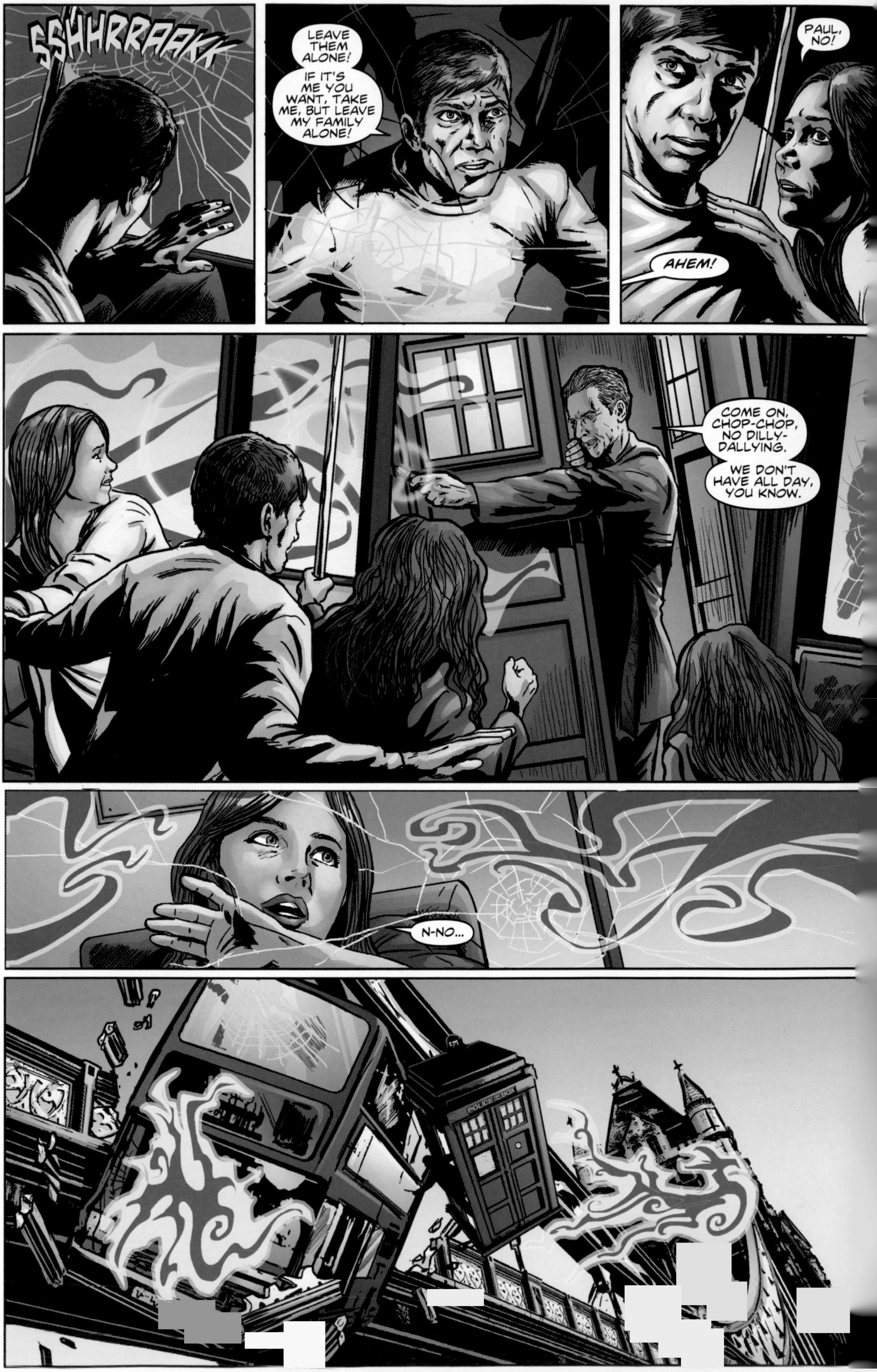
SSHHRRAAKK
LEAVE THEM ALONE!
IF IT'S ME YOU WANT, TAKE ME, BUT LEAVE MY FAMILY ALONE!
PAUL, NO!
AHEM!
COME ON, CHOP-CHOP, NO DILLY-DALLYING.
WE DON'T HAVE ALL DAY, YOU KNOW.
N-NO...
POLICE BOX

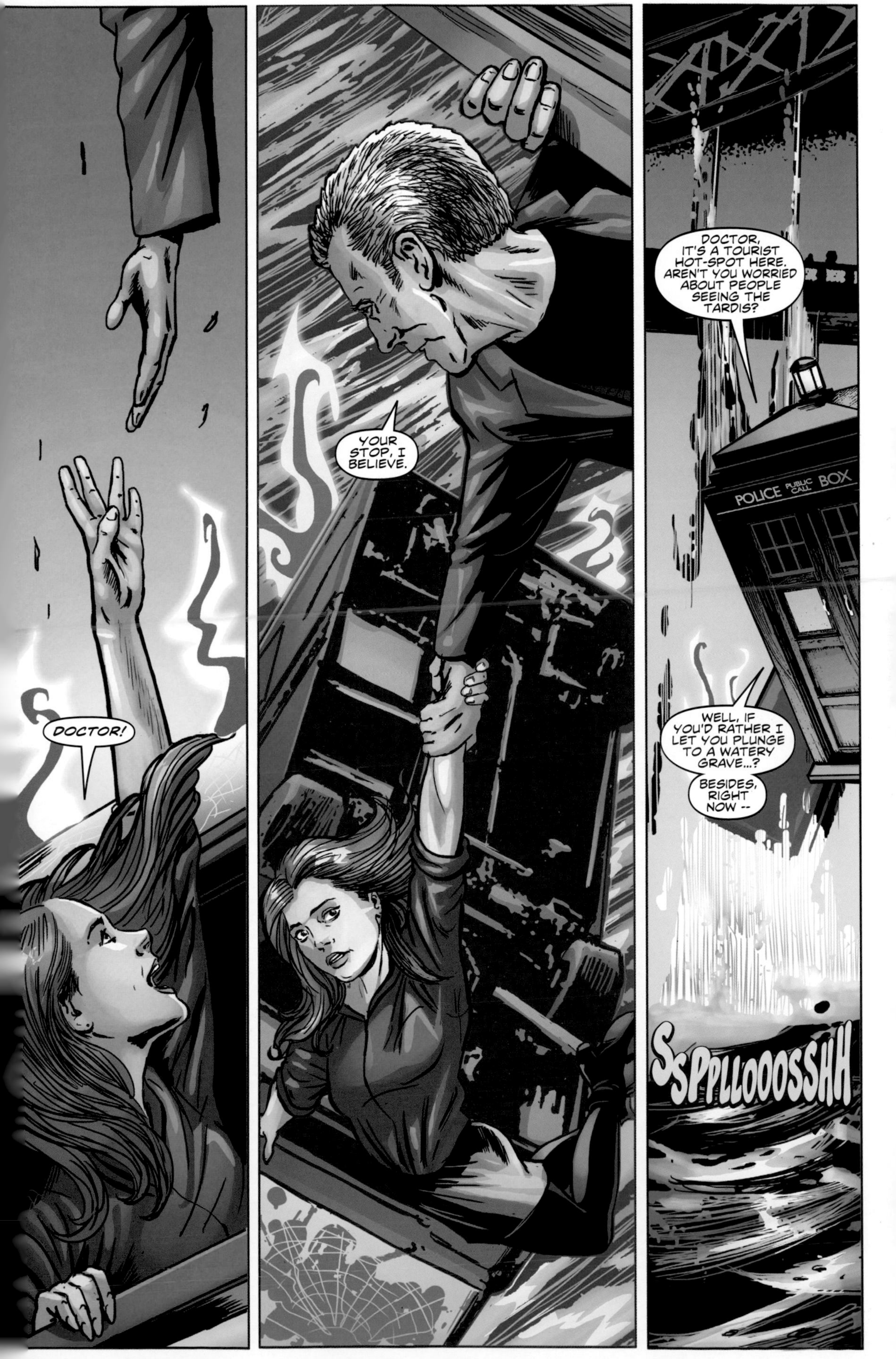
DOCTOR!
YOUR STOP, I BELIEVE.
DOCTOR, IT'S A TOURIST HOT-SPOT HERE. AREN'T YOU WORRIED ABOUT PEOPLE SEEING THE TARDIS?
POLICE PUBLIC CALL BOX
WELL, IF YOU'D RATHER I LET YOU PLUNGE TO A WATERY GRAVE...?
BESIDES, RIGHT NOW --
SSPPLLOOOSSHH

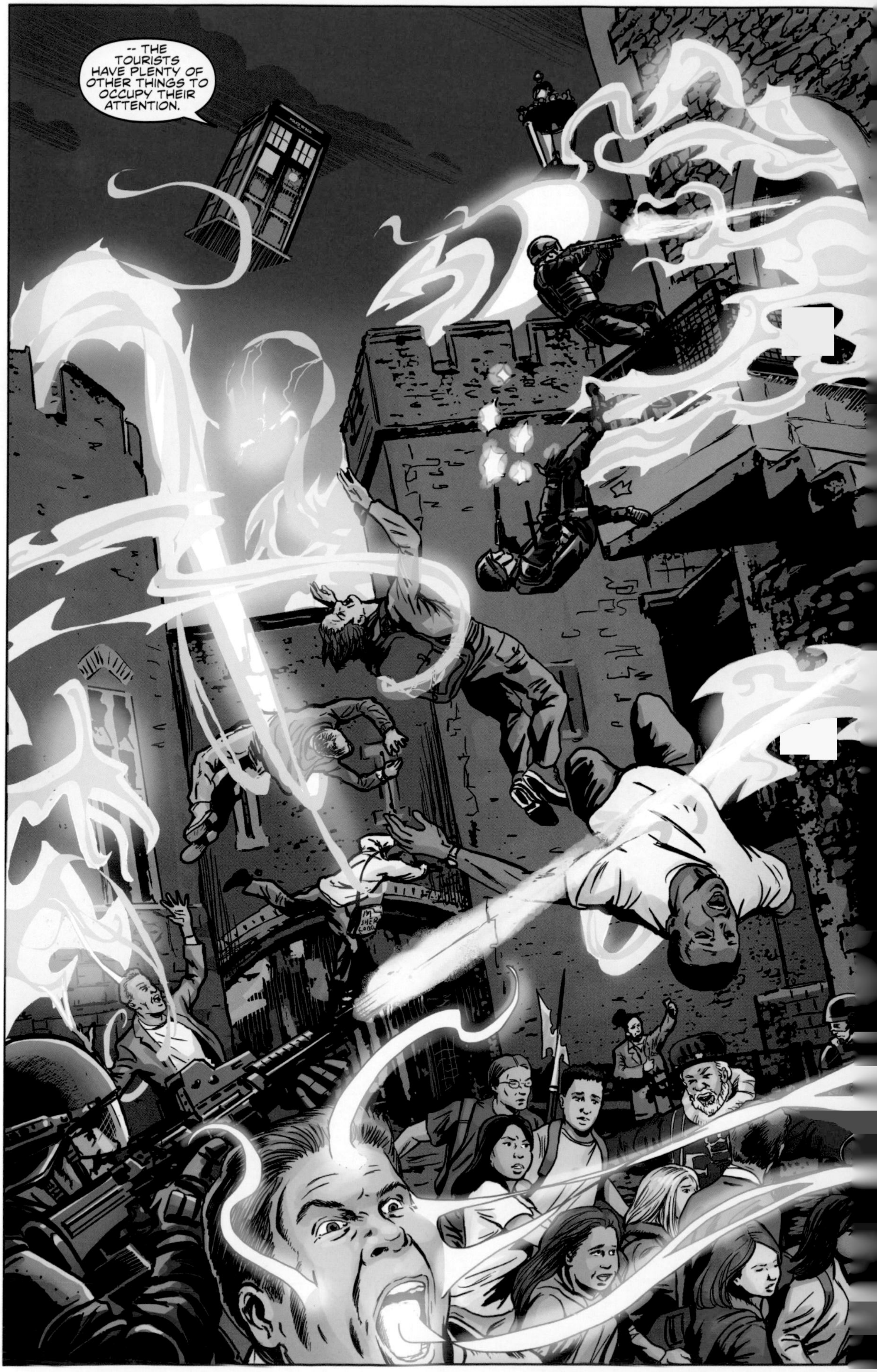
-- THE TOURISTS HAVE PLENTY OF OTHER THINGS TO OCCUPY THEIR ATTENTION.

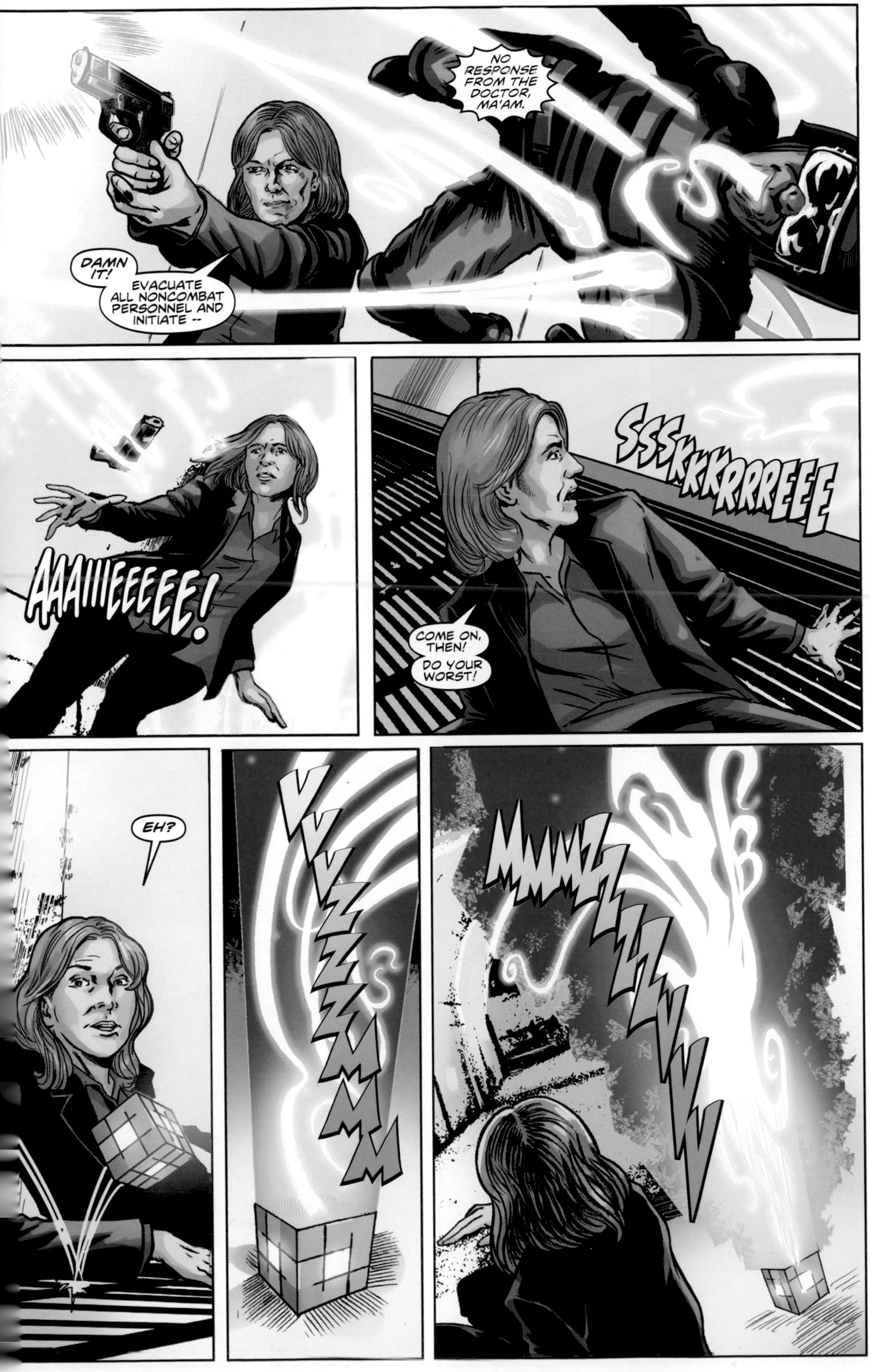
NO RESPONSE FROM THE DOCTOR, MA'AM.
DAMN IT!
EVACUATE ALL NONCOMBAT PERSONNEL AND INITIATE --
AAAIIIEEEEEE!
SSSKKKRRRREEEE
COME ON, THEN!
DO YOUR WORST!
EH?
VVVZZZZMMM
MMMZZZZVVVV

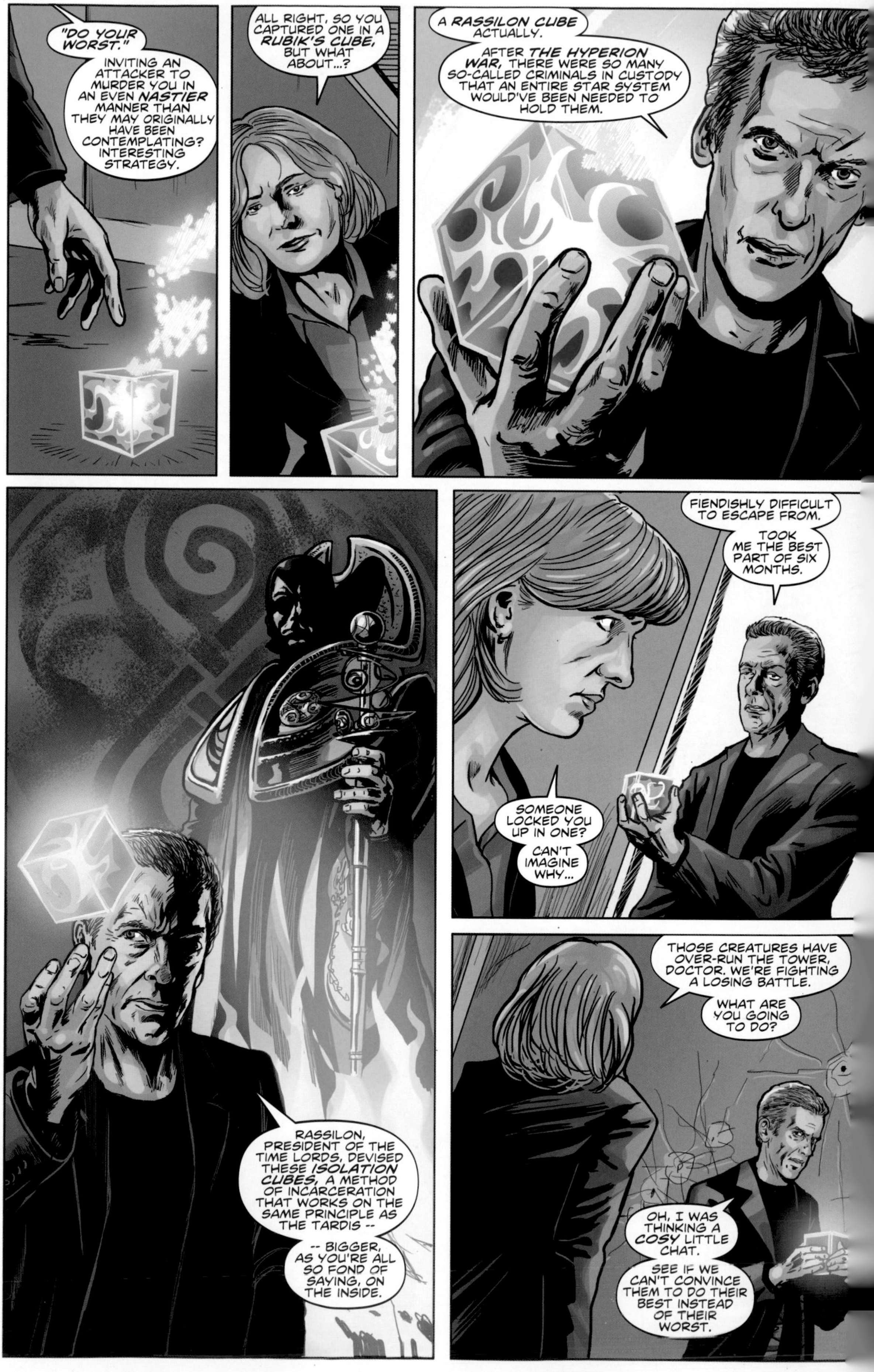
"DO YOUR WORST."
INVITING AN ATTACKER TO MURDER YOU IN AN EVEN NASTIER MANNER THAN THEY MAY HAVE ORIGINALLY BEEN CONTEMPLATING? INTERESTING STRATEGY.
ALL RIGHT, SO YOU CAPTURED ONE IN A RUBIK'S CUBE, BUT WHAT ABOUT...?
A RASSILON CUBE ACTUALLY.
AFTER THE HYPERION WAR, THERE WERE SO MANY SO-CALLED CRIMINALS IN CUSTODY THAT AN ENTIRE STAR SYSTEM WOULD'VE BEEN NEEDED TO HOLD THEM.
RASSILON, PRESIDENT OF THE TIME LORDS, DEVISED THESE ISOLATION CUBES, A METHOD OF INCARCERATION THAT WORKS ON THE SAME PRINCIPLE AS THE TARDIS --
-- BIGGER, AS YOU'RE ALL SO FOND OF SAYING, ON THE INSIDE.
FIENDISHLY DIFFICULT TO ESCAPE FROM.
TOOK ME THE BEST PART OF SIX MONTHS.
SOMEONE LOCKED YOU UP IN ONE?
CAN'T IMAGINE WHY...
THOSE CREATURES HAVE OVER-RUN THE TOWER, DOCTOR. WE'RE FIGHTING A LOSING BATTLE.
WHAT ARE YOU GOING TO DO?
OH, I WAS THINKING A COSY LITTLE CHAT.
SEE IF WE CAN'T CONVINCE THEM TO DO THEIR BEST INSTEAD OF THEIR WORST.

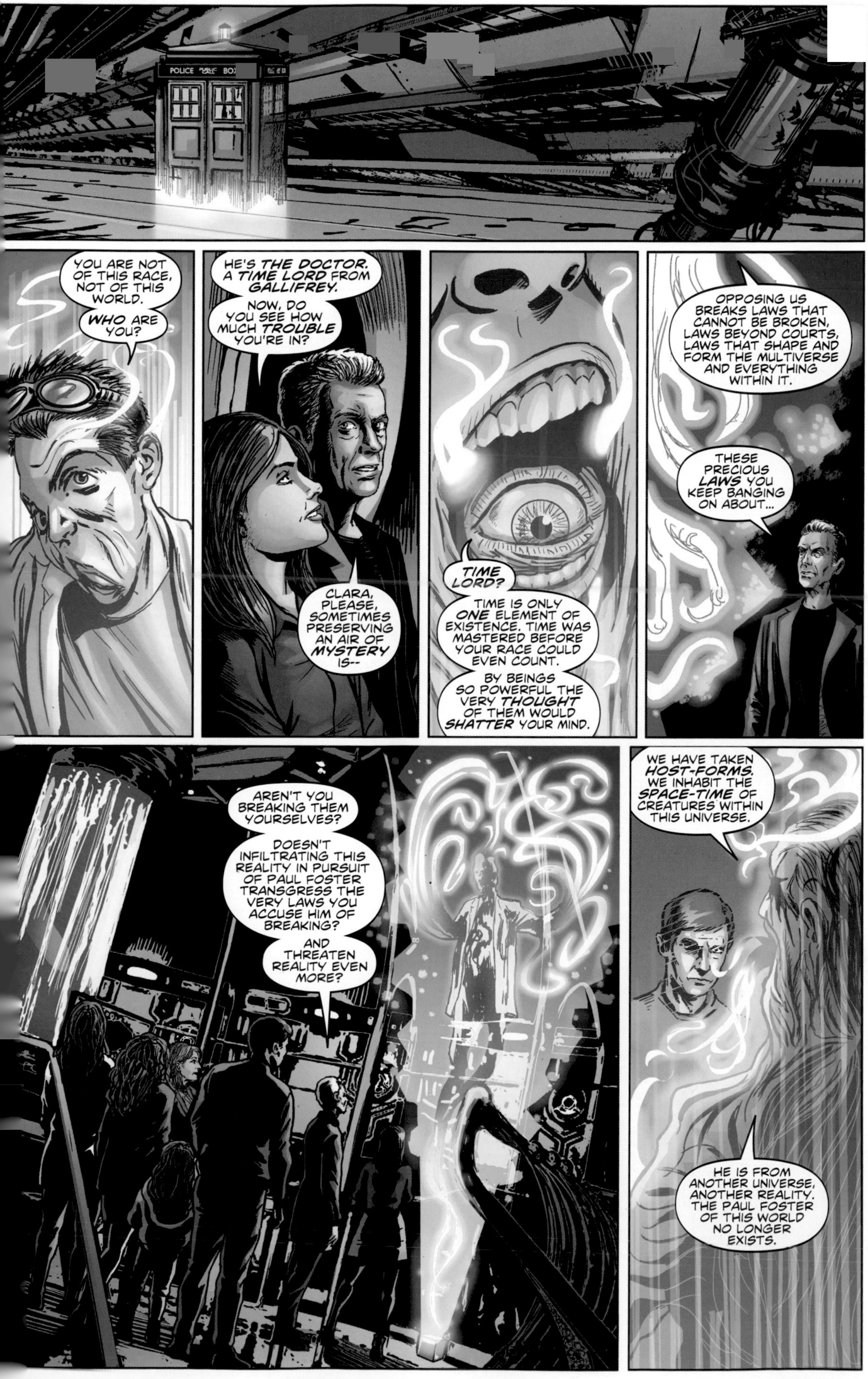
POLICE PUBLIC CALL BOX
YOU ARE NOT OF THIS RACE, NOT OF THIS WORLD.
WHO ARE YOU?
HE'S THE DOCTOR. A TIME LORD FROM GALLIFREY.
NOW, DO YOU SEE HOW MUCH TROUBLE YOU'RE IN?
CLARA, PLEASE, SOMETIMES PRESERVING AN AIR OF MYSTERY IS--
TIME LORD?
TIME IS ONLY ONE ELEMENT OF EXISTENCE. TIME WAS MASTERED BEFORE YOUR RACE COULD EVEN COUNT.
BY BEINGS SO POWERFUL THE VERY THOUGHT OF THEM WOULD SHATTER YOUR MIND.
OPPOSING US BREAKS LAWS THAT CANNOT BE BROKEN, LAWS BEYOND COURTS, LAWS THAT SHAPE AND FORM THE MULTIVERSE AND EVERYTHING WITHIN IT.
THESE PRECIOUS LAWS YOU KEEP BANGING ON ABOUT...
AREN'T YOU BREAKING THEM YOURSELVES?
DOESN'T INFILTRATING THIS REALITY IN PURSUIT OF PAUL FOSTER TRANSGRESS THE VERY LAWS YOU ACCUSE HIM OF BREAKING?
AND THREATEN REALITY EVEN MORE?
WE HAVE TAKEN HOST-FORMS. WE INHABIT THE SPACE-TIME OF CREATURES WITHIN THIS UNIVERSE.
HE IS FROM ANOTHER UNIVERSE, ANOTHER REALITY. THE PAUL FOSTER OF THIS WORLD NO LONGER EXISTS.

SO, YOUR PRESENCE HERE IS A FORM OF *TEMPORAL DISPLACEMENT.*

YOU FORCE YOUR WAY INTO THIS WORLD, WHILE SIMULTANEOUSLY FORCING YOUR SO-CALLED HOSTS OUT OF IT.

YOU STEAL THEIR FORMS, INHABIT THEIR THREE-DIMENSIONAL SPACE, WHILE TRAPPING THEM IN YOURS.

"IN THE *VOID.*

"NOT EXACTLY THE HOLIDAY OF A LIFETIME FOR THEM."

A NECESSARY EVIL. REALITY MUST BE --

THERE! THAT'S IT. THAT'S THE WORD.

NECESSARY OR NOT, WE ALWAYS HAVE TO AT LEAST TRY TO DO BETTER THAN 'EVIL'.

THANKS, YOU'VE BEEN VERY HELPFUL. I KNOW EXACTLY WHAT I HAVE TO DO.

BACK IN YOUR BOX NOW.

NO! OPPOSE US AND ALL THE POWER OF EXISTENCE WILL BE AGAINST YOU!

AGAINST *YOU,* DOCTOR!

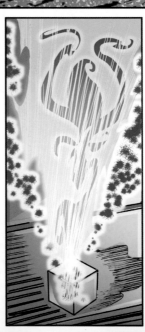

SO, YOU KNOW *EXACTLY* WHAT TO DO?.

OF COURSE! STILL MORE BRAIN IN HERE THAN PUDDING.

MIND SHARING? I AM MEANT TO BE IN CHARGE HERE...

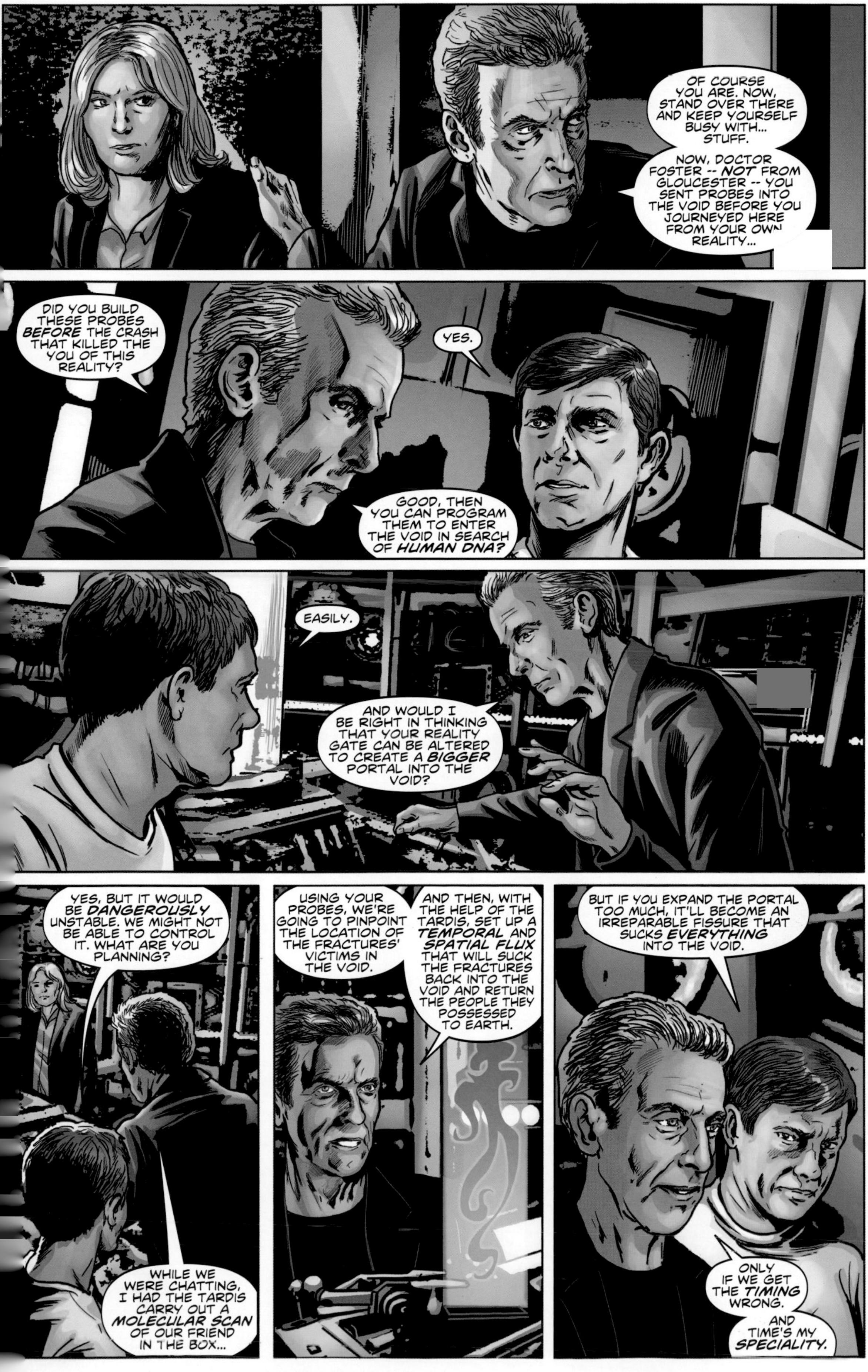
OF COURSE YOU ARE. NOW, STAND OVER THERE AND KEEP YOURSELF BUSY WITH... STUFF.
NOW, DOCTOR FOSTER -- NOT FROM GLOUCESTER -- YOU SENT PROBES INTO THE VOID BEFORE YOU JOURNEYED HERE FROM YOUR OWN REALITY...
DID YOU BUILD THESE PROBES BEFORE THE CRASH THAT KILLED THE YOU OF THIS REALITY?
YES.
GOOD, THEN YOU CAN PROGRAM THEM TO ENTER THE VOID IN SEARCH OF HUMAN DNA?
EASILY.
AND WOULD I BE RIGHT IN THINKING THAT YOUR REALITY GATE CAN BE ALTERED TO CREATE A BIGGER PORTAL INTO THE VOID?
YES, BUT IT WOULD BE DANGEROUSLY UNSTABLE. WE MIGHT NOT BE ABLE TO CONTROL IT. WHAT ARE YOU PLANNING?
WHILE WE WERE CHATTING, I HAD THE TARDIS CARRY OUT A MOLECULAR SCAN OF OUR FRIEND IN THE BOX...
USING YOUR PROBES, WE'RE GOING TO PINPOINT THE LOCATION OF THE FRACTURES' VICTIMS IN THE VOID.
AND THEN, WITH THE HELP OF THE TARDIS, SET UP A TEMPORAL AND SPATIAL FLUX THAT WILL SUCK THE FRACTURES BACK INTO THE VOID AND RETURN THE PEOPLE THEY POSSESSED TO EARTH.
BUT IF YOU EXPAND THE PORTAL TOO MUCH, IT'LL BECOME AN IRREPARABLE FISSURE THAT SUCKS EVERYTHING INTO THE VOID.
ONLY IF WE GET THE TIMING WRONG.
AND TIME'S MY SPECIALITY.

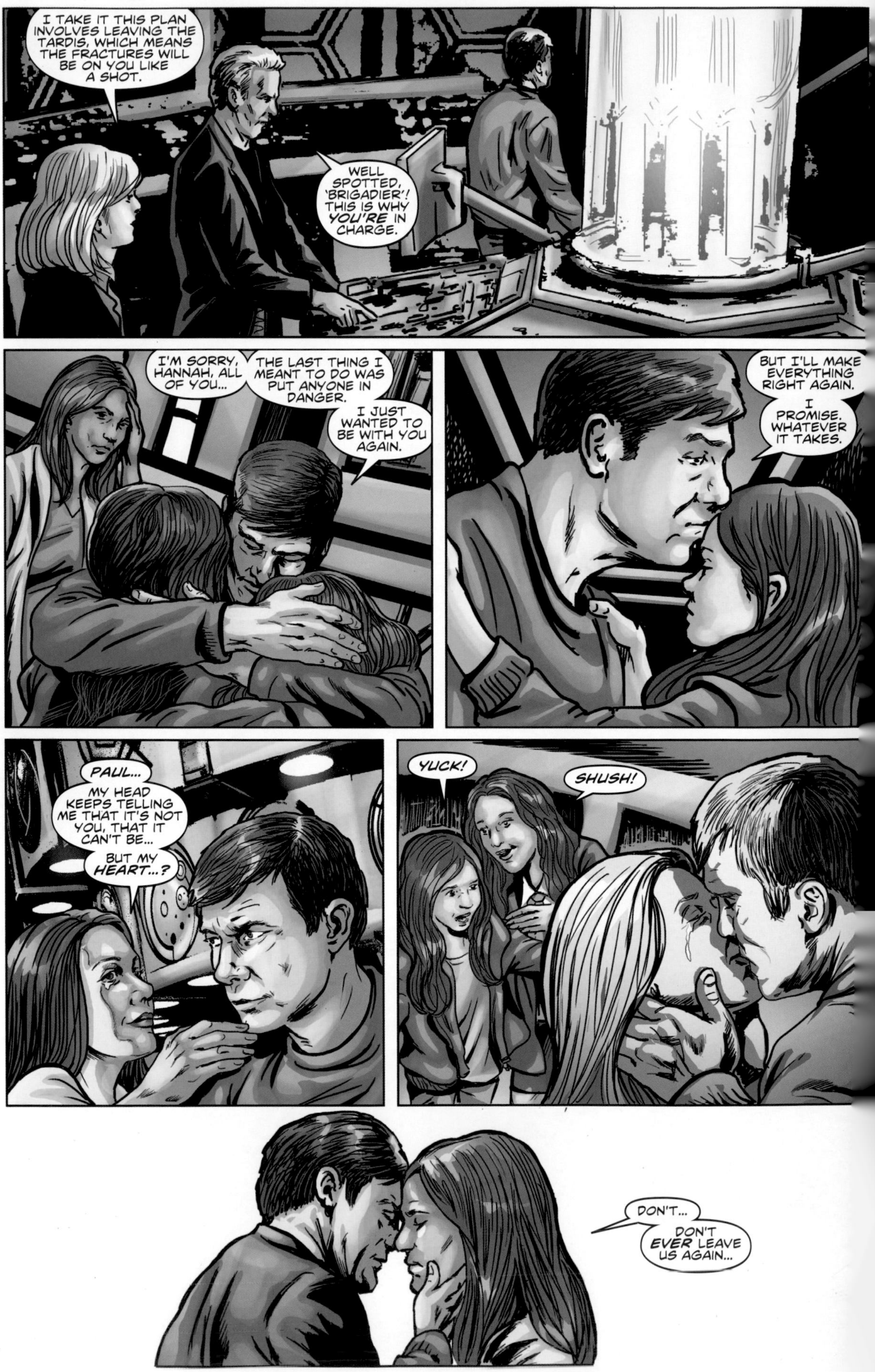

I TAKE IT THIS PLAN INVOLVES LEAVING THE TARDIS, WHICH MEANS THE FRACTURES WILL BE ON YOU LIKE A SHOT.
WELL SPOTTED, 'BRIGADIER'! THIS IS WHY YOU'RE IN CHARGE.
I'M SORRY, HANNAH, ALL OF YOU...
THE LAST THING I MEANT TO DO WAS PUT ANYONE IN DANGER.
I JUST WANTED TO BE WITH YOU AGAIN.
BUT I'LL MAKE EVERYTHING RIGHT AGAIN.
I PROMISE. WHATEVER IT TAKES.
PAUL...
MY HEAD KEEPS TELLING ME THAT IT'S NOT YOU, THAT IT CAN'T BE...
BUT MY HEART...?
YUCK!
SHUSH!
DON'T...
DON'T EVER LEAVE US AGAIN...

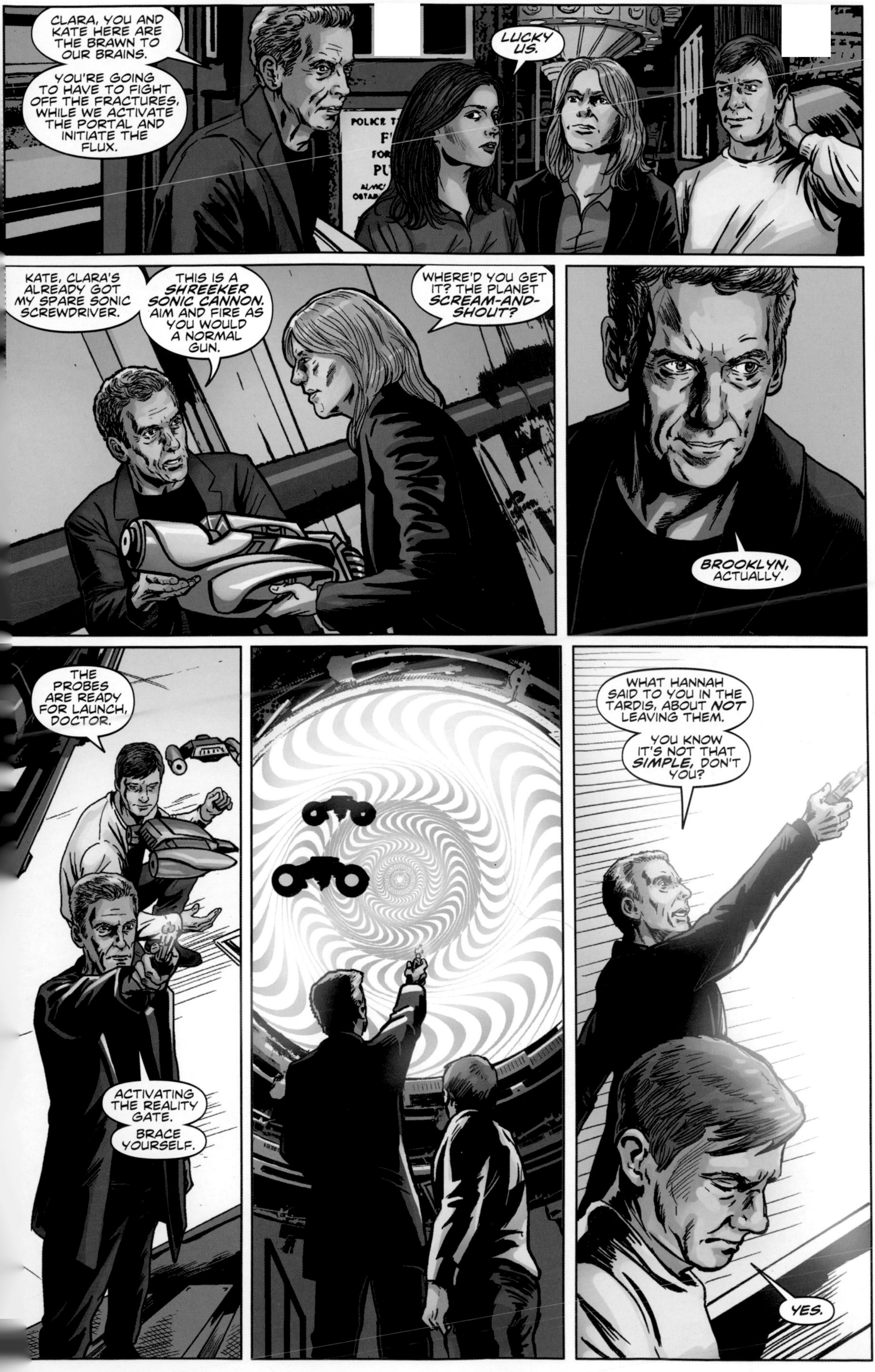
CLARA, YOU AND KATE HERE ARE THE BRAWN TO OUR BRAINS.
YOU'RE GOING TO HAVE TO FIGHT OFF THE FRACTURES, WHILE WE ACTIVATE THE PORTAL AND INITIATE THE FLUX.
LUCKY US.
KATE, CLARA'S ALREADY GOT MY SPARE SONIC SCREWDRIVER.
THIS IS A SHREEKER SONIC CANNON. AIM AND FIRE AS YOU WOULD A NORMAL GUN.
WHERE'D YOU GET IT? THE PLANET SCREAM-AND-SHOUT?
BROOKLYN, ACTUALLY.
THE PROBES ARE READY FOR LAUNCH, DOCTOR.
ACTIVATING THE REALITY GATE.
BRACE YOURSELF.
WHAT HANNAH SAID TO YOU IN THE TARDIS, ABOUT NOT LEAVING THEM.
YOU KNOW IT'S NOT THAT SIMPLE, DON'T YOU?
YES.

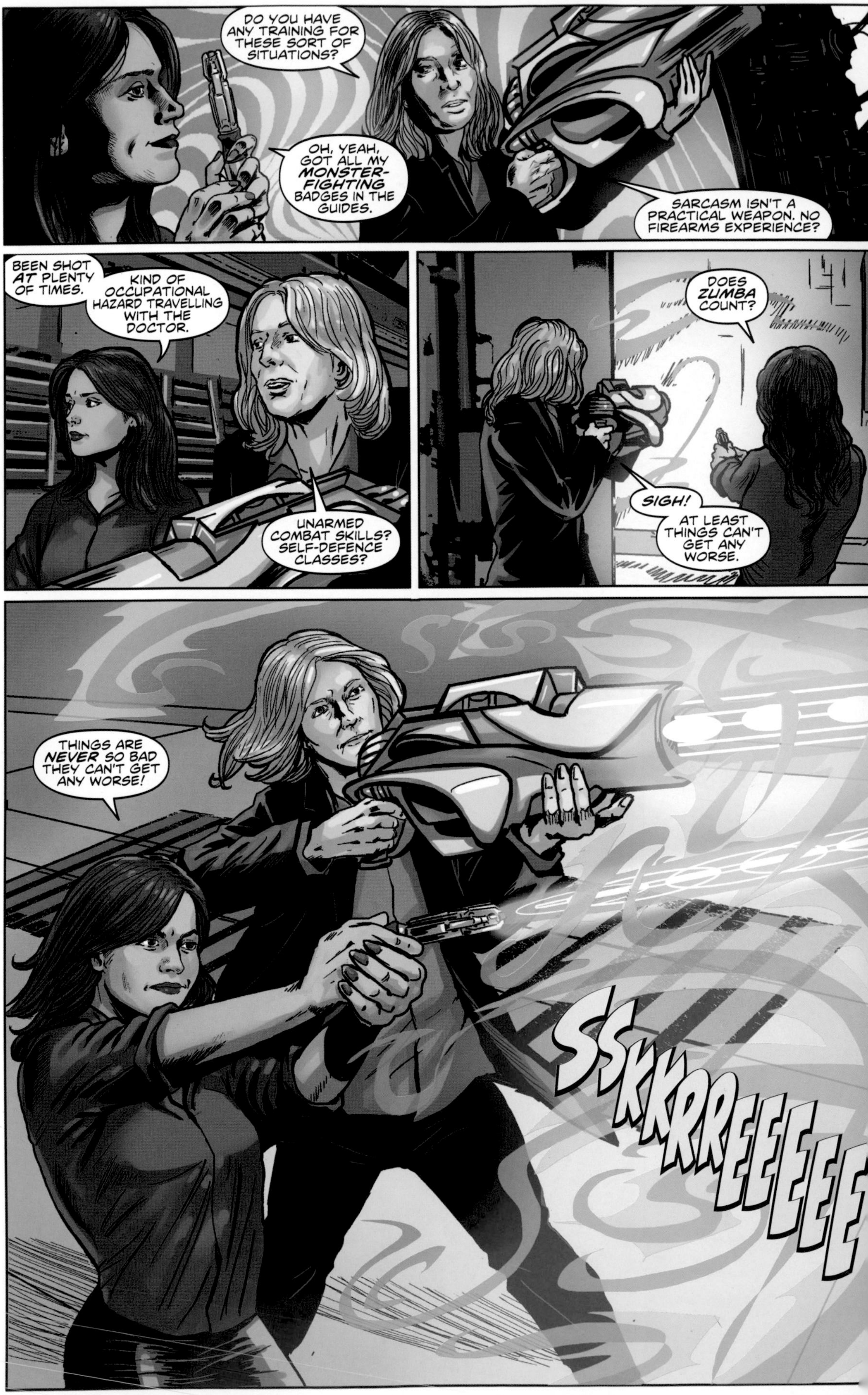
DO YOU HAVE ANY TRAINING FOR THESE SORT OF SITUATIONS?
OH, YEAH, GOT ALL MY MONSTER-FIGHTING BADGES IN THE GUIDES.
SARCASM ISN'T A PRACTICAL WEAPON. NO FIREARMS EXPERIENCE?
BEEN SHOT AT PLENTY OF TIMES.
KIND OF OCCUPATIONAL HAZARD TRAVELLING WITH THE DOCTOR.
UNARMED COMBAT SKILLS? SELF-DEFENCE CLASSES?
DOES ZUMBA COUNT?
SIGH!
AT LEAST THINGS CAN'T GET ANY WORSE.
THINGS ARE NEVER SO BAD THEY CAN'T GET ANY WORSE!
SSKKRREEEEEE

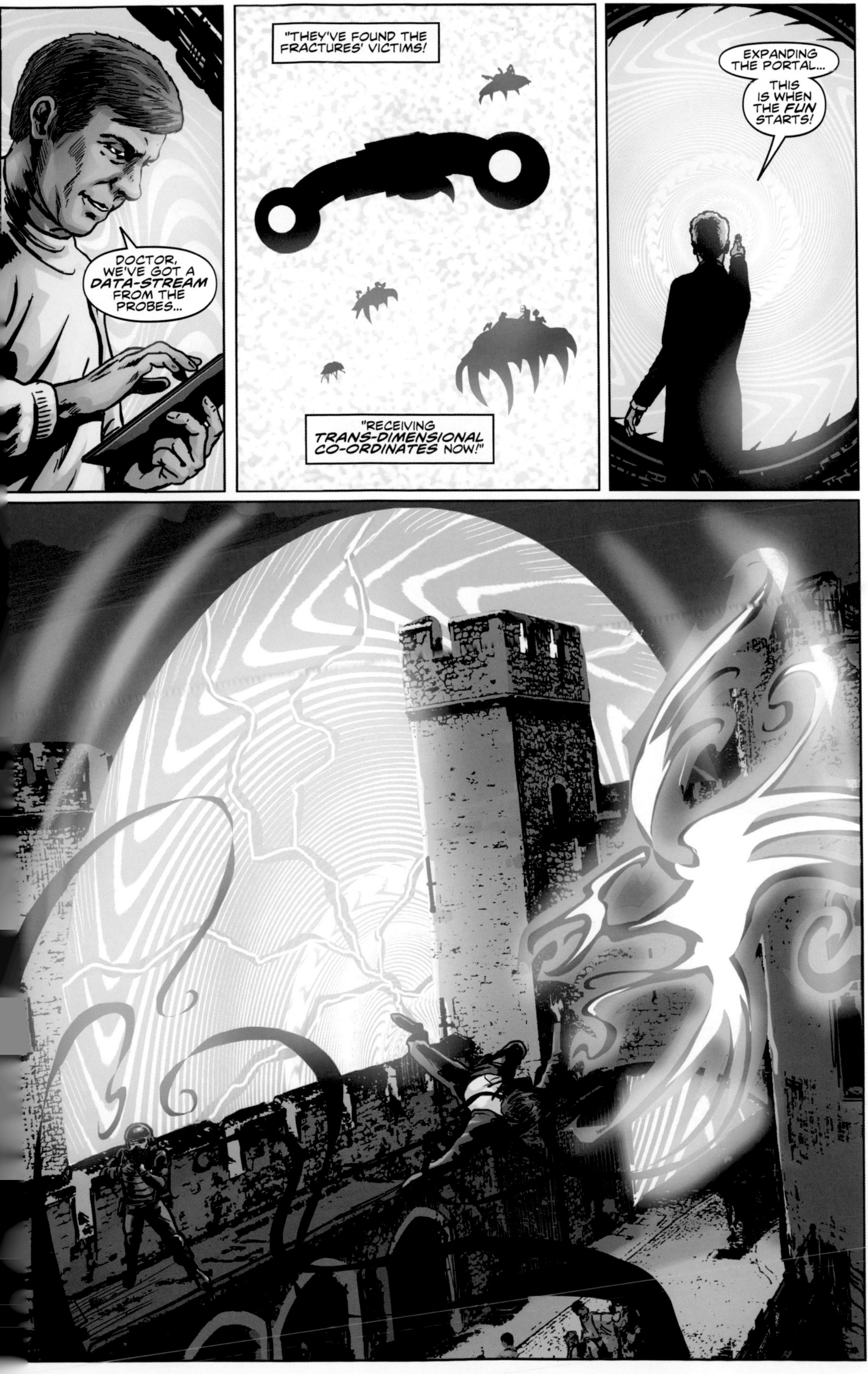
DOCTOR, WE'VE GOT A DATA-STREAM FROM THE PROBES...
"THEY'VE FOUND THE FRACTURES' VICTIMS!
"RECEIVING TRANS-DIMENSIONAL CO-ORDINATES NOW!"
EXPANDING THE PORTAL...
THIS IS WHEN THE FUN STARTS!

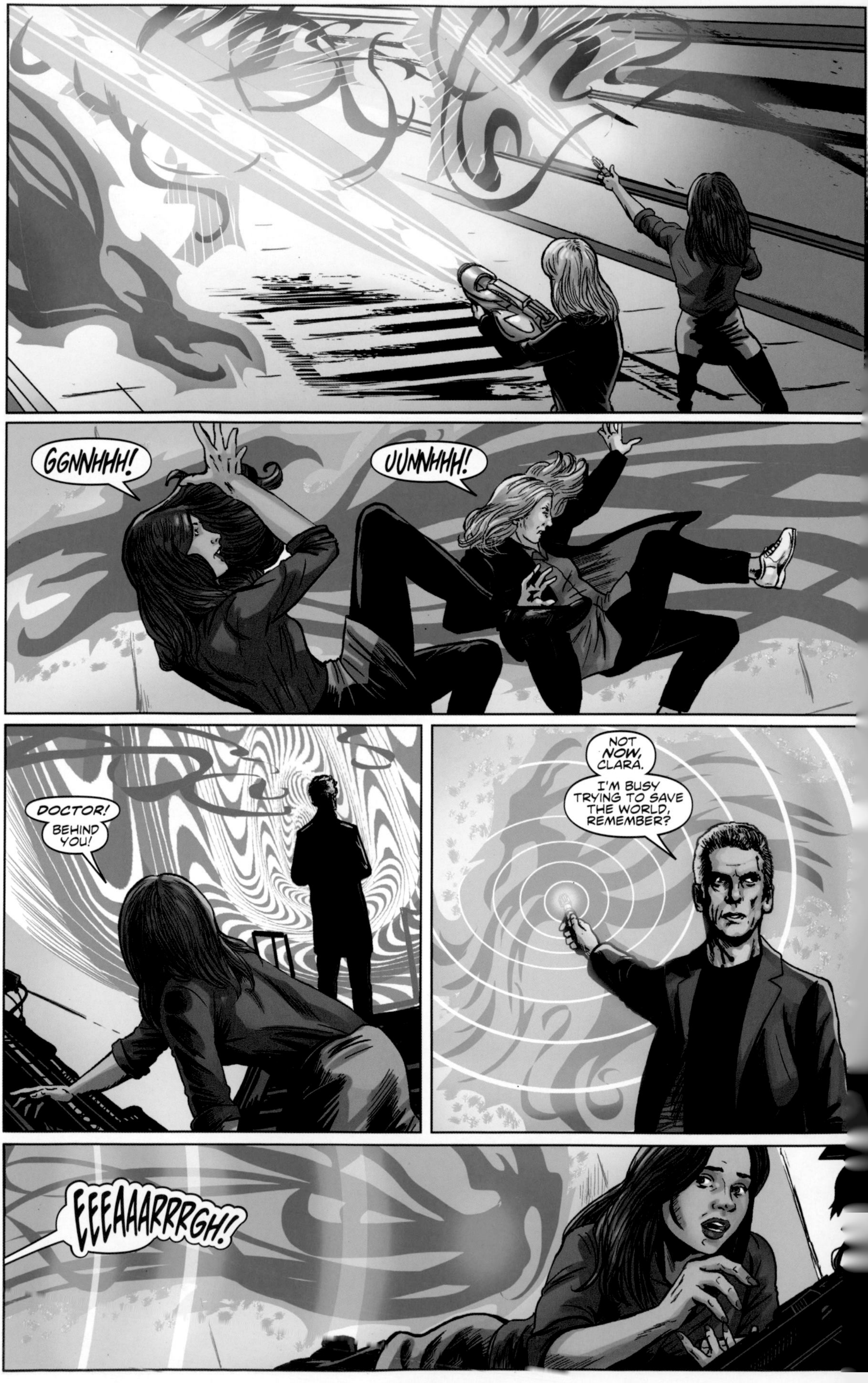
GGNHHH!
UUNHHH!
DOCTOR! BEHIND YOU!
NOT NOW, CLARA.
I'M BUSY TRYING TO SAVE THE WORLD, REMEMBER?
EEEAAARRRGH!

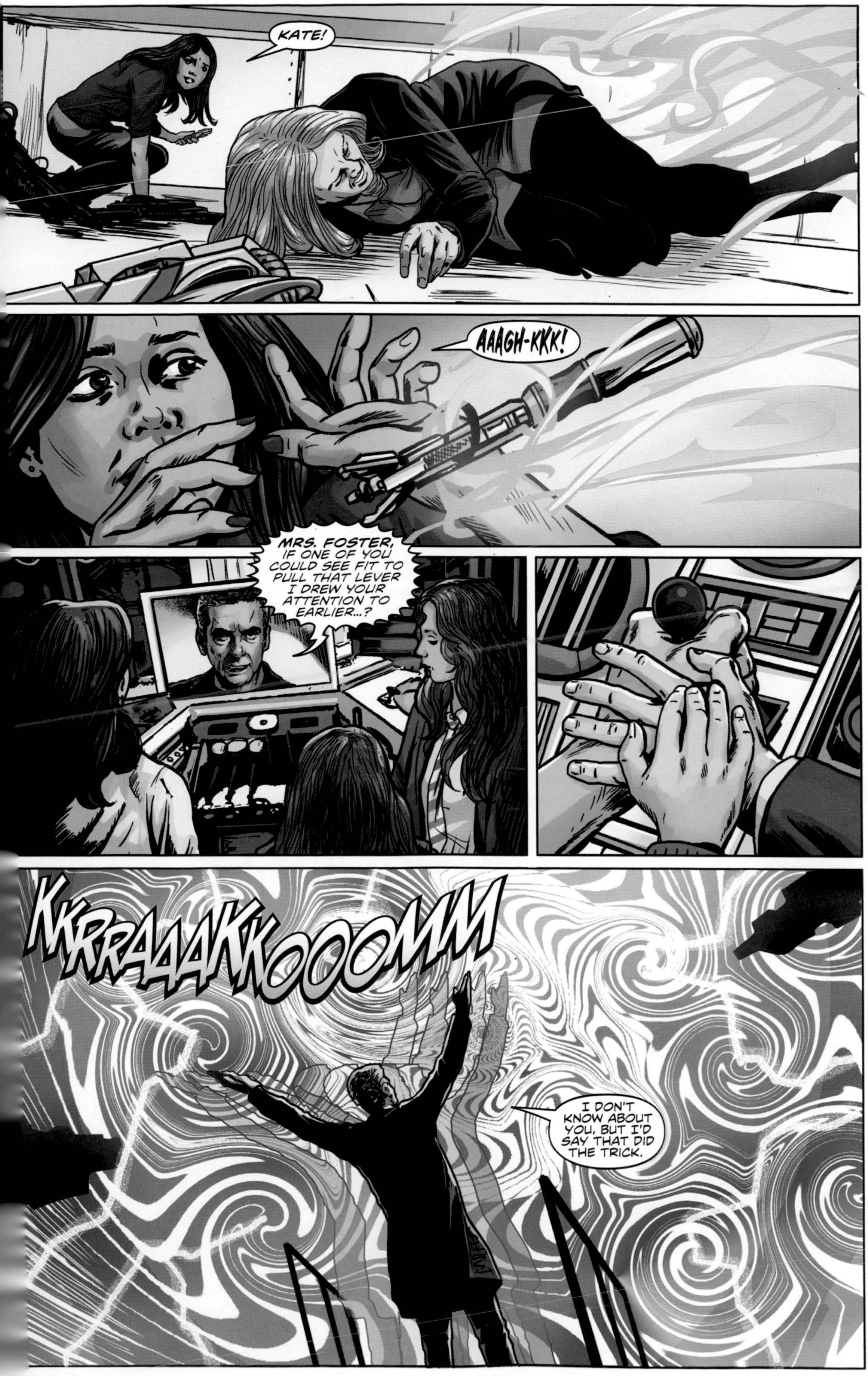
KATE!
AAAGH-KKK!
MRS. FOSTER, IF ONE OF YOU COULD SEE FIT TO PULL THAT LEVER I DREW YOUR ATTENTION TO EARLIER...?
KKRRAAAKKOOOOMM
I DON'T KNOW ABOUT YOU, BUT I'D SAY THAT DID THE TRICK.

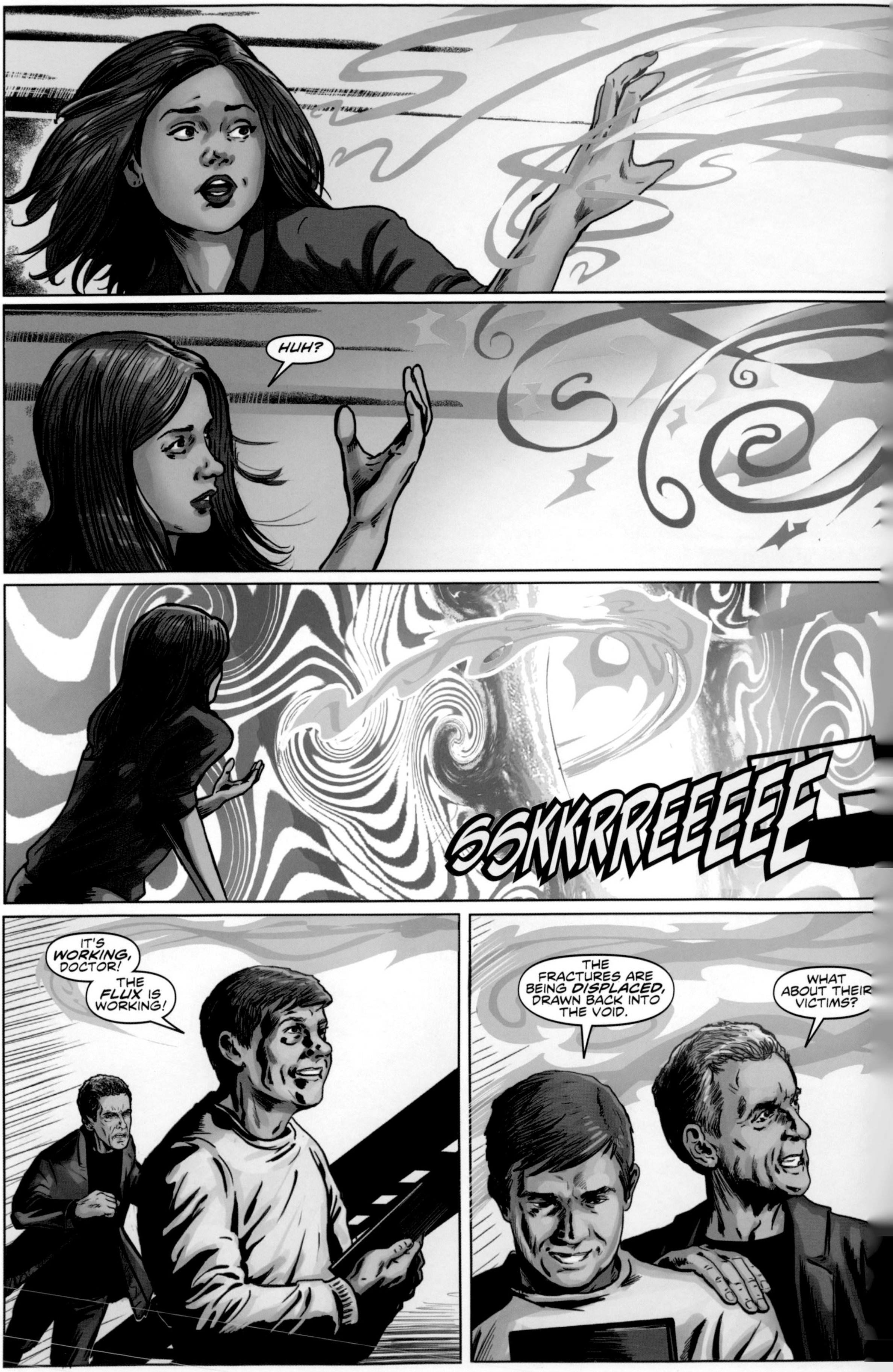
HUH?
SSKKRREEEEEE
IT'S WORKING, DOCTOR!
THE FLUX IS WORKING!
THE FRACTURES ARE BEING DISPLACED, DRAWN BACK INTO THE VOID.
WHAT ABOUT THEIR VICTIMS?

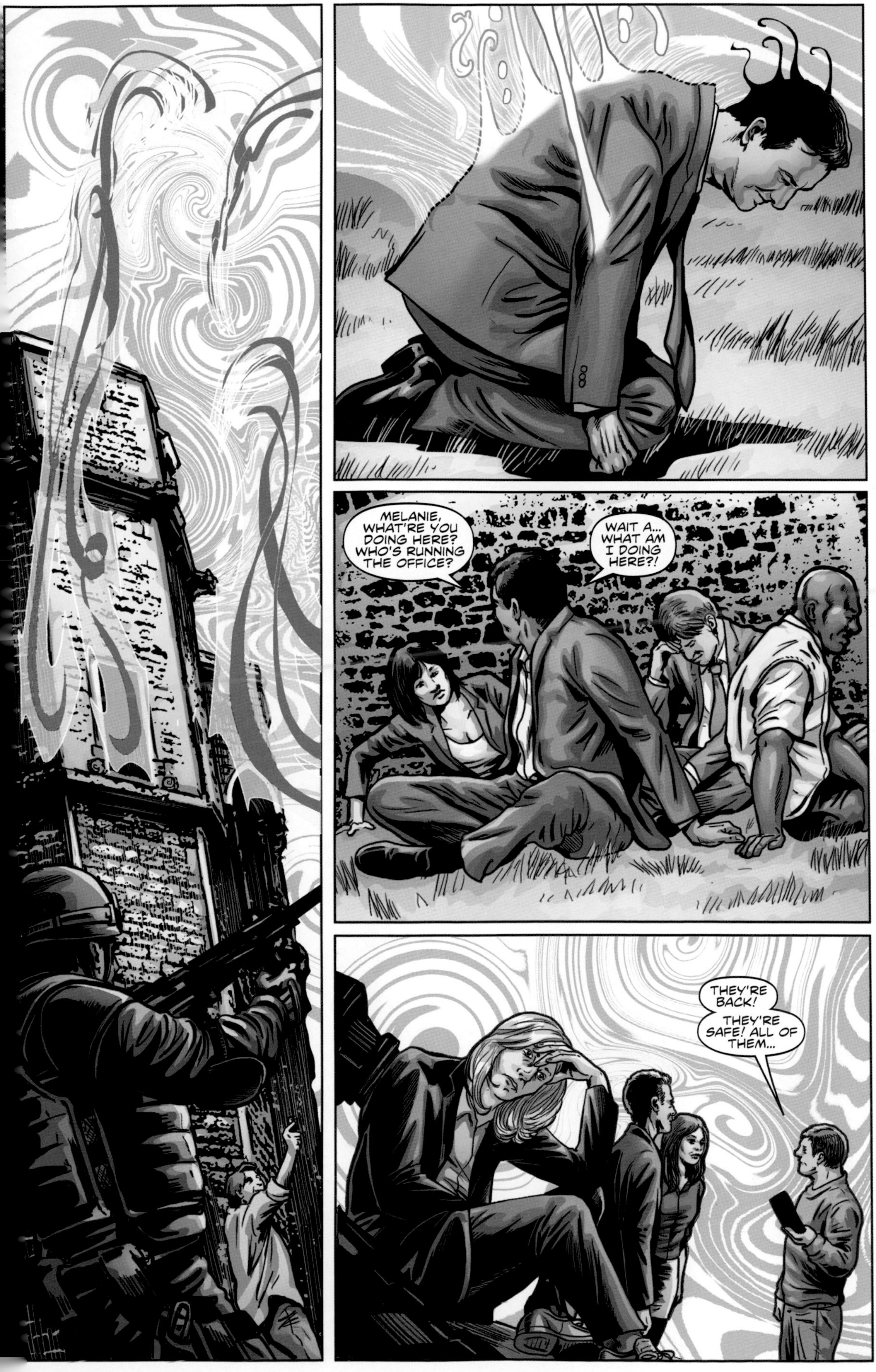
MELANIE, WHAT'RE YOU DOING HERE? WHO'S RUNNING THE OFFICE?
WAIT A... WHAT AM I DOING HERE?!
THEY'RE BACK!
THEY'RE SAFE! ALL OF THEM...

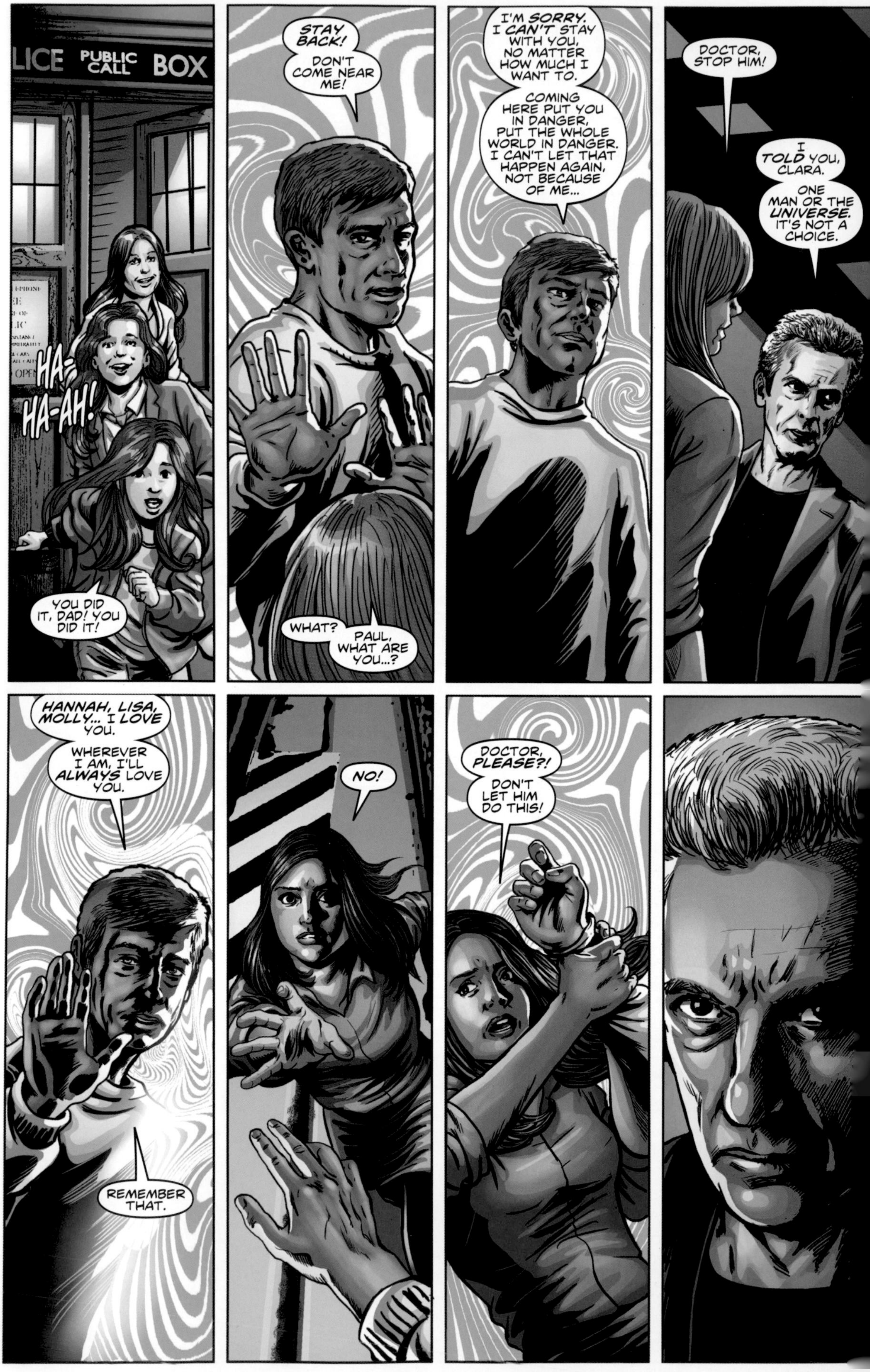
LICE PUBLIC CALL BOX
HA-HA-AH!
YOU DID IT, DAD! YOU DID IT!
STAY BACK!
DON'T COME NEAR ME!
WHAT?
PAUL, WHAT ARE YOU...?
I'M SORRY. I CAN'T STAY WITH YOU, NO MATTER HOW MUCH I WANT TO.
COMING HERE PUT YOU IN DANGER, PUT THE WHOLE WORLD IN DANGER. I CAN'T LET THAT HAPPEN AGAIN, NOT BECAUSE OF ME...
DOCTOR, STOP HIM!
I TOLD YOU, CLARA.
ONE MAN OR THE UNIVERSE. IT'S NOT A CHOICE.
HANNAH, LISA, MOLLY... I LOVE YOU.
WHEREVER I AM, I'LL ALWAYS LOVE YOU.
REMEMBER THAT.
NO!
DOCTOR, PLEASE?!
DON'T LET HIM DO THIS!

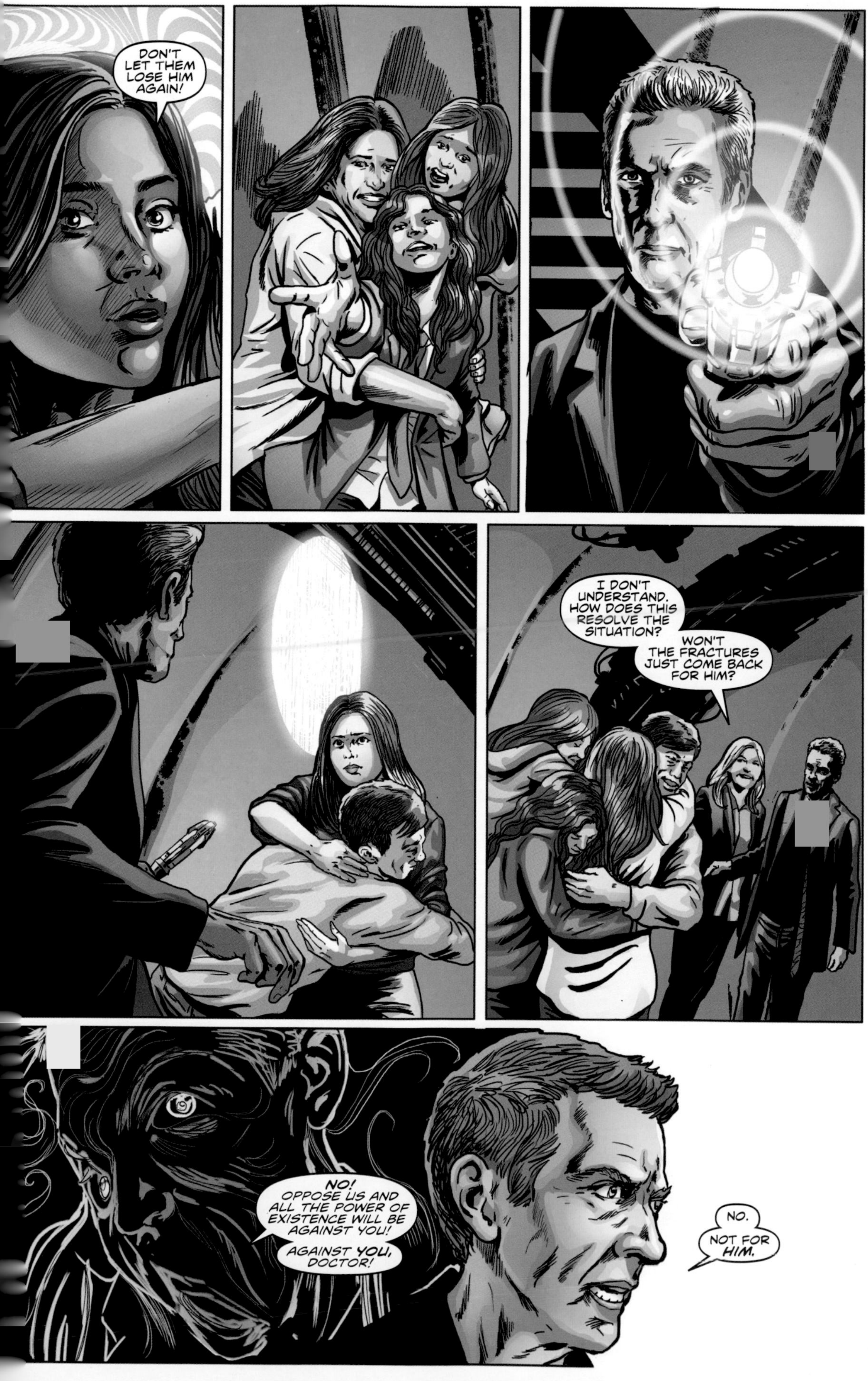
DON'T LET THEM LOSE HIM AGAIN!
I DON'T UNDERSTAND. HOW DOES THIS RESOLVE THE SITUATION?
WON'T THE FRACTURES JUST COME BACK FOR HIM?
NO! OPPOSE US AND ALL THE POWER OF EXISTENCE WILL BE AGAINST YOU!
AGAINST **YOU**, DOCTOR!
NO.
NOT FOR ***HIM.***

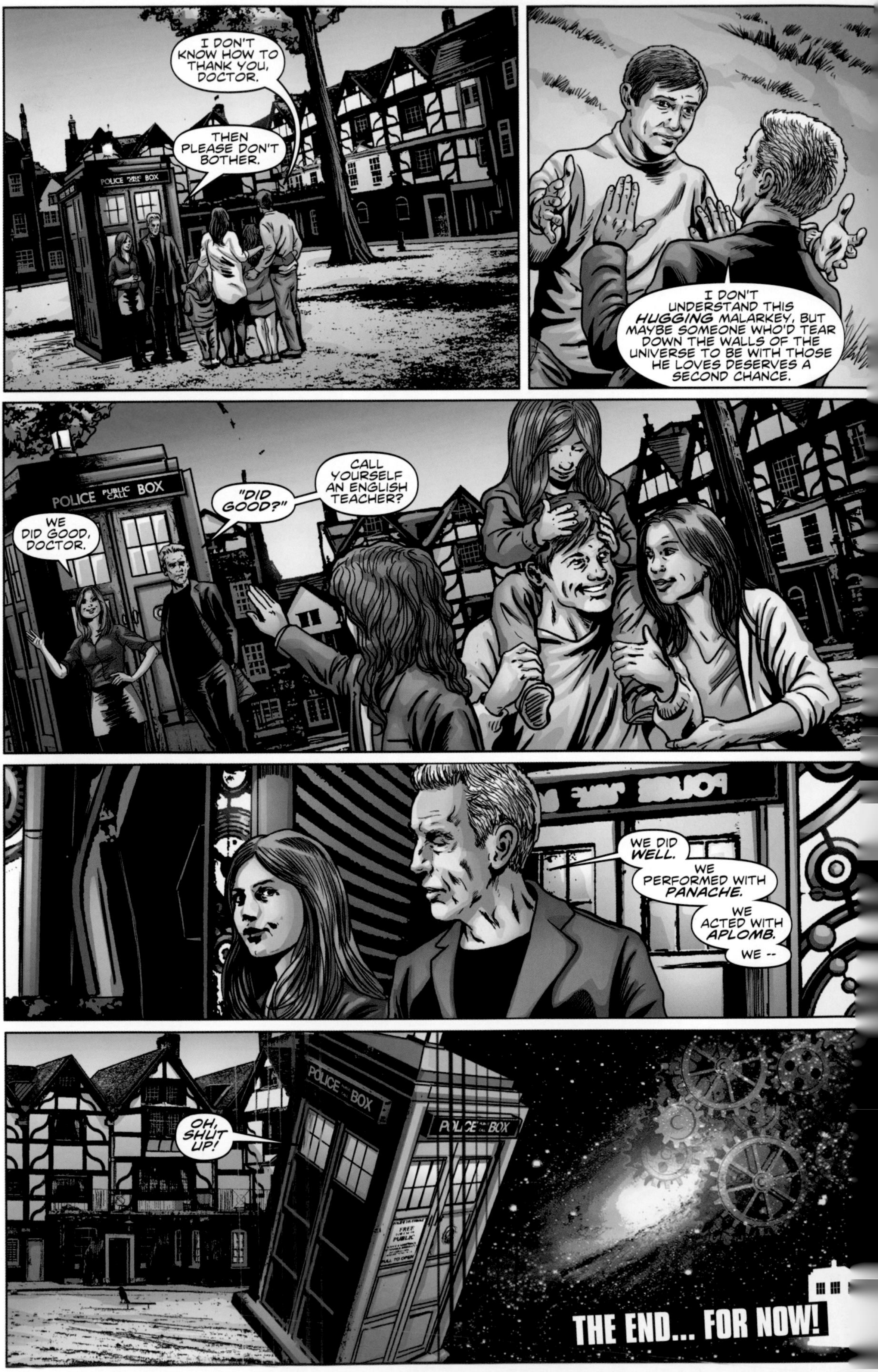
I DON'T KNOW HOW TO THANK YOU, DOCTOR.
THEN PLEASE DON'T BOTHER.
POLICE PUBLIC CALL BOX
I DON'T UNDERSTAND THIS HUGGING MALARKEY, BUT MAYBE SOMEONE WHO'D TEAR DOWN THE WALLS OF THE UNIVERSE TO BE WITH THOSE HE LOVES DESERVES A SECOND CHANCE.
POLICE PUBLIC CALL BOX
WE DID GOOD, DOCTOR.
"DID GOOD?"
CALL YOURSELF AN ENGLISH TEACHER?
WE DID WELL.
WE PERFORMED WITH PANACHE.
WE ACTED WITH APLOMB.
WE --
POLICE PUBLIC CALL BOX
OH, SHUT UP!
THE END... FOR NOW!

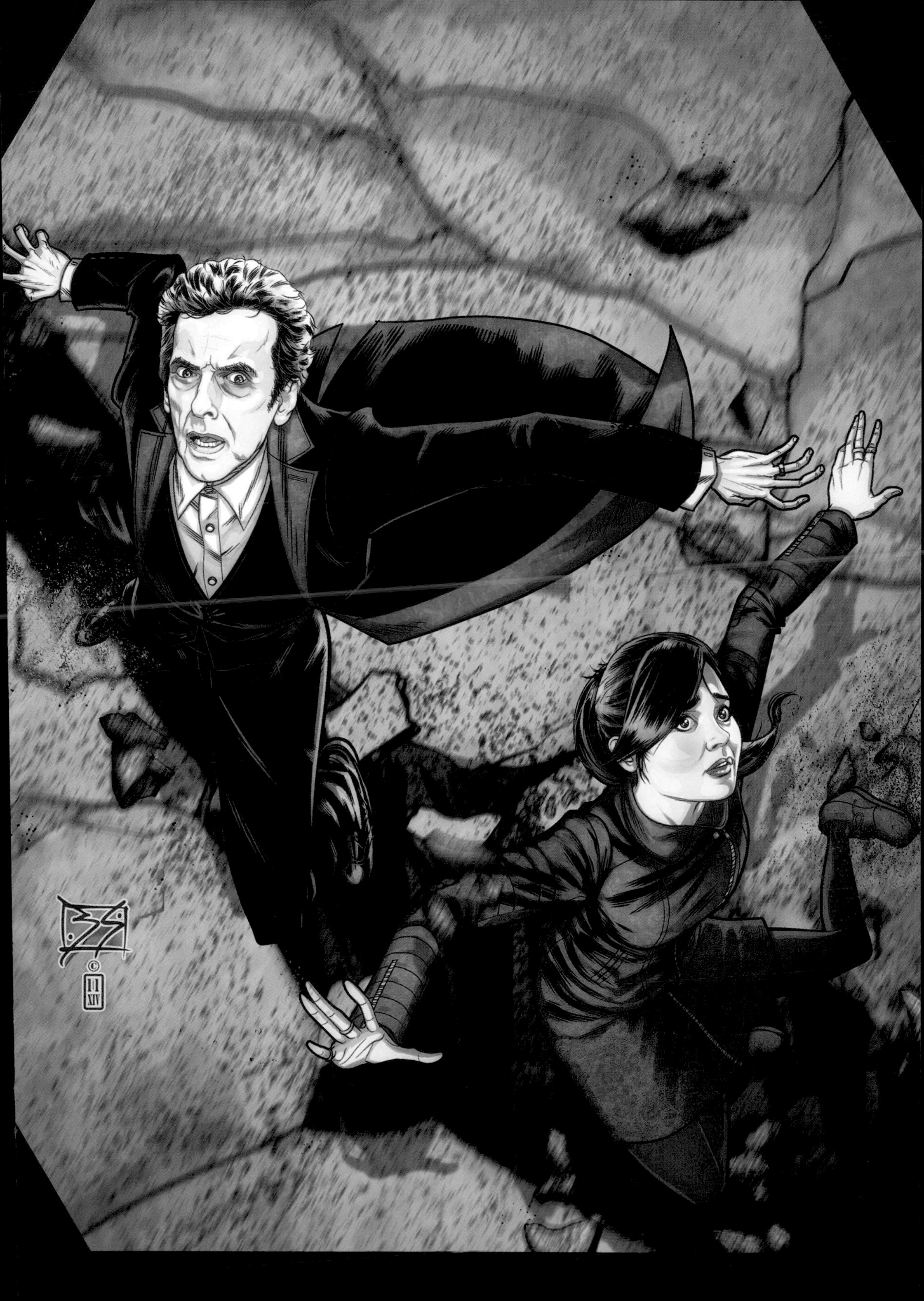

12D #7 Cover Art by Blair Shedd

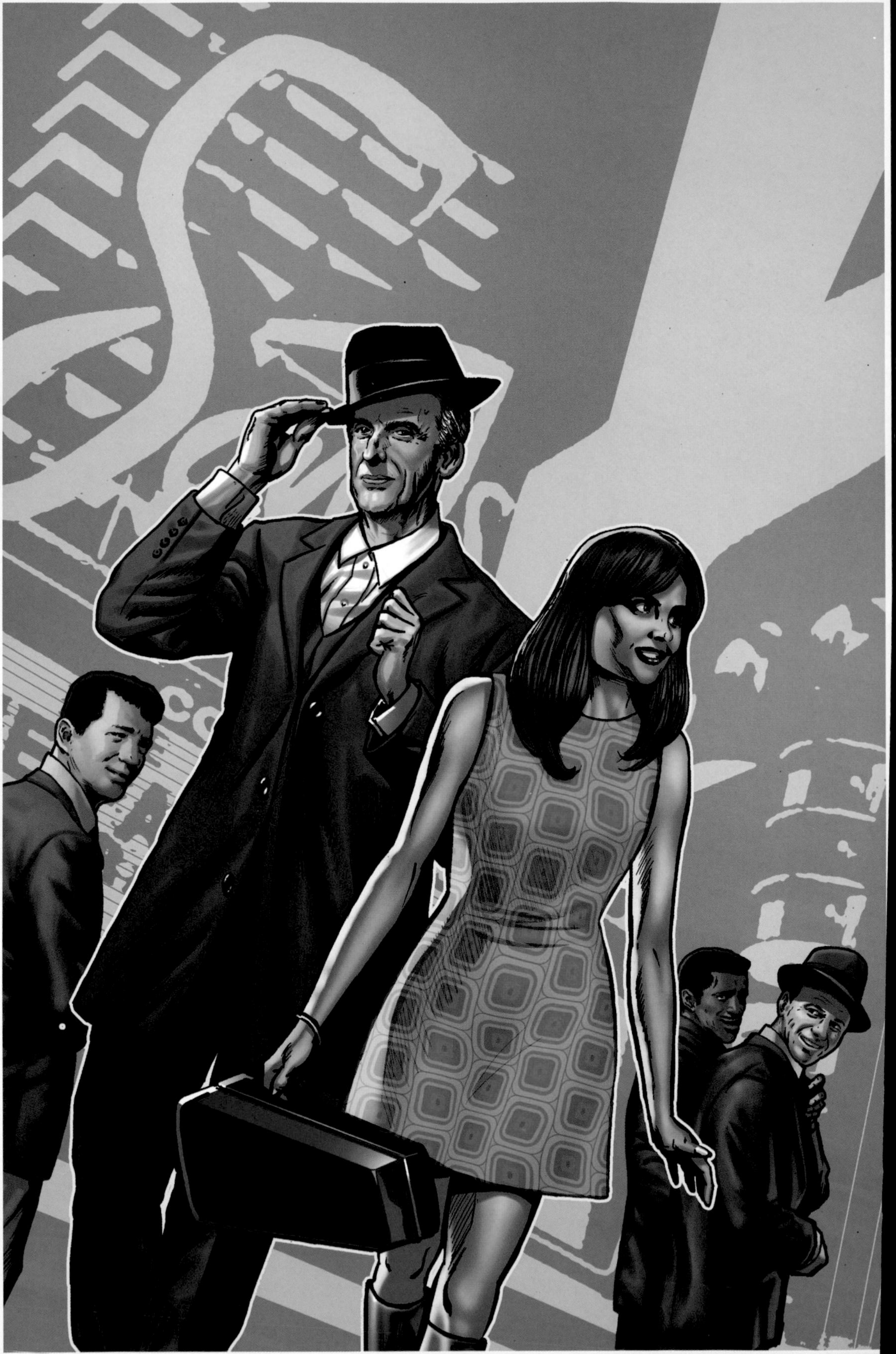

GANGLAND Cover: Brian Williamson & Luis Guerrero

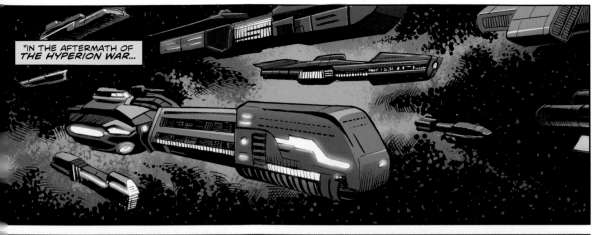

"IN THE AFTERMATH OF *THE HYPERION WAR...*

"THE ALLIANCE OF RACES, LED BY *RASSILON*, PRESIDENT OF THE TIME LORDS, EMBARKED ON A PURGE OF OTHER FORCES THAT POSED A THREAT TO UNIVERSAL HARMONY.

"ONE OF THEIR TARGETS WAS *COUNT D'IF*, RULER OF *THE CYBOCK IMPERIUM,* WHICH HAD SEIZED CONTROL OF SEVERAL PEACEFUL STAR SYSTEMS.

"D'IF WAS A DEADLY FOE, A CUNNING, RUTHLESS TYRANT, BUT HE HAD ONE WEAKNESS.

"HE WAS A NOTORIOUS *GAMBLER.*

"WITH THEIR FORCES LOCKED IN *STALEMATE,* RASSILON, ADEPT AT MANIPULATING THE FLAWS OF BOTH FRIENDS AND ENEMIES, CHALLENGED D'IF TO A GAME OF CHANCE.

"A GAME OF *DEATH.*

"AND *MORE* THAN DEATH."

"A GAME THAT BECAME KNOWN AS *RASSILON'S ROULETTE*.

"PLAYED IN THE SAME WAY AS THE MORE COMMONLY-KNOWN RUSSIAN VERSION, BUT WITH *A TIME-GUN*."

"ONLY ONE CHAMBER OF THE WEAPON IS LOADED, BUT NOT WITH ANY ORDINARY BULLET, WITH A *TIME-BOMB*.

"A PROJECTILE THAT EXTINGUISHES ITS VICTIM'S ENTIRE *TIMELINE*, EFFECTIVELY WIPING THEM FROM EXISTENCE."

CLICK

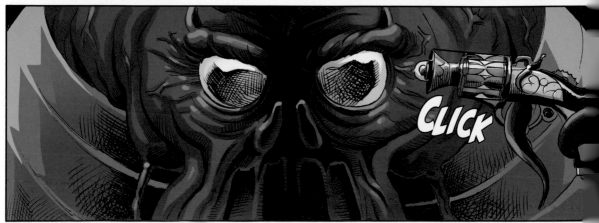

CLICK

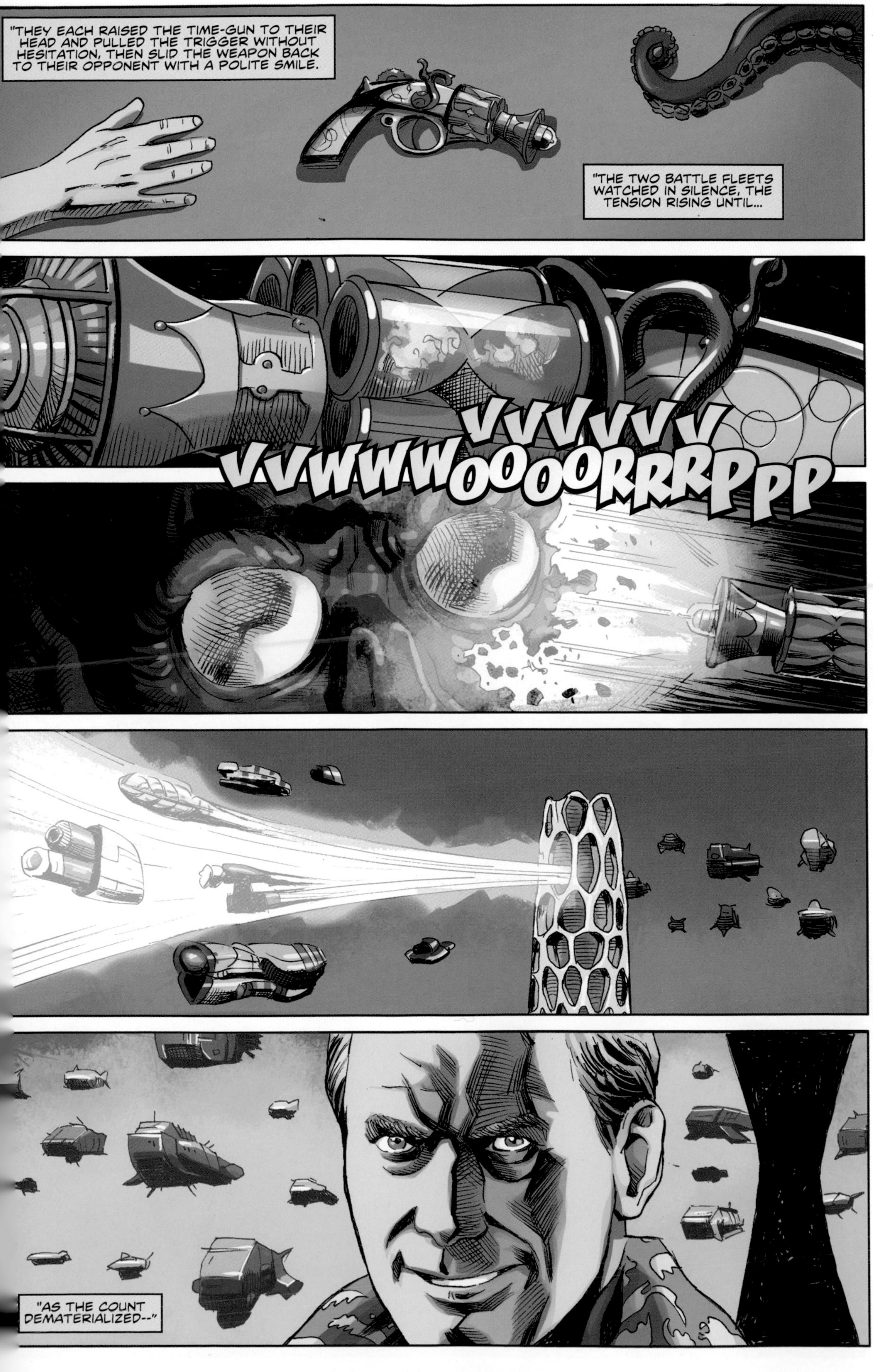
"THEY EACH RAISED THE TIME-GUN TO THEIR HEAD AND PULLED THE TRIGGER WITHOUT HESITATION, THEN SLID THE WEAPON BACK TO THEIR OPPONENT WITH A POLITE SMILE.
"THE TWO BATTLE FLEETS WATCHED IN SILENCE, THE TENSION RISING UNTIL...
VVVVVVVVWWWWOOOORRRPPP
"AS THE COUNT DEMATERIALIZED--"

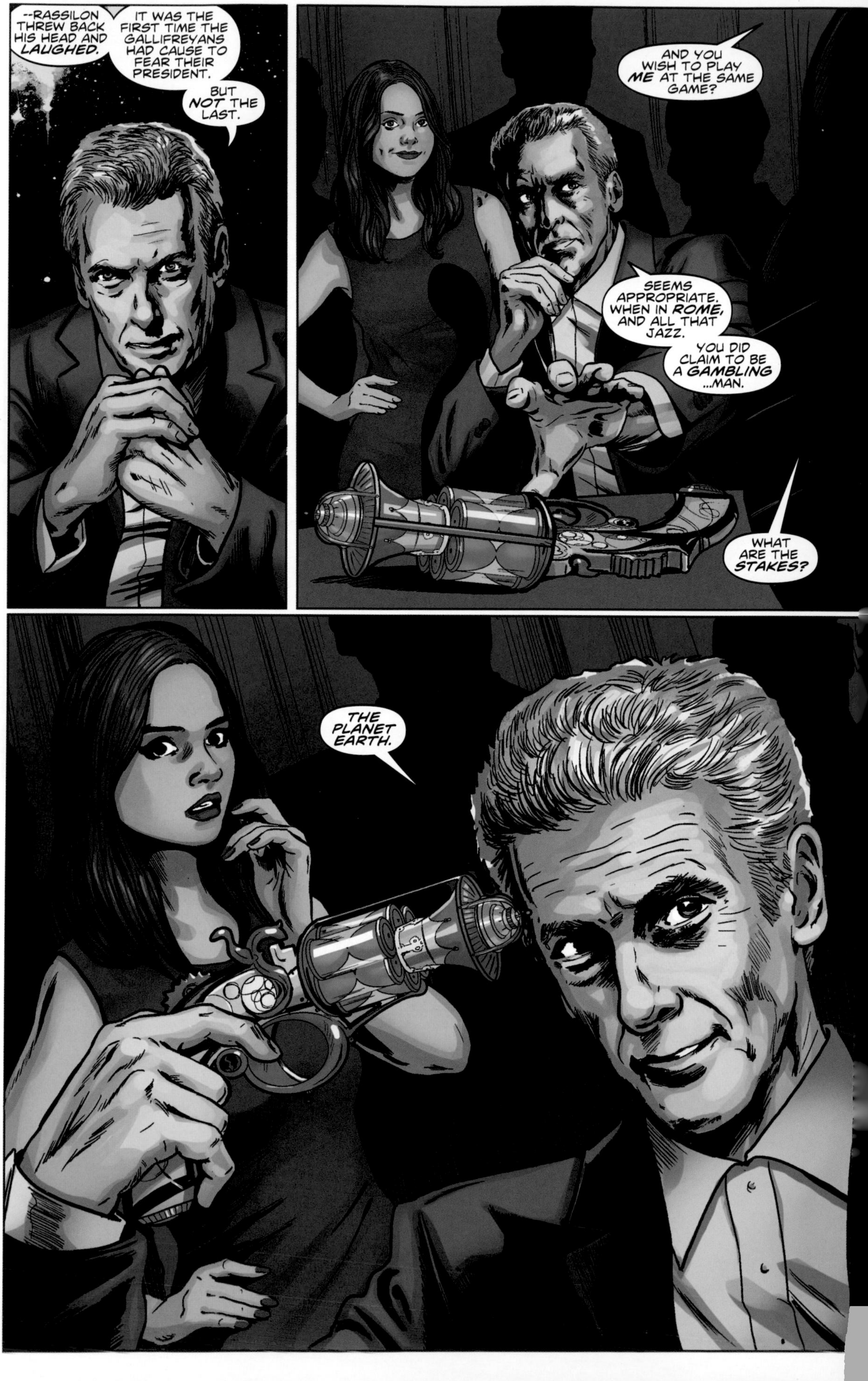
--RASSILON THREW BACK HIS HEAD AND *LAUGHED.*
IT WAS THE FIRST TIME THE GALLIFREYANS HAD CAUSE TO FEAR THEIR PRESIDENT.
BUT *NOT* THE LAST.
AND YOU WISH TO PLAY *ME* AT THE SAME GAME?
SEEMS APPROPRIATE. WHEN IN *ROME,* AND ALL THAT JAZZ.
YOU DID CLAIM TO BE A *GAMBLING* ...MAN.
WHAT ARE THE *STAKES?*
THE PLANET EARTH.

GANGLAND

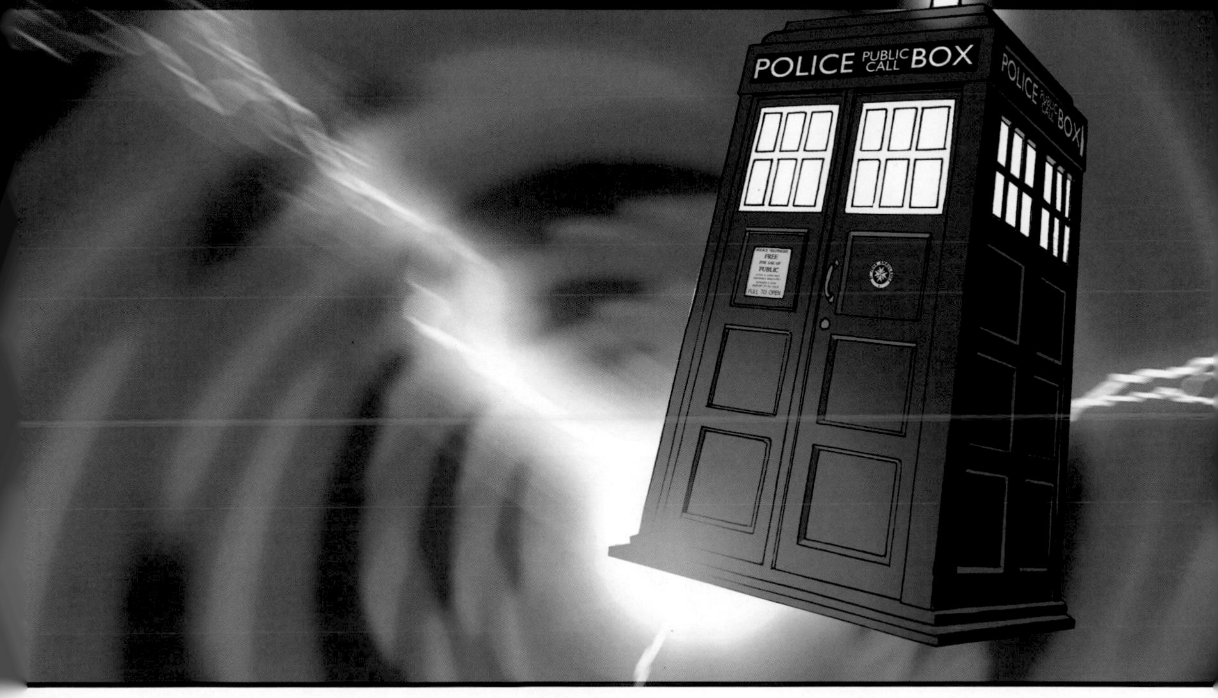
POLICE PUBLIC CALL BOX

WRITER
ROBBIE MORRISON

ARTISTS
BRIAN WILLIAMSON
& MARIANO LACLAUSTRA

COLORIST
HI-FI

LETTERER
RICHARD STARKINGS AND COMICRAFT'S JIMMY BETANCOURT

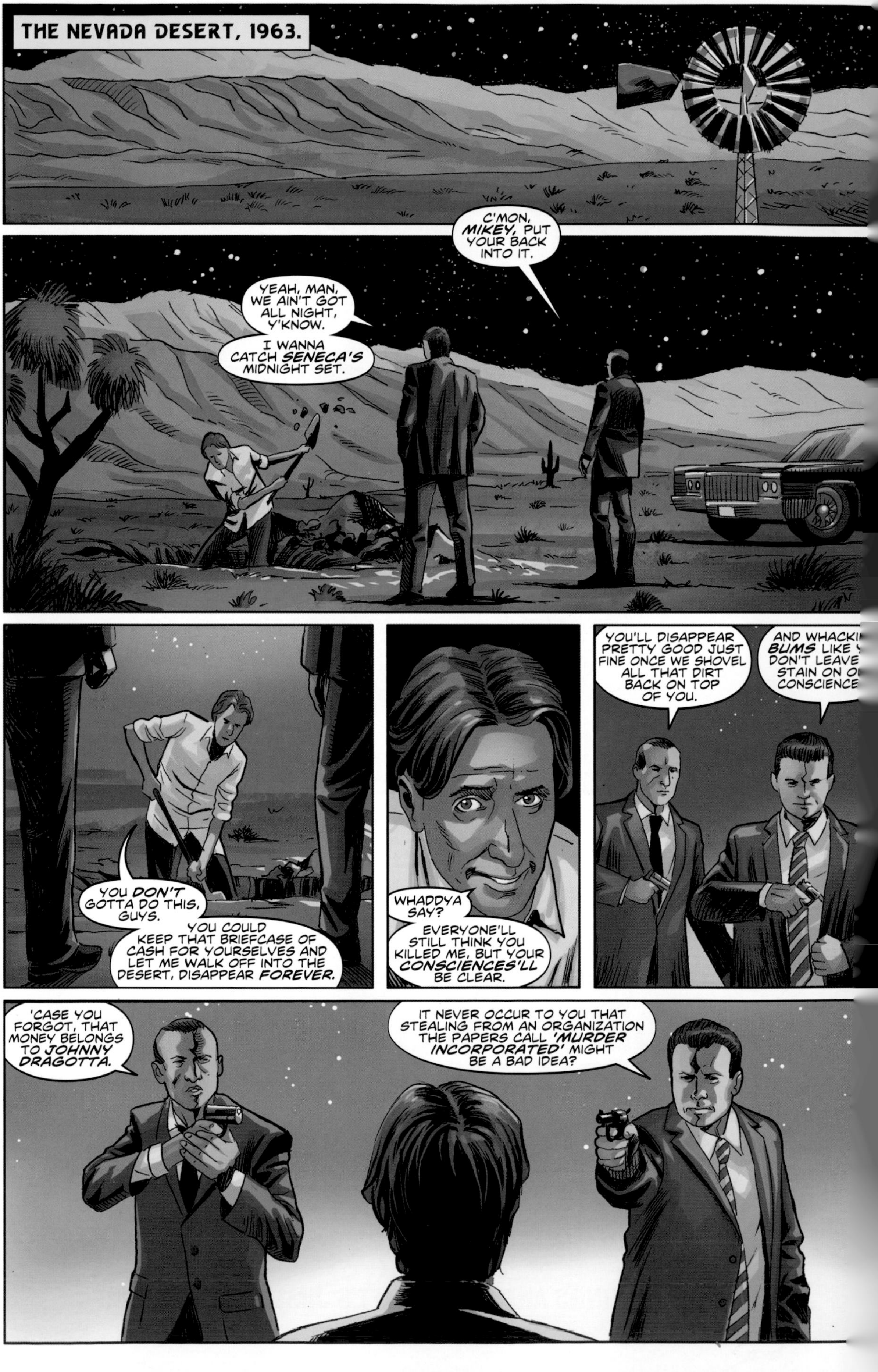
THE NEVADA DESERT, 1963.
C'MON, MIKEY, PUT YOUR BACK INTO IT.
YEAH, MAN, WE AIN'T GOT ALL NIGHT, Y'KNOW.
I WANNA CATCH SENECA'S MIDNIGHT SET.
YOU DON'T GOTTA DO THIS, GUYS.
YOU COULD KEEP THAT BRIEFCASE OF CASH FOR YOURSELVES AND LET ME WALK OFF INTO THE DESERT, DISAPPEAR FOREVER.
WHADDYA SAY?
EVERYONE'LL STILL THINK YOU KILLED ME, BUT YOUR CONSCIENCES'LL BE CLEAR.
YOU'LL DISAPPEAR PRETTY GOOD JUST FINE ONCE WE SHOVEL ALL THAT DIRT BACK ON TOP OF YOU.
AND WHACKIN BUMS LIKE DON'T LEAVE STAIN ON O CONSCIENCE
'CASE YOU FORGOT, THAT MONEY BELONGS TO JOHNNY DRAGOTTA.
IT NEVER OCCUR TO YOU THAT STEALING FROM AN ORGANIZATION THE PAPERS CALL 'MURDER INCORPORATED' MIGHT BE A BAD IDEA?

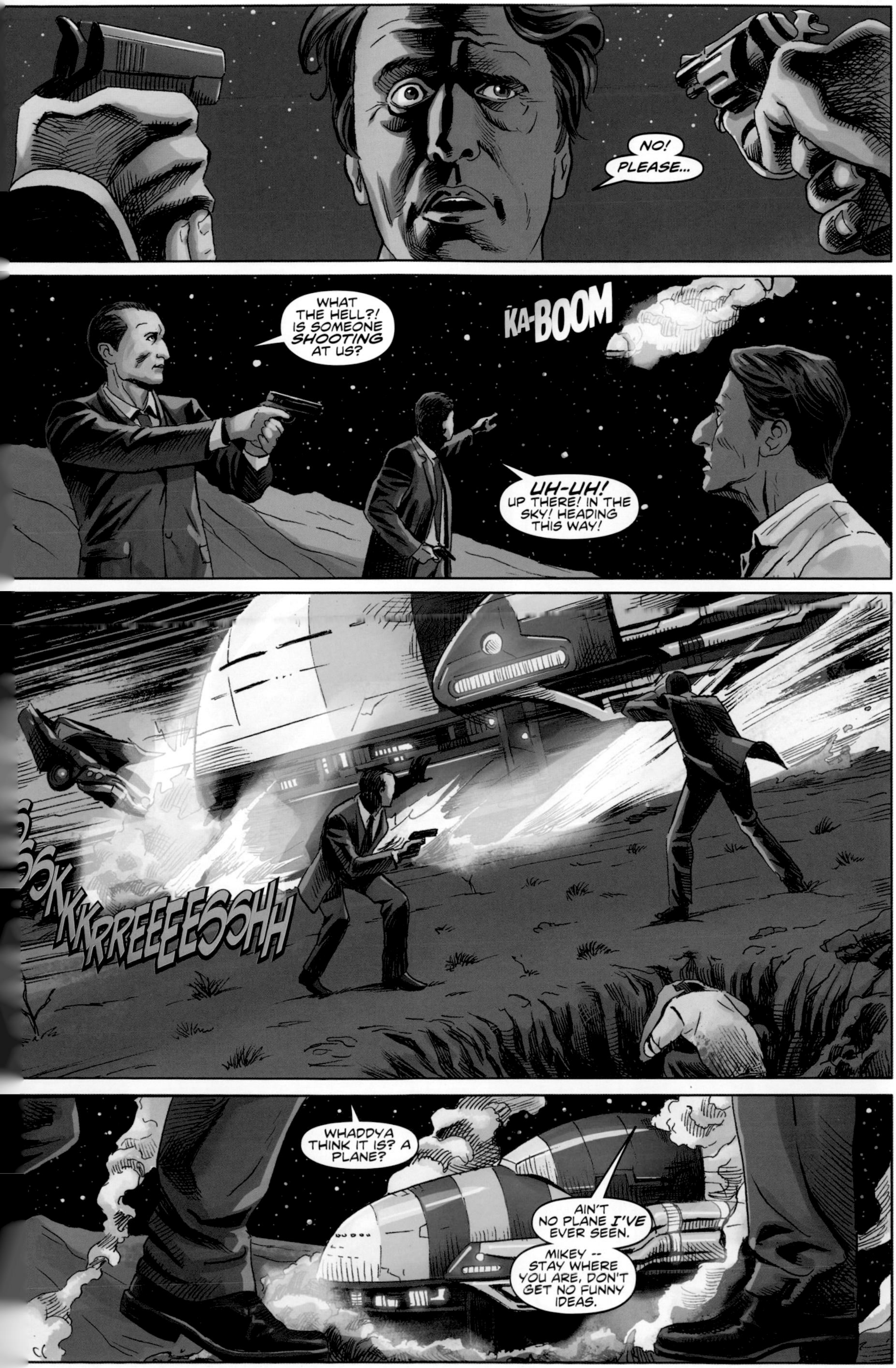
NO! PLEASE...
WHAT THE HELL?! IS SOMEONE SHOOTING AT US?
KA-BOOM
UH-UH! UP THERE! IN THE SKY! HEADING THIS WAY!
SKKKRREEEEESSHH
WHADDYA THINK IT IS? A PLANE?
AIN'T NO PLANE I'VE EVER SEEN.
MIKEY -- STAY WHERE YOU ARE, DON'T GET NO FUNNY IDEAS.

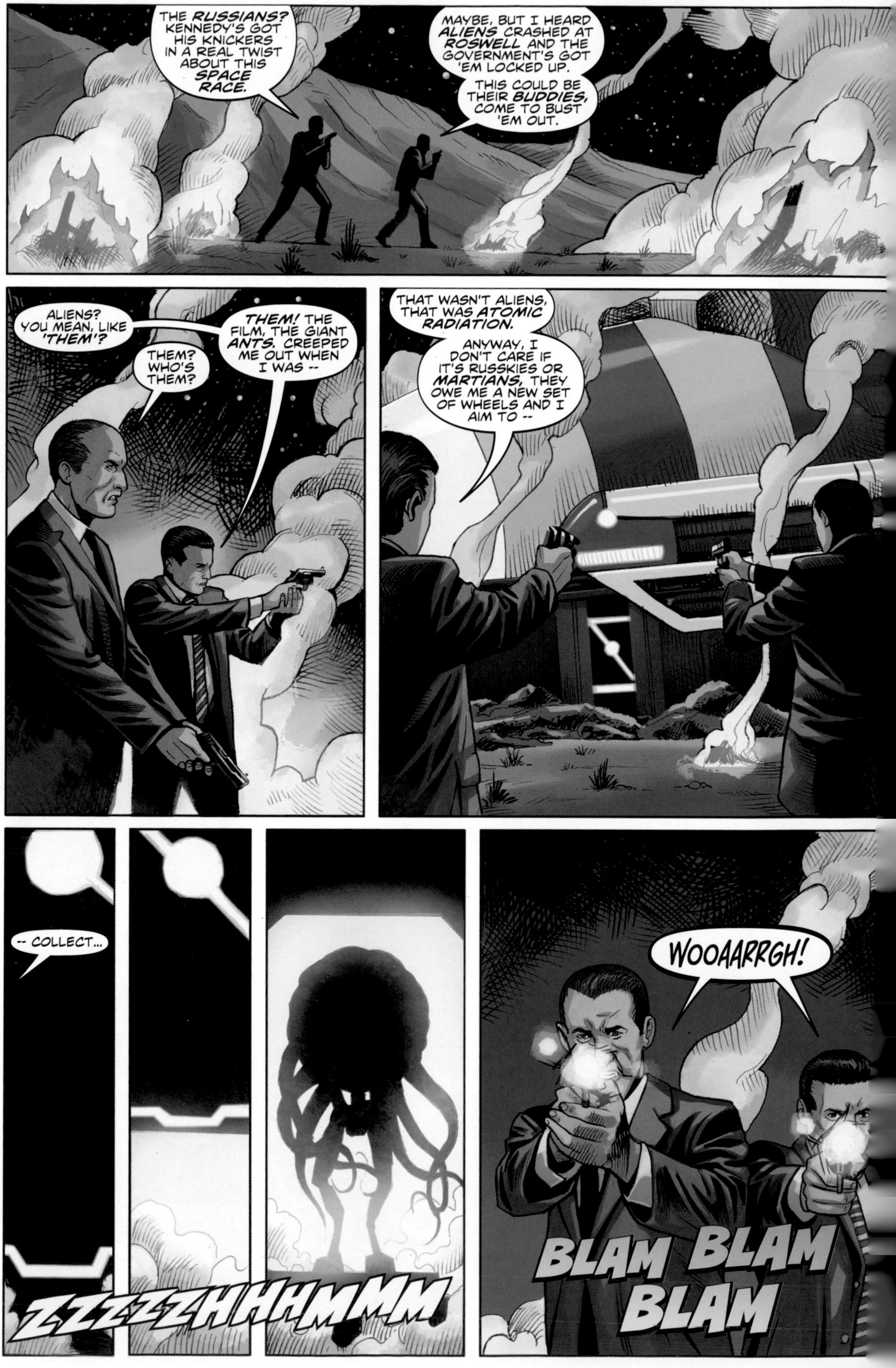
THE RUSSIANS? KENNEDY'S GOT HIS KNICKERS IN A REAL TWIST ABOUT THIS SPACE RACE.
MAYBE, BUT I HEARD ALIENS CRASHED AT ROSWELL AND THE GOVERNMENT'S GOT 'EM LOCKED UP.
THIS COULD BE THEIR BUDDIES, COME TO BUST 'EM OUT.
ALIENS? YOU MEAN, LIKE 'THEM'?
THEM? WHO'S THEM?
THEM! THE FILM, THE GIANT ANTS. CREEPED ME OUT WHEN I WAS --
THAT WASN'T ALIENS, THAT WAS ATOMIC RADIATION.
ANYWAY, I DON'T CARE IF IT'S RUSSKIES OR MARTIANS, THEY OWE ME A NEW SET OF WHEELS AND I AIM TO --
-- COLLECT...
ZZZZZHHHHMMMM
WOOAARRGH!
BLAM BLAM BLAM

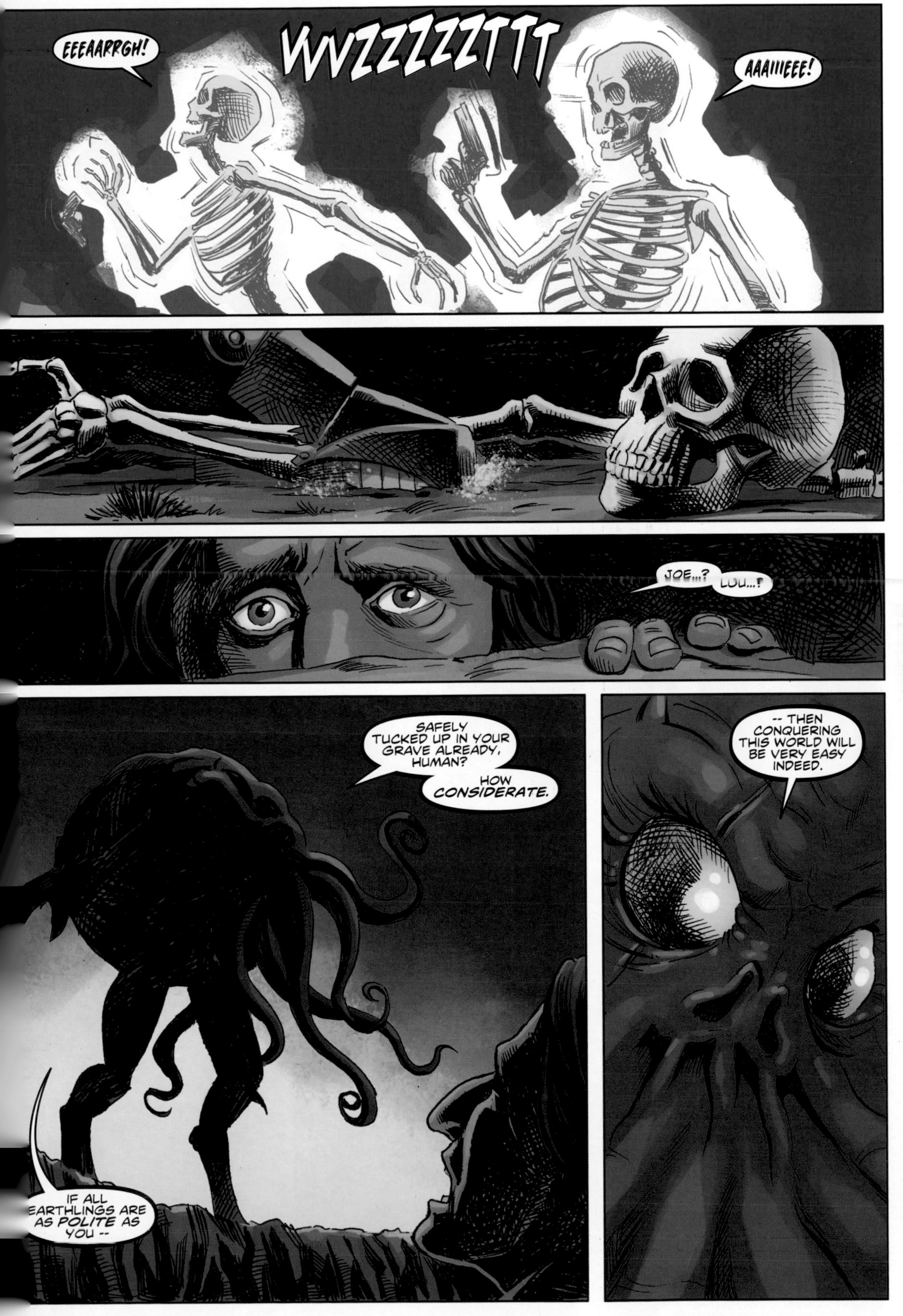
EEEAARRGH!
VVVZZZZZTTT
AAAIIIEEE!
JOE...?
LOU...?
SAFELY TUCKED UP IN YOUR GRAVE ALREADY, HUMAN?
HOW CONSIDERATE.
IF ALL EARTHLINGS ARE AS POLITE AS YOU --
-- THEN CONQUERING THIS WORLD WILL BE VERY EASY INDEED.

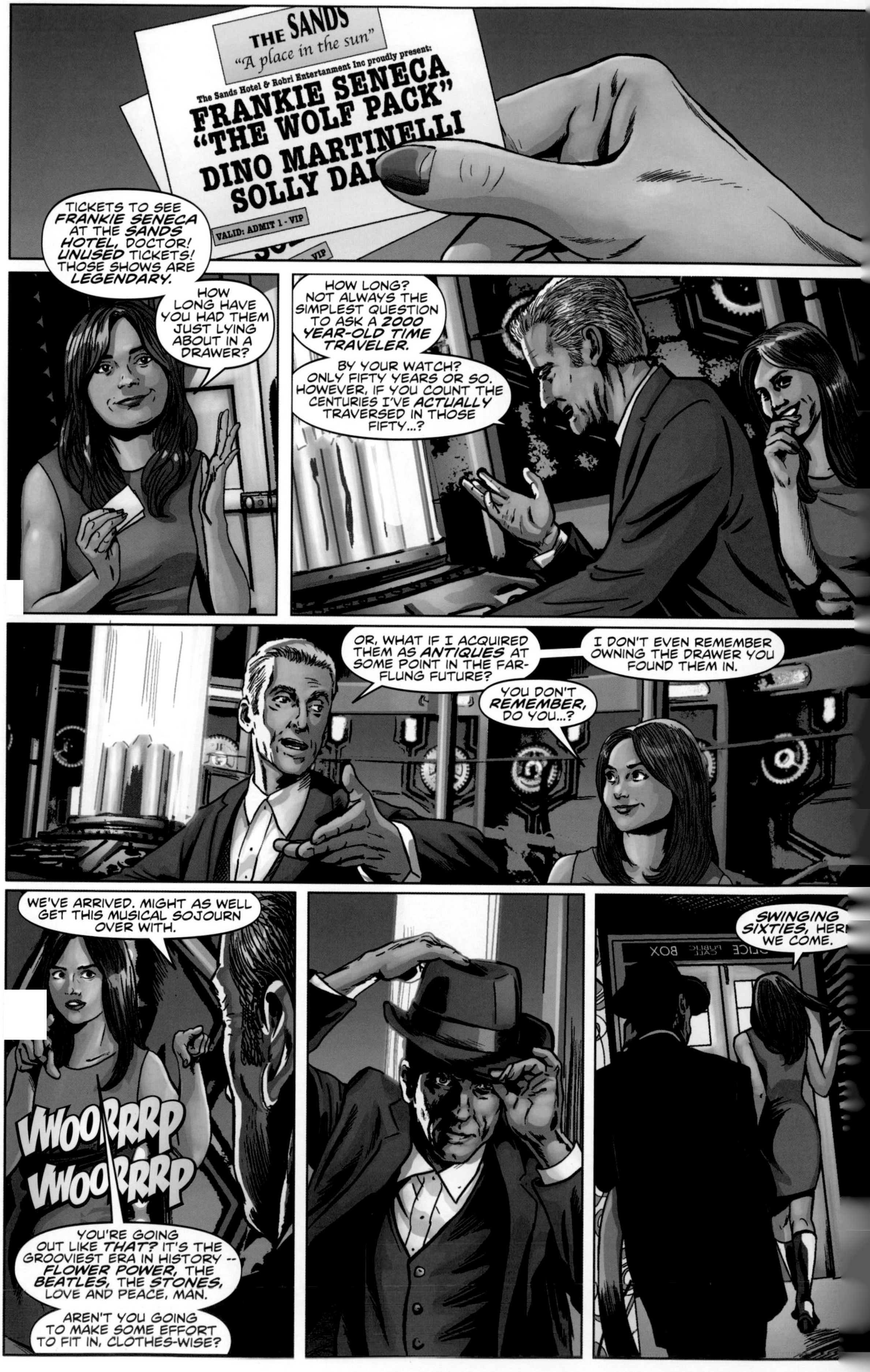
THE SANDS
"A place in the sun"
The Sands Hotel & Robri Entertainment Inc proudly present:
FRANKIE SENECA
"THE WOLF PACK"
DINO MARTINELLI
SOLLY
VALID: ADMIT 1 - VIP
TICKETS TO SEE FRANKIE SENECA AT THE SANDS HOTEL, DOCTOR! UNUSED TICKETS! THOSE SHOWS ARE LEGENDARY.
HOW LONG HAVE YOU HAD THEM JUST LYING ABOUT IN A DRAWER?
HOW LONG? NOT ALWAYS THE SIMPLEST QUESTION TO ASK A 2000 YEAR-OLD TIME TRAVELER.
BY YOUR WATCH? ONLY FIFTY YEARS OR SO. HOWEVER, IF YOU COUNT THE CENTURIES I'VE ACTUALLY TRAVERSED IN THOSE FIFTY...?
OR, WHAT IF I ACQUIRED THEM AS ANTIQUES AT SOME POINT IN THE FAR-FLUNG FUTURE?
I DON'T EVEN REMEMBER OWNING THE DRAWER YOU FOUND THEM IN.
YOU DON'T REMEMBER, DO YOU...?
WE'VE ARRIVED. MIGHT AS WELL GET THIS MUSICAL SOJOURN OVER WITH.
VWOORRRP
VWOORRRP
YOU'RE GOING OUT LIKE THAT? IT'S THE GROOVIEST ERA IN HISTORY -- FLOWER POWER, THE BEATLES, THE STONES, LOVE AND PEACE, MAN.
AREN'T YOU GOING TO MAKE SOME EFFORT TO FIT IN, CLOTHES-WISE?
SWINGING SIXTIES, HERE WE COME.

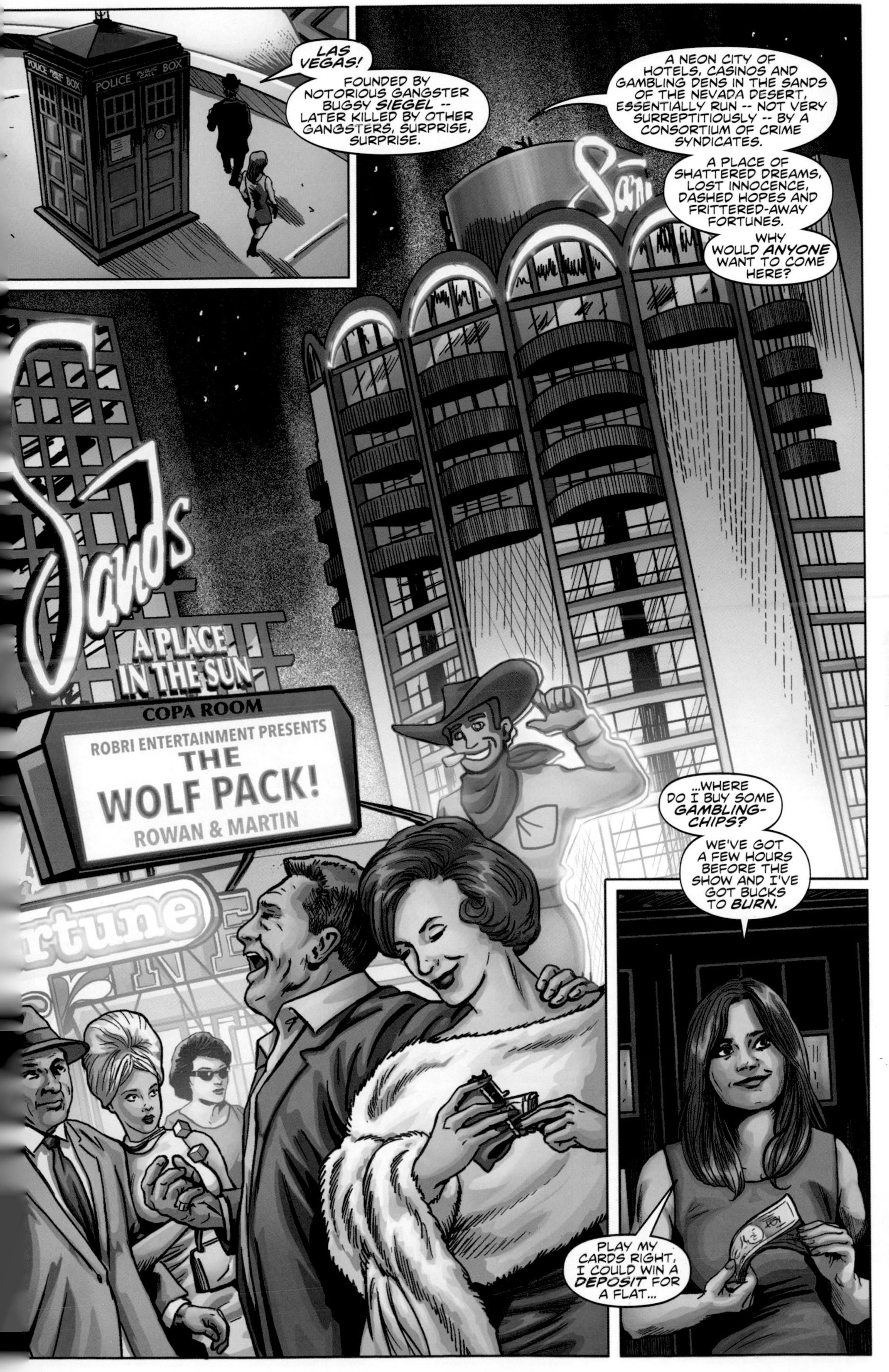

POLICE PUBLIC CALL BOX
LAS VEGAS!
FOUNDED BY NOTORIOUS GANGSTER BUGSY SIEGEL -- LATER KILLED BY OTHER GANGSTERS, SURPRISE, SURPRISE.
A NEON CITY OF HOTELS, CASINOS AND GAMBLING DENS IN THE SANDS OF THE NEVADA DESERT, ESSENTIALLY RUN -- NOT VERY SURREPTITIOUSLY -- BY A CONSORTIUM OF CRIME SYNDICATES.
A PLACE OF SHATTERED DREAMS, LOST INNOCENCE, DASHED HOPES AND FRITTERED-AWAY FORTUNES.
WHY WOULD ANYONE WANT TO COME HERE?
Sands
A PLACE IN THE SUN
COPA ROOM
ROBRI ENTERTAINMENT PRESENTS
THE WOLF PACK!
ROWAN & MARTIN
...WHERE DO I BUY SOME GAMBLING-CHIPS?
WE'VE GOT A FEW HOURS BEFORE THE SHOW AND I'VE GOT BUCKS TO BURN.
PLAY MY CARDS RIGHT, I COULD WIN A DEPOSIT FOR A FLAT...

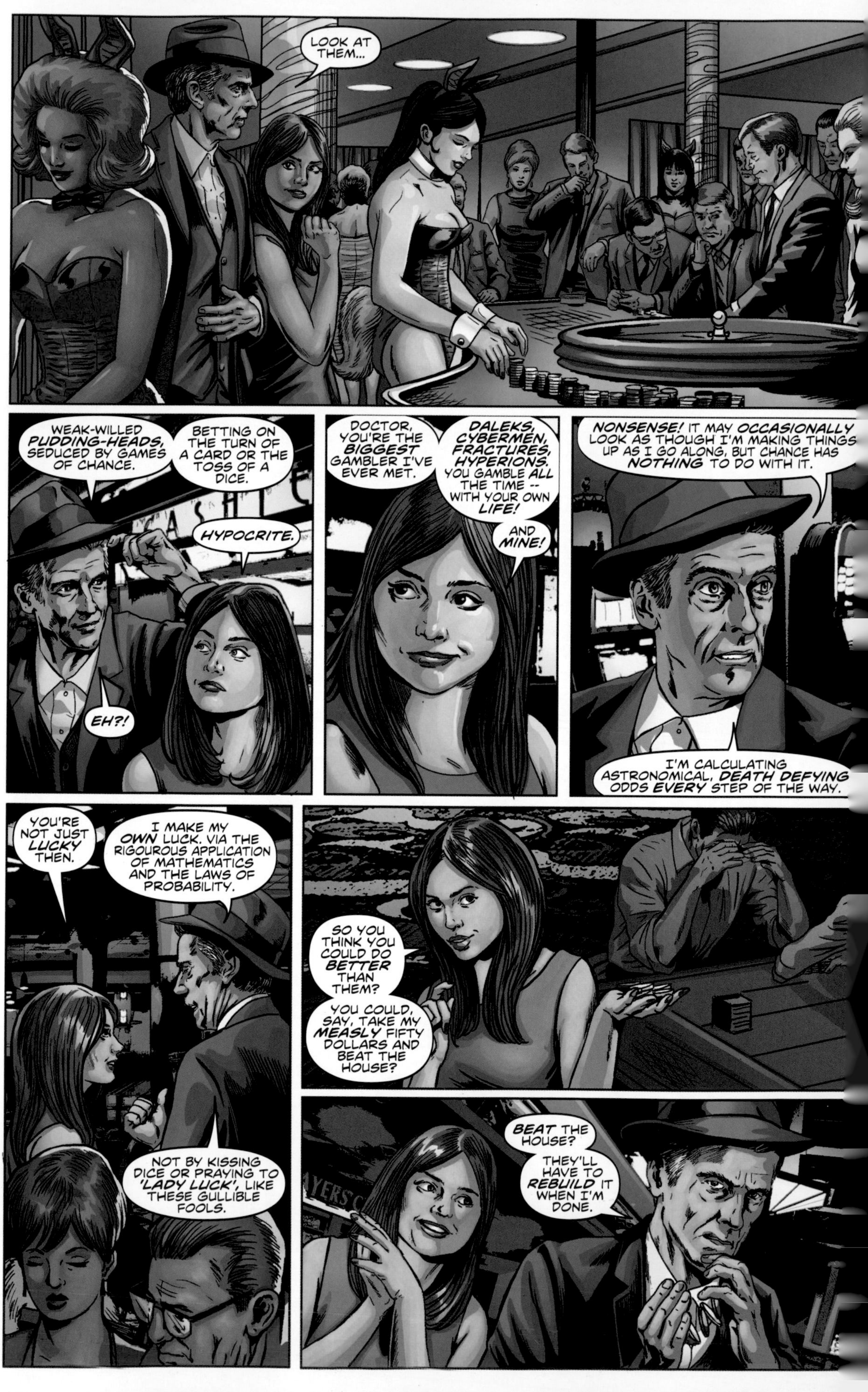
LOOK AT THEM...
WEAK-WILLED PUDDING-HEADS, SEDUCED BY GAMES OF CHANCE.
BETTING ON THE TURN OF A CARD OR THE TOSS OF A DICE.
HYPOCRITE.
EH?!
DOCTOR, YOU'RE THE BIGGEST GAMBLER I'VE EVER MET.
DALEKS, CYBERMEN, FRACTURES, HYPERIONS. YOU GAMBLE ALL THE TIME -- WITH YOUR OWN LIFE!
AND MINE!
NONSENSE! IT MAY OCCASIONALLY LOOK AS THOUGH I'M MAKING THINGS UP AS I GO ALONG, BUT CHANCE HAS NOTHING TO DO WITH IT.
I'M CALCULATING ASTRONOMICAL, DEATH DEFYING ODDS EVERY STEP OF THE WAY.
YOU'RE NOT JUST LUCKY THEN.
I MAKE MY OWN LUCK. VIA THE RIGOUROUS APPLICATION OF MATHEMATICS AND THE LAWS OF PROBABILITY.
NOT BY KISSING DICE OR PRAYING TO 'LADY LUCK', LIKE THESE GULLIBLE FOOLS.
SO YOU THINK YOU COULD DO BETTER THAN THEM?
YOU COULD, SAY, TAKE MY MEASLY FIFTY DOLLARS AND BEAT THE HOUSE?
BEAT THE HOUSE?
THEY'LL HAVE TO REBUILD IT WHEN I'M DONE.

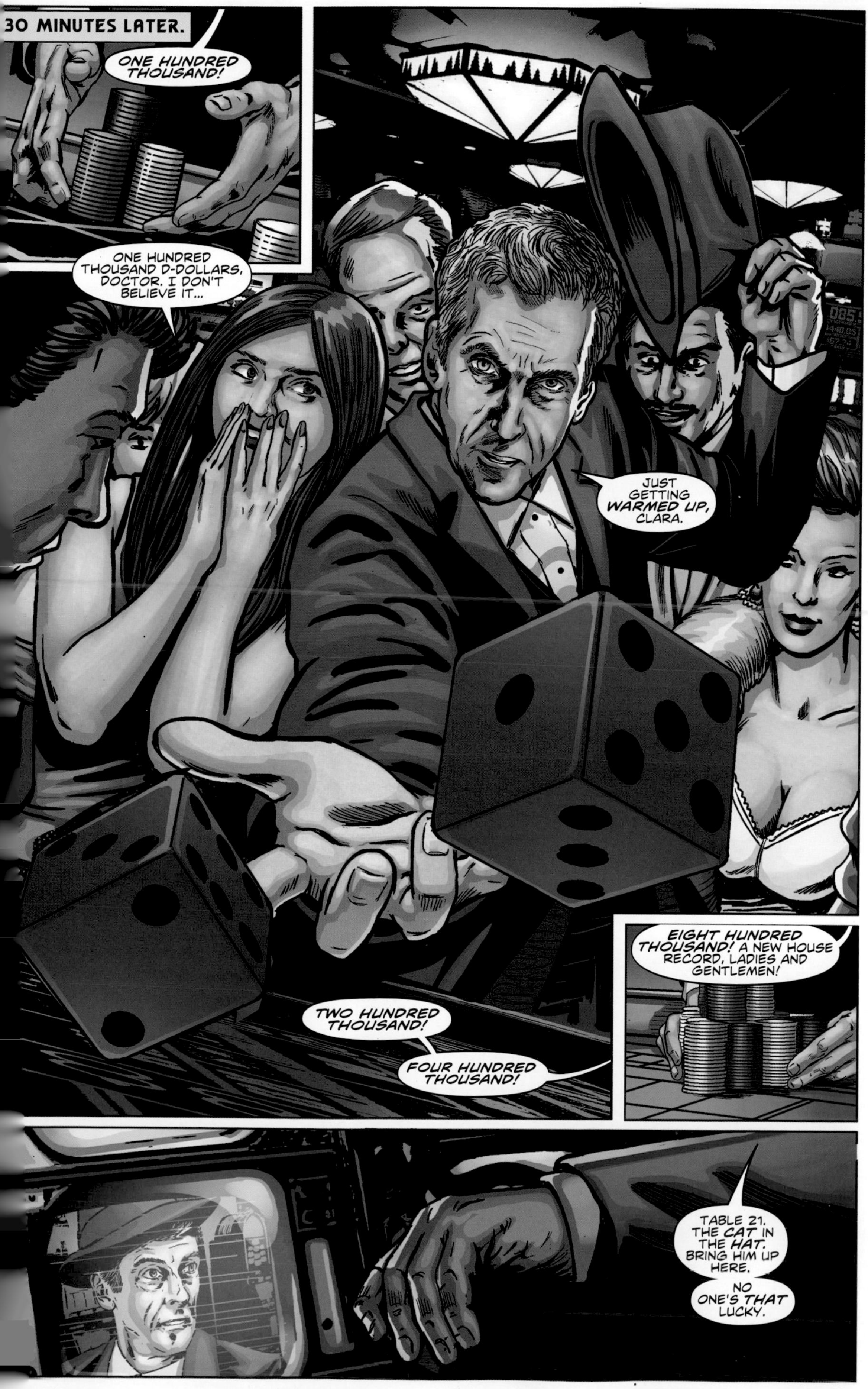
30 MINUTES LATER.
ONE HUNDRED THOUSAND!
ONE HUNDRED THOUSAND D-DOLLARS, DOCTOR. I DON'T BELIEVE IT...
JUST GETTING WARMED UP, CLARA.
TWO HUNDRED THOUSAND!
FOUR HUNDRED THOUSAND!
EIGHT HUNDRED THOUSAND! A NEW HOUSE RECORD, LADIES AND GENTLEMEN!
TABLE 21. THE CAT IN THE HAT. BRING HIM UP HERE.
NO ONE'S THAT LUCKY.

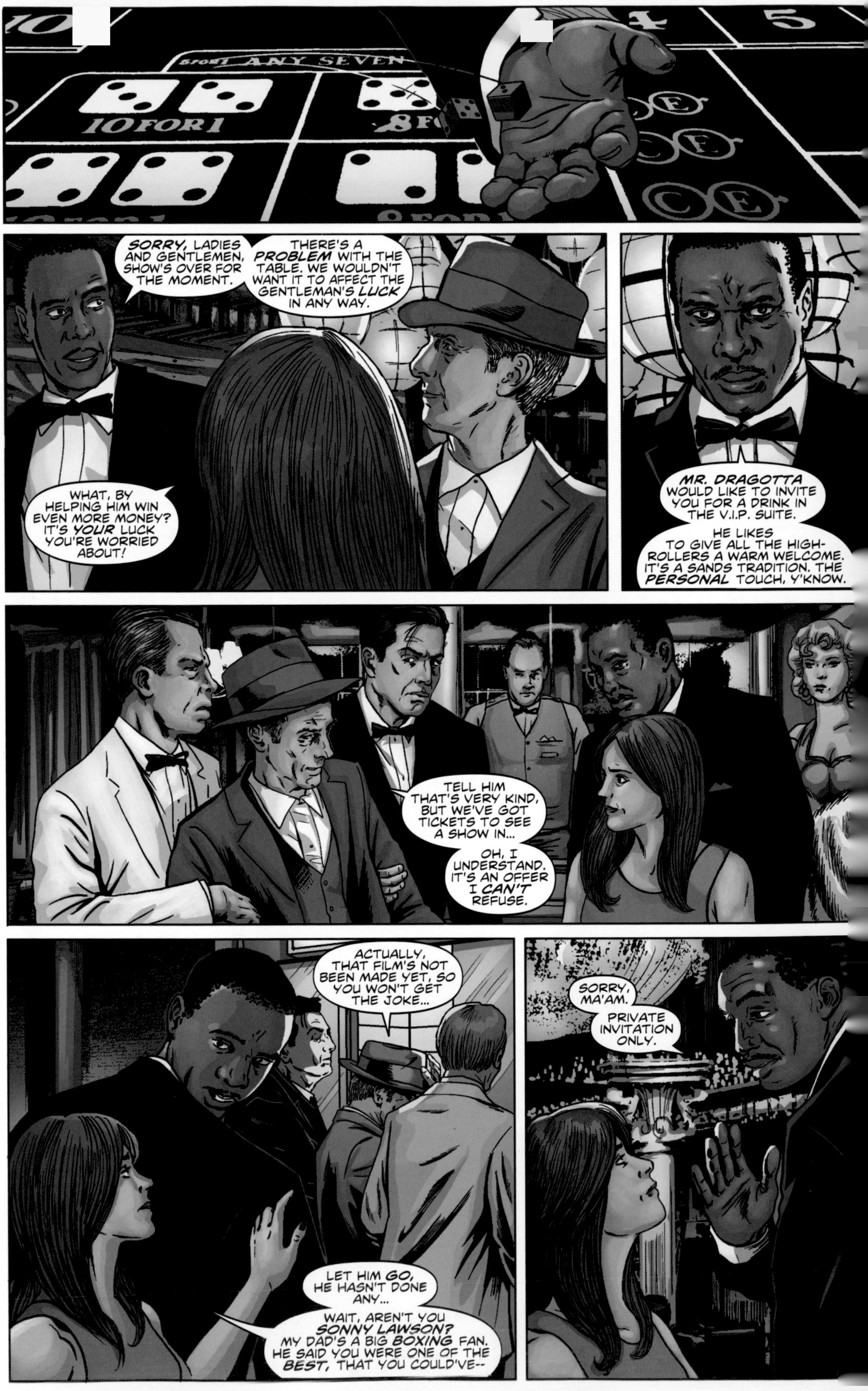
ANY SEVEN
10 FOR 1
SORRY, LADIES AND GENTLEMEN, SHOW'S OVER FOR THE MOMENT.
THERE'S A PROBLEM WITH THE TABLE. WE WOULDN'T WANT IT TO AFFECT THE GENTLEMAN'S LUCK IN ANY WAY.
WHAT, BY HELPING HIM WIN EVEN MORE MONEY? IT'S YOUR LUCK YOU'RE WORRIED ABOUT!
MR. DRAGOTTA WOULD LIKE TO INVITE YOU FOR A DRINK IN THE V.I.P. SUITE.
HE LIKES TO GIVE ALL THE HIGH-ROLLERS A WARM WELCOME. IT'S A SANDS TRADITION. THE PERSONAL TOUCH, Y'KNOW.
TELL HIM THAT'S VERY KIND, BUT WE'VE GOT TICKETS TO SEE A SHOW IN...
OH, I UNDERSTAND. IT'S AN OFFER I CAN'T REFUSE.
ACTUALLY, THAT FILM'S NOT BEEN MADE YET, SO YOU WON'T GET THE JOKE...
LET HIM GO, HE HASN'T DONE ANY...
WAIT, AREN'T YOU SONNY LAWSON? MY DAD'S A BIG BOXING FAN. HE SAID YOU WERE ONE OF THE BEST, THAT YOU COULD'VE--
SORRY, MA'AM.
PRIVATE INVITATION ONLY.

YOU CAN PUT ME *DOWN* NOW, IF YOU LIKE.

SHADDUP.

OR NOT, IF YOU'RE ENJOYING THE EXERCISE.

HEY, GLAD YOU COULD *MAKE* IT. THE BOYS TREATING YOU ALRIGHT, MAKING YOU FEEL WANTED? 'COURSE THEY ARE.

NAME'S *DRAGOTTA*, JOHNNY DRAGOTTA, MAIN MAN IN THIS ESTABLISHMENT.

WE GOTTA TALK, MISTER...?

DOCTOR.

DOCTOR! AN *EDUCATED* MAN -- HOW ABOUT THAT, BOYS?

EDUCATION'S A *WONDERFUL* THING, EXCEPT THAT SOMETIMES IT DOESN'T EXACTLY GIVE YOU *COMMON SENSE* --

-- OTHERWISE YOU WOULDN'T BE *CRAZY* ENOUGH TO TRY AND *CHEAT* ME!

CHEAT? OUTRAGEOUS!

IF YOU LOOK *CLOSELY*, I THINK YOU'LL FIND I WAS PLAYING FAIR AND SQUARE.

YOU JUST WON *800,000 DOLLARS* IN LESS THAN AN HOUR! YOU'RE EITHER THE *CROOKEDEST* MAN ALIVE -- OR THE *LUCKIEST!*

IF YOU DON'T TELL ME YOUR SYSTEM, SONNY HERE IS GONNA HANG YOU UP AND USE YOU AS A *PUNCHING-BAG!*

OH, WELL, SEEING AS YOU ASKED SO *NICELY*...

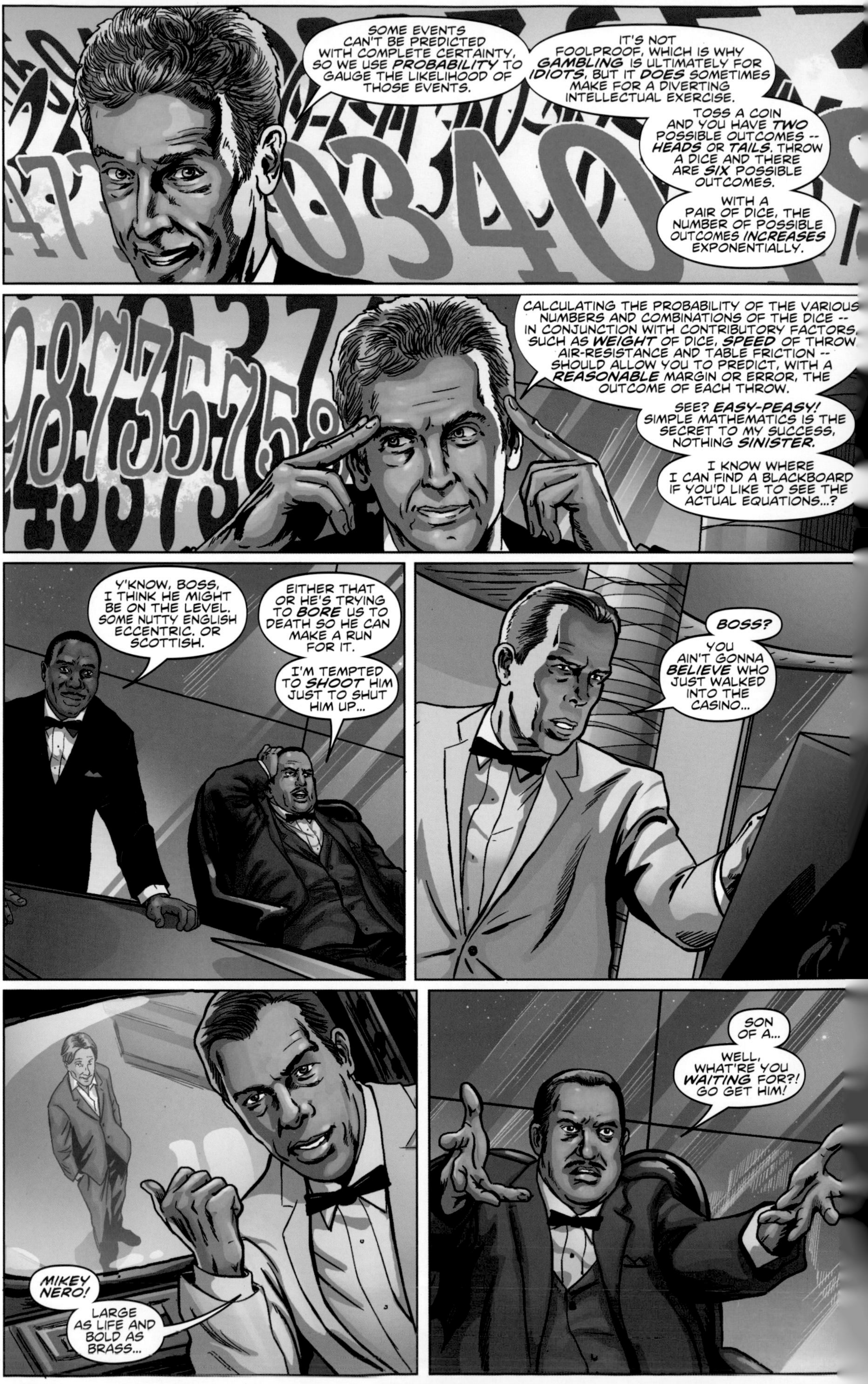
SOME EVENTS CAN'T BE PREDICTED WITH COMPLETE CERTAINTY, SO WE USE PROBABILITY TO GAUGE THE LIKELIHOOD OF THOSE EVENTS.
IT'S NOT FOOLPROOF, WHICH IS WHY GAMBLING IS ULTIMATELY FOR IDIOTS, BUT IT DOES SOMETIMES MAKE FOR A DIVERTING INTELLECTUAL EXERCISE.
TOSS A COIN AND YOU HAVE TWO POSSIBLE OUTCOMES -- HEADS OR TAILS. THROW A DICE AND THERE ARE SIX POSSIBLE OUTCOMES.
WITH A PAIR OF DICE, THE NUMBER OF POSSIBLE OUTCOMES INCREASES EXPONENTIALLY.
CALCULATING THE PROBABILITY OF THE VARIOUS NUMBERS AND COMBINATIONS OF THE DICE -- IN CONJUNCTION WITH CONTRIBUTORY FACTORS, SUCH AS WEIGHT OF DICE, SPEED OF THROW, AIR-RESISTANCE AND TABLE FRICTION -- SHOULD ALLOW YOU TO PREDICT, WITH A REASONABLE MARGIN OR ERROR, THE OUTCOME OF EACH THROW.
SEE? EASY-PEASY! SIMPLE MATHEMATICS IS THE SECRET TO MY SUCCESS, NOTHING SINISTER.
I KNOW WHERE I CAN FIND A BLACKBOARD IF YOU'D LIKE TO SEE THE ACTUAL EQUATIONS...?
Y'KNOW, BOSS, I THINK HE MIGHT BE ON THE LEVEL. SOME NUTTY ENGLISH ECCENTRIC. OR SCOTTISH.
EITHER THAT OR HE'S TRYING TO BORE US TO DEATH SO HE CAN MAKE A RUN FOR IT.
I'M TEMPTED TO SHOOT HIM JUST TO SHUT HIM UP...
BOSS?
YOU AIN'T GONNA BELIEVE WHO JUST WALKED INTO THE CASINO...
MIKEY NERO!
LARGE AS LIFE AND BOLD AS BRASS...
SON OF A...
WELL, WHAT'RE YOU WAITING FOR?! GO GET HIM!

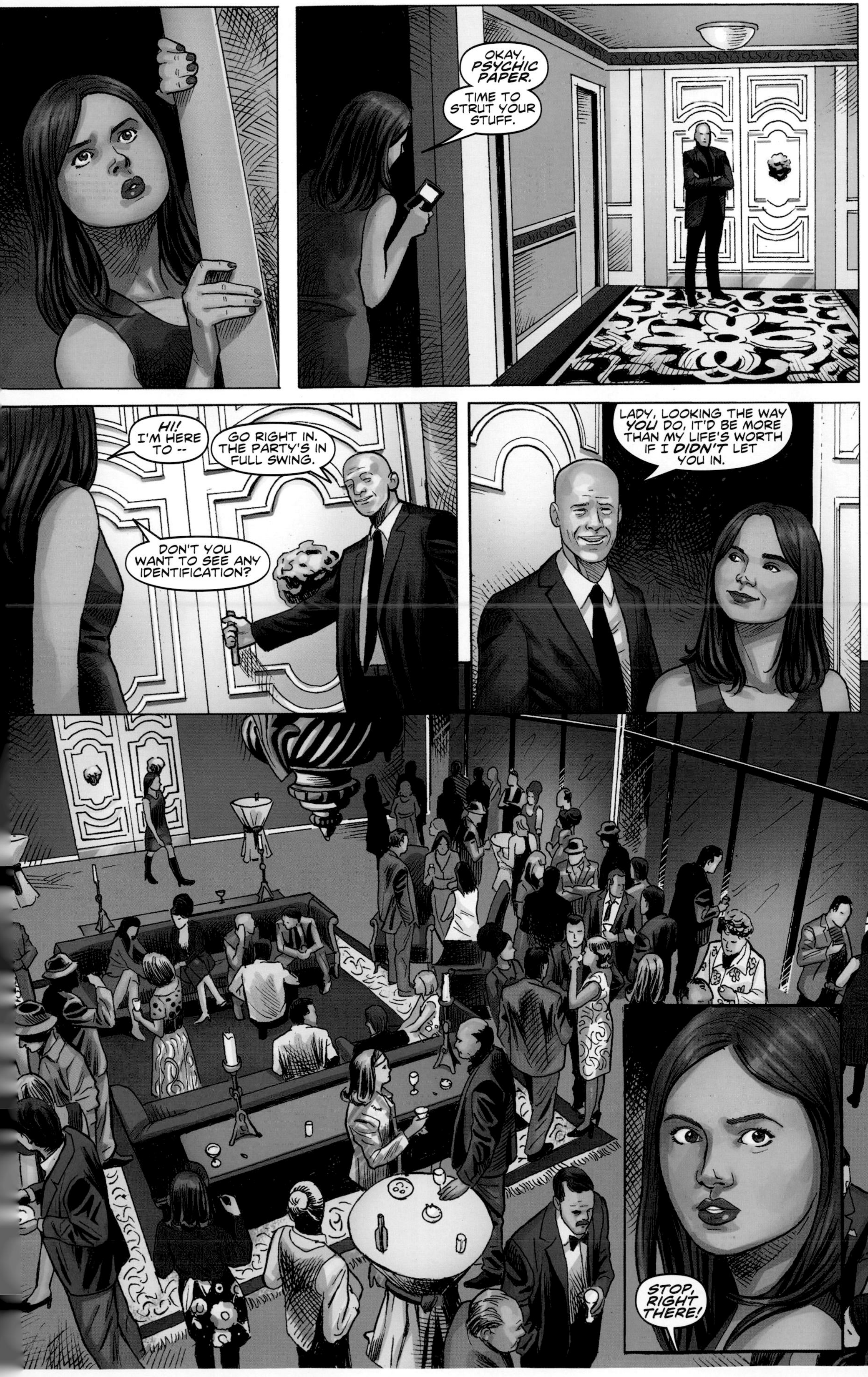
OKAY, PSYCHIC PAPER.
TIME TO STRUT YOUR STUFF.
HI! I'M HERE TO --
GO RIGHT IN. THE PARTY'S IN FULL SWING.
DON'T YOU WANT TO SEE ANY IDENTIFICATION?
LADY, LOOKING THE WAY YOU DO, IT'D BE MORE THAN MY LIFE'S WORTH IF I DIDN'T LET YOU IN.
STOP, RIGHT THERE!

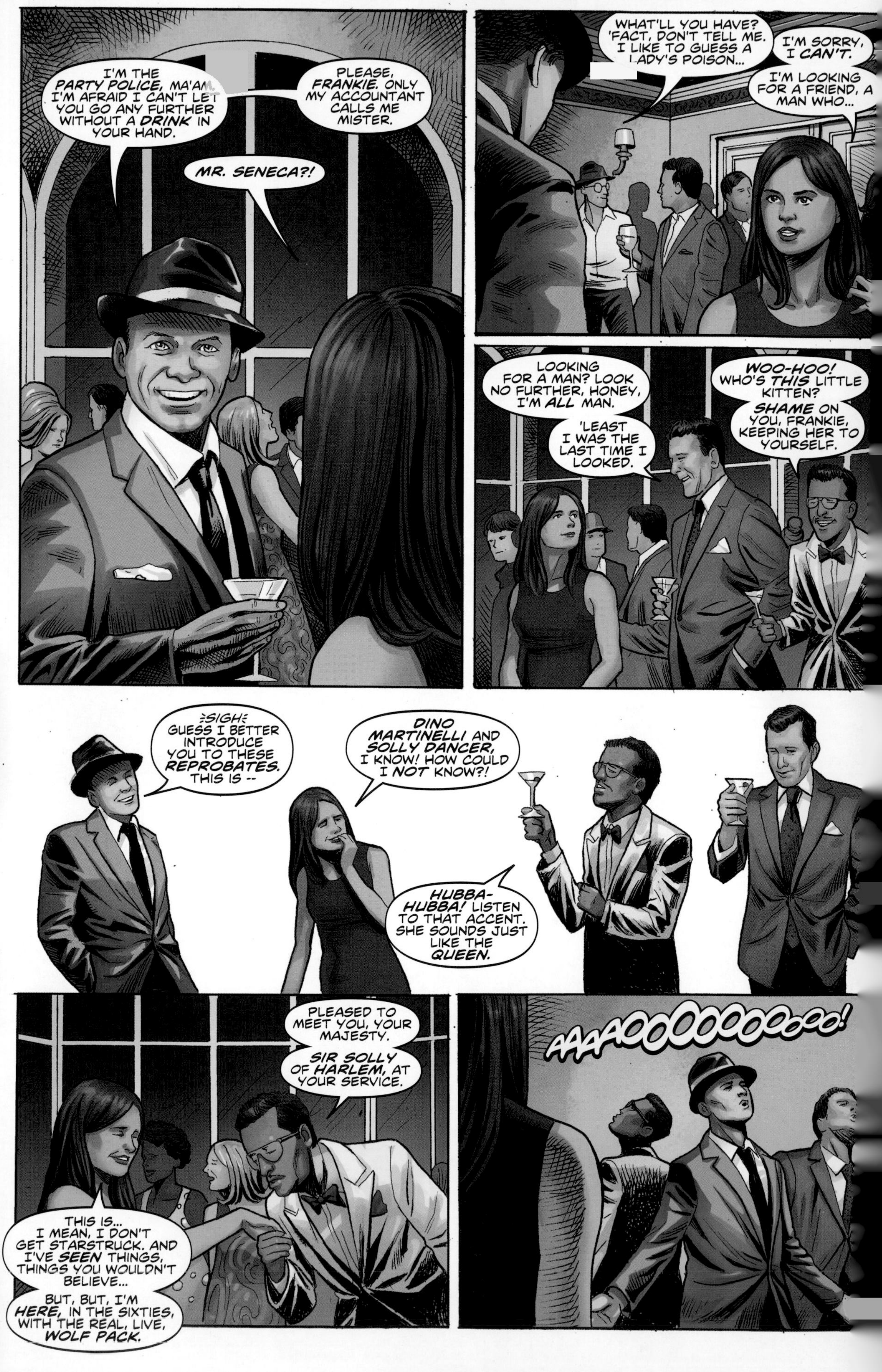
I'M THE PARTY POLICE, MA'AM. I'M AFRAID I CAN'T LET YOU GO ANY FURTHER WITHOUT A DRINK IN YOUR HAND.
MR. SENECA?!
PLEASE, FRANKIE. ONLY MY ACCOUNTANT CALLS ME MISTER.
WHAT'LL YOU HAVE? 'FACT, DON'T TELL ME. I LIKE TO GUESS A LADY'S POISON...
I'M SORRY, I CAN'T.
I'M LOOKING FOR A FRIEND, A MAN WHO...
LOOKING FOR A MAN? LOOK NO FURTHER, HONEY, I'M ALL MAN.
'LEAST I WAS THE LAST TIME I LOOKED.
WOO-HOO! WHO'S THIS LITTLE KITTEN?
SHAME ON YOU, FRANKIE, KEEPING HER TO YOURSELF.
SIGH GUESS I BETTER INTRODUCE YOU TO THESE REPROBATES. THIS IS --
DINO MARTINELLI AND SOLLY DANCER, I KNOW! HOW COULD I NOT KNOW?!
HUBBA-HUBBA! LISTEN TO THAT ACCENT. SHE SOUNDS JUST LIKE THE QUEEN.
PLEASED TO MEET YOU, YOUR MAJESTY.
SIR SOLLY OF HARLEM, AT YOUR SERVICE.
THIS IS... I MEAN, I DON'T GET STARSTRUCK. AND I'VE SEEN THINGS, THINGS YOU WOULDN'T BELIEVE...
BUT, BUT, I'M HERE, IN THE SIXTIES, WITH THE REAL, LIVE, WOLF PACK.
AAAAOOOOOOOOooo!

WELL, I DON'T KNOW ABOUT *YOU*, MIKEY, BUT I FIGURE YOU'VE GOT SOME MAJOR EXPLAINING TO DO.

STARTING WITH...

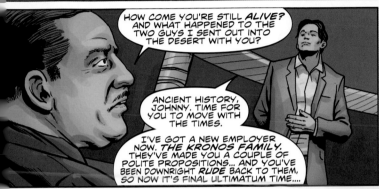

HOW COME YOU'RE STILL *ALIVE?* AND WHAT HAPPENED TO THE TWO GUYS I SENT OUT INTO THE DESERT WITH YOU?

ANCIENT HISTORY, JOHNNY. TIME FOR YOU TO MOVE WITH THE TIMES.

I'VE GOT A NEW EMPLOYER NOW. *THE KRONOS FAMILY.* THEY'VE MADE YOU A COUPLE OF POLITE PROPOSITIONS... AND YOU'VE BEEN DOWNRIGHT *RUDE* BACK TO THEM, SO NOW IT'S FINAL ULTIMATUM TIME....

HAND OVER CONTROL OF THE SANDS HOTEL AND ALL YOUR RACKETS, OR YOU AND YOUR ENTIRE ORGANIZATION WILL BE *WIPED* FROM EXISTENCE.

LITERALLY.

S *TALK* FROM A CHEAP, O-BIT HUSTLER. WHAT'RE YOU GONNA *DO?*

TAKE ON THE WHOLE *MAFIA?*

MISTER AGOTTA, IS *ISN'T* MAN YOU KNOW.

IN FACT...

HE MAY NOT EVEN BE *HUMAN!*

GGRRRAAAAGH! HHHHHH!

WHOA! WHAT IS THIS?

GET OUTTA HERE, YOU FREELOADING BUMS!

THESE GUYS HAVE GOT A SHOW TO DO, Y'HEAR?

YOU TOO, SWEETHEART.

UH-UH, *ARTIE.* SHE'S WITH US.

A DAMSEL IN DISTRESS.

AND WE'RE HER GUARDIAN ANGELS.

WATCH THE SHOW FROM BACKSTAGE, KID.

ONCE WE'VE DONE AN ENCORE, WE'LL TRACK DOWN THIS DISAPPEARING DOCTOR OF YOURS.

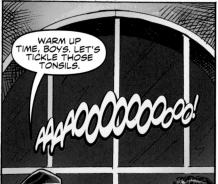

WARM UP TIME, BOYS. LET'S TICKLE THOSE TONSILS.

SSSKKKAAASSSHHH

AAAAOOOOOOOOOooo!

WELL, AIN'T THAT A *KICK* IN THE HEAD.

WE MUST'VE HIT A REAL *HIGH* NOTE.

SOMEHOW, I DON'T THINK IT WAS *YOUR* DULCET TONES.

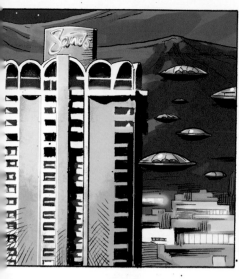

OUTTA
SIGHT...

OUTTA
THIS
WORLD...

OUTTA
HERE, AS
IN, LET'S
GET...

STAGE
FRIGHT, LADIES AND
GENTLEMEN?

I HOPE
NOT.

THE
SHOW'S JUST
BEGINNING.

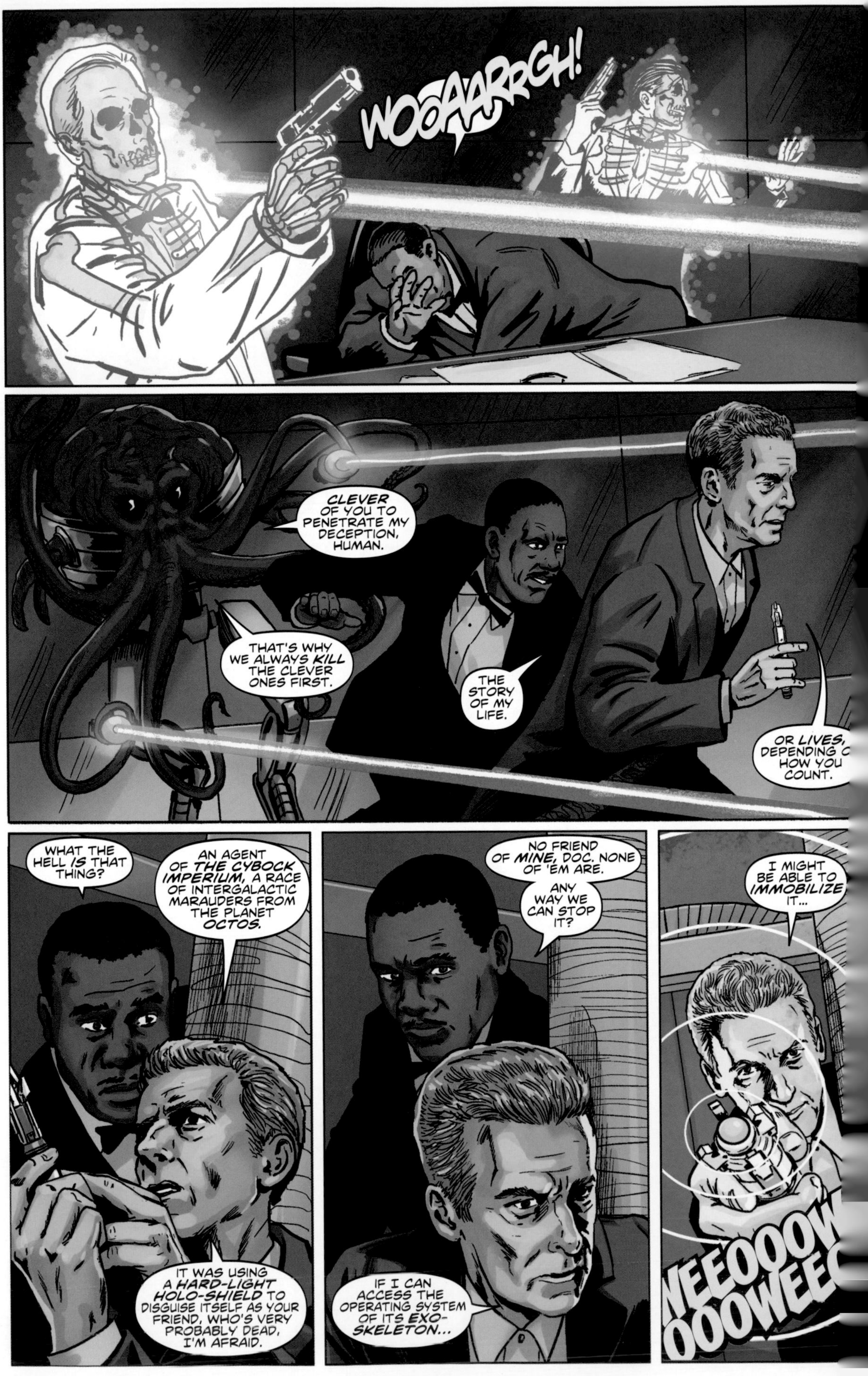
WOOAARRGH!
CLEVER OF YOU TO PENETRATE MY DECEPTION, HUMAN.
THAT'S WHY WE ALWAYS KILL THE CLEVER ONES FIRST.
THE STORY OF MY LIFE.
OR LIVES, DEPENDING O HOW YOU COUNT.
WHAT THE HELL IS THAT THING?
AN AGENT OF THE CYBOCK IMPERIUM, A RACE OF INTERGALACTIC MARAUDERS FROM THE PLANET OCTOS.
IT WAS USING A HARD-LIGHT HOLO-SHIELD TO DISGUISE ITSELF AS YOUR FRIEND, WHO'S VERY PROBABLY DEAD, I'M AFRAID.
NO FRIEND OF MINE, DOC. NONE OF 'EM ARE.
ANY WAY WE CAN STOP IT?
IF I CAN ACCESS THE OPERATING SYSTEM OF ITS EXO-SKELETON...
I MIGHT BE ABLE TO IMMOBILIZE IT...
NEEOOOW OOOWEE

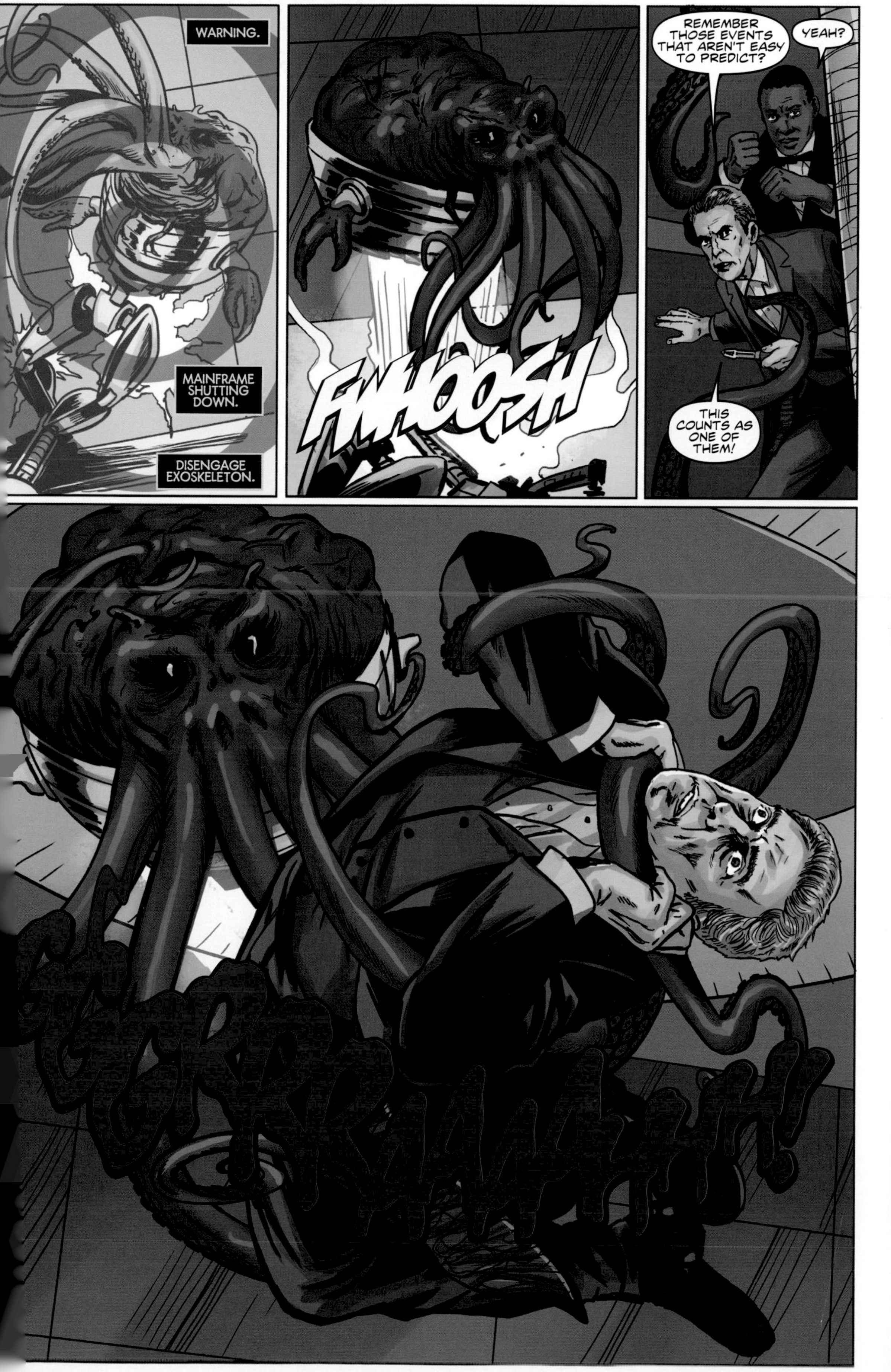
WARNING.
MAINFRAME SHUTTING DOWN.
DISENGAGE EXOSKELETON.
FWHOOSH
REMEMBER THOSE EVENTS THAT AREN'T EASY TO PREDICT?
YEAH?
THIS COUNTS AS ONE OF THEM!

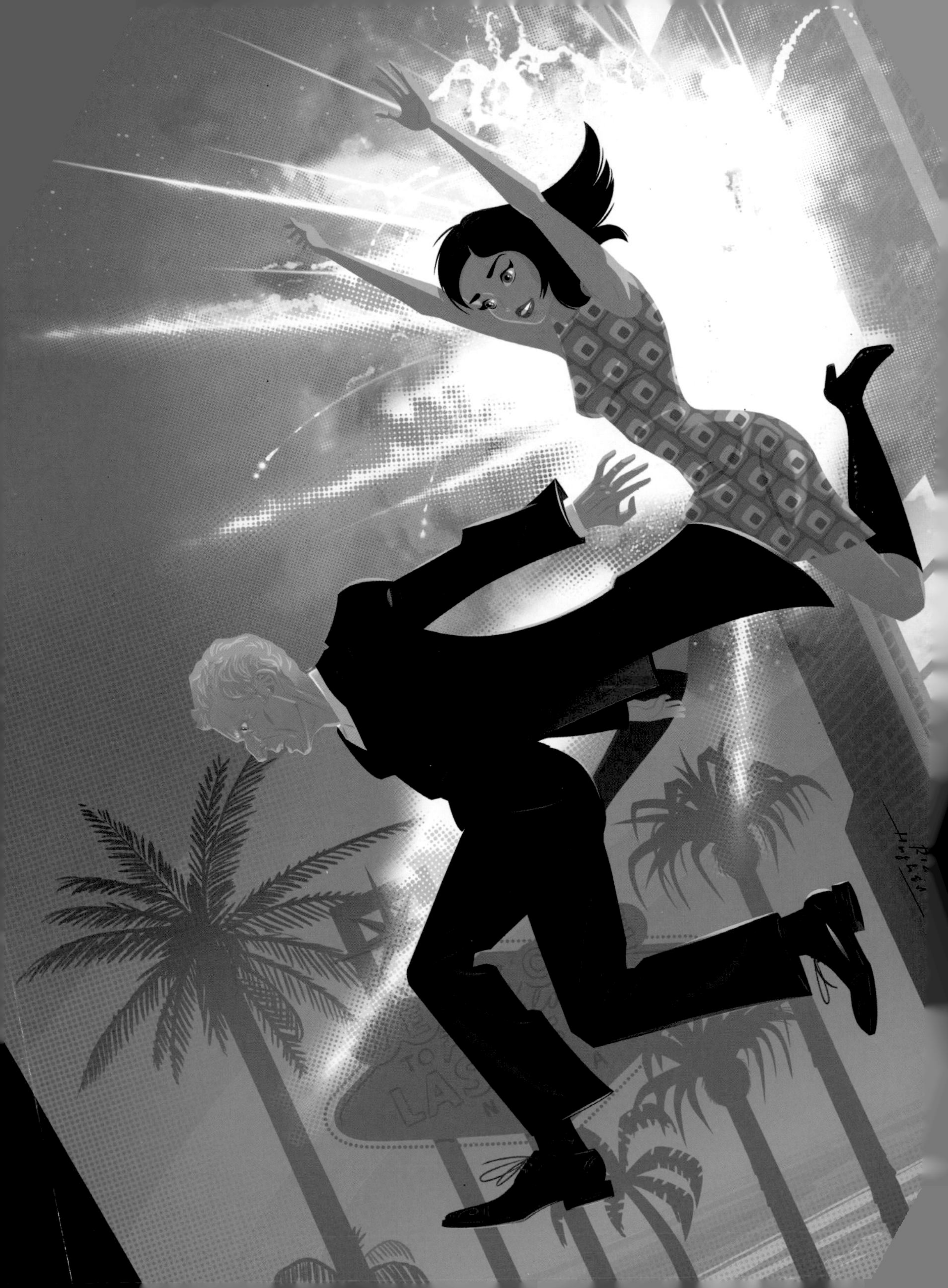
TO
LAS

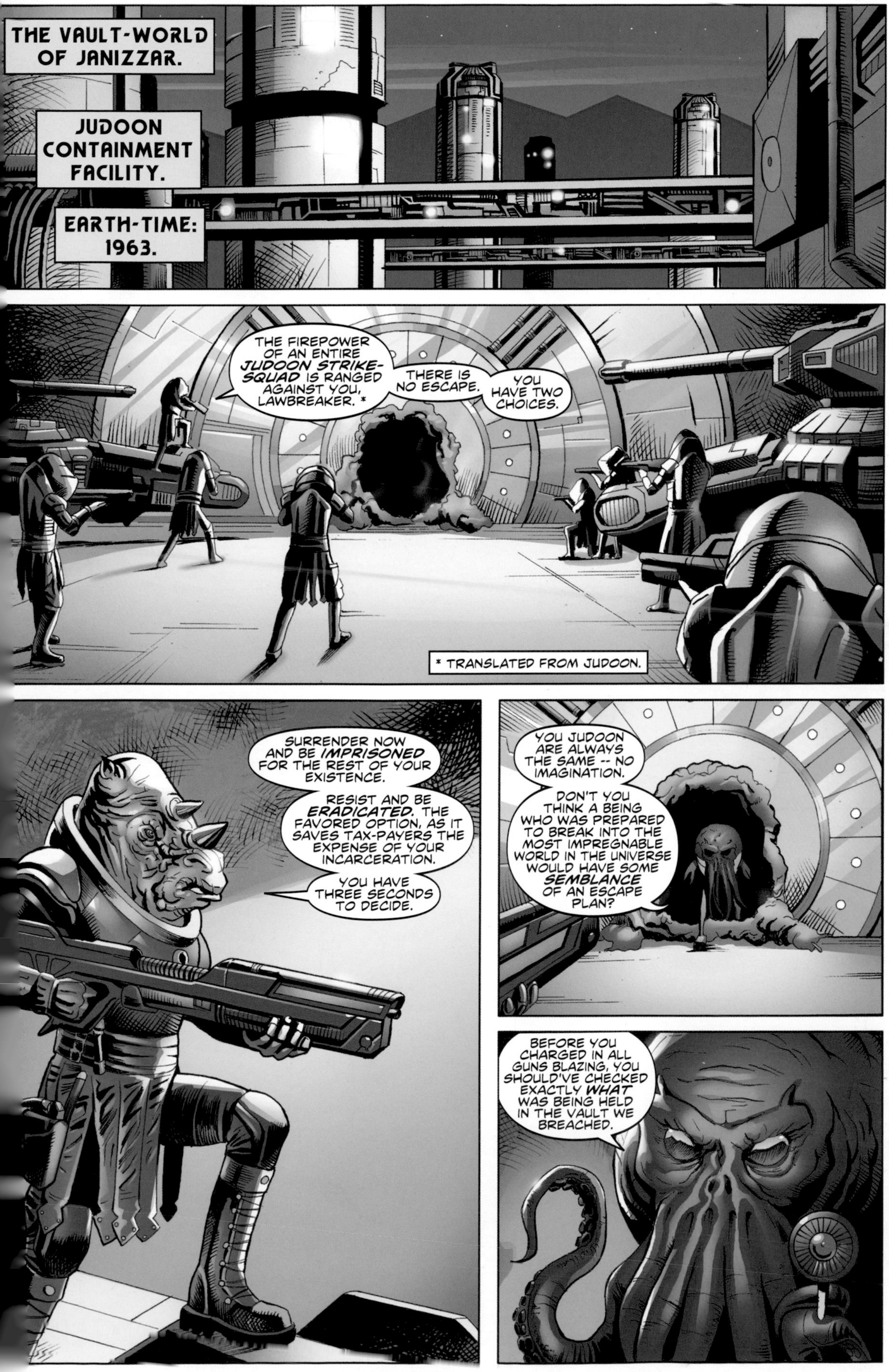
THE VAULT-WORLD OF JANIZZAR.
JUDOON CONTAINMENT FACILITY.
EARTH-TIME: 1963.
THE FIREPOWER OF AN ENTIRE JUDOON STRIKE-SQUAD IS RANGED AGAINST YOU, LAWBREAKER. *
THERE IS NO ESCAPE.
YOU HAVE TWO CHOICES.
* TRANSLATED FROM JUDOON.
SURRENDER NOW AND BE IMPRISONED FOR THE REST OF YOUR EXISTENCE.
RESIST AND BE ERADICATED. THE FAVORED OPTION, AS IT SAVES TAX-PAYERS THE EXPENSE OF YOUR INCARCERATION.
YOU HAVE THREE SECONDS TO DECIDE.
YOU JUDOON ARE ALWAYS THE SAME -- NO IMAGINATION.
DON'T YOU THINK A BEING WHO WAS PREPARED TO BREAK INTO THE MOST IMPREGNABLE WORLD IN THE UNIVERSE WOULD HAVE SOME SEMBLANCE OF AN ESCAPE PLAN?
BEFORE YOU CHARGED IN ALL GUNS BLAZING, YOU SHOULD'VE CHECKED EXACTLY WHAT WAS BEING HELD IN THE VAULT WE BREACHED.

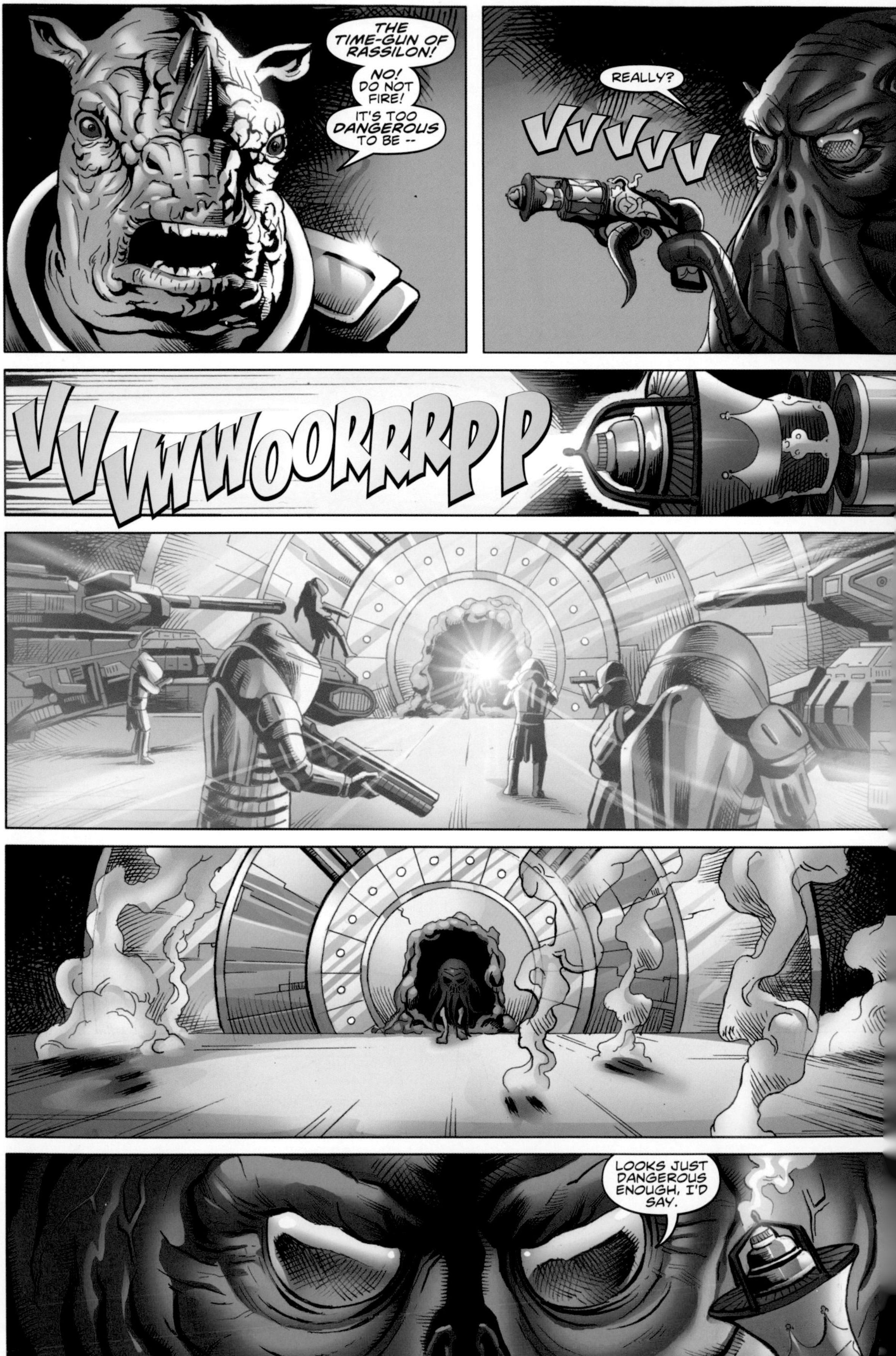
THE TIME-GUN OF RASSILON!
NO! DO NOT FIRE!
IT'S TOO DANGEROUS TO BE --
REALLY?
VVVVVV
VVVWWWOORRRPP
LOOKS JUST DANGEROUS ENOUGH, I'D SAY.

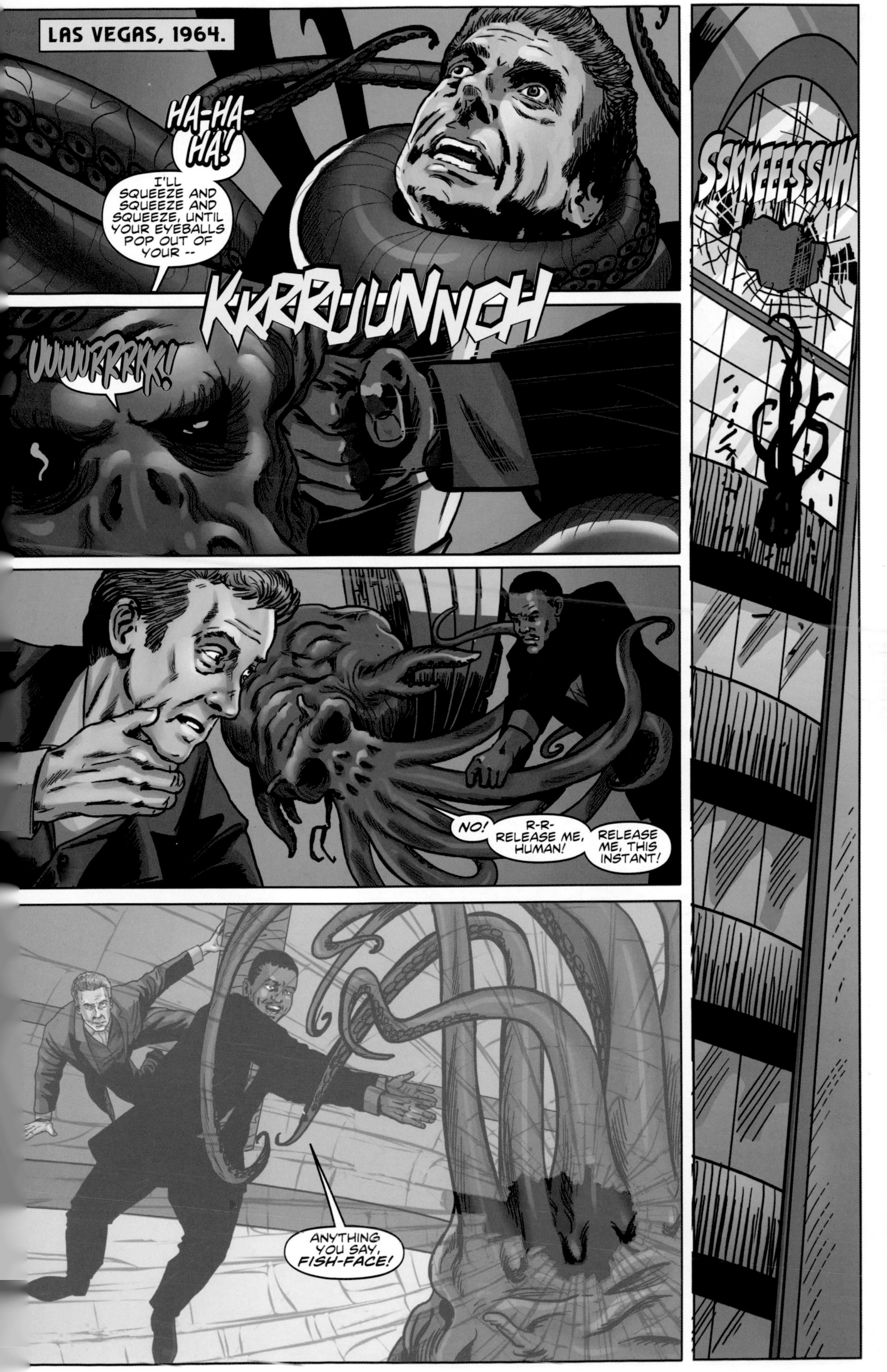
LAS VEGAS, 1964.
HA-HA-HA!
I'LL SQUEEZE AND SQUEEZE AND SQUEEZE, UNTIL YOUR EYEBALLS POP OUT OF YOUR --
KKRRUUNNCH
UUUURRRK!
NO!
R-R-RELEASE ME, HUMAN!
RELEASE ME, THIS INSTANT!
ANYTHING YOU SAY, *FISH-FACE!*
SSKKEEEESSHH

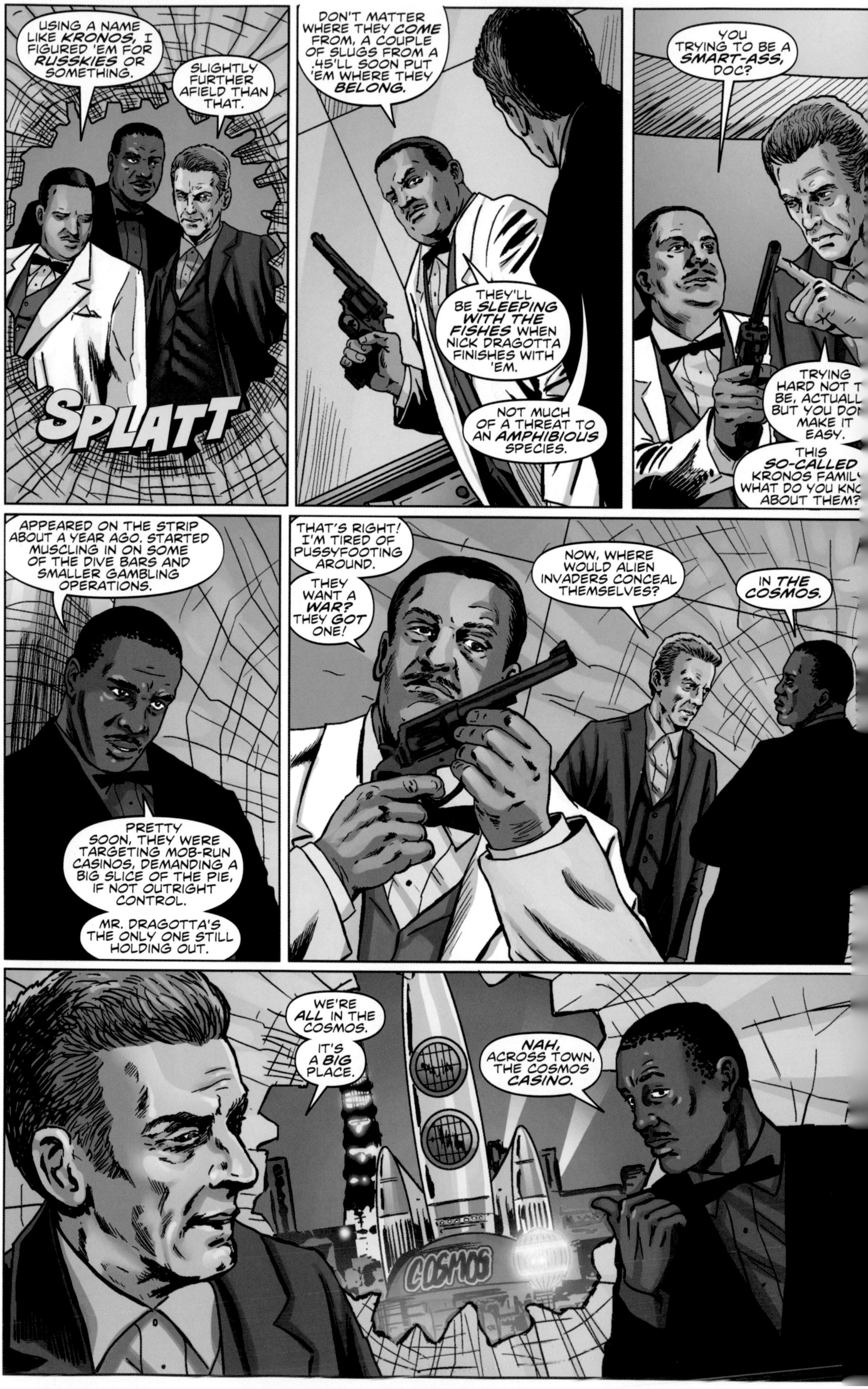
USING A NAME LIKE KRONOS, I FIGURED 'EM FOR RUSSKIES OR SOMETHING.
SLIGHTLY FURTHER AFIELD THAN THAT.
SPLATT
DON'T MATTER WHERE THEY COME FROM, A COUPLE OF SLUGS FROM A .45'LL SOON PUT 'EM WHERE THEY BELONG.
THEY'LL BE SLEEPING WITH THE FISHES WHEN NICK DRAGOTTA FINISHES WITH 'EM.
NOT MUCH OF A THREAT TO AN AMPHIBIOUS SPECIES.
YOU TRYING TO BE A SMART-ASS, DOC?
TRYING HARD NOT T BE, ACTUALL BUT YOU DO MAKE IT EASY.
THIS SO-CALLED KRONOS FAMIL WHAT DO YOU KN ABOUT THEM?
APPEARED ON THE STRIP ABOUT A YEAR AGO. STARTED MUSCLING IN ON SOME OF THE DIVE BARS AND SMALLER GAMBLING OPERATIONS.
PRETTY SOON, THEY WERE TARGETING MOB-RUN CASINOS, DEMANDING A BIG SLICE OF THE PIE, IF NOT OUTRIGHT CONTROL.
MR. DRAGOTTA'S THE ONLY ONE STILL HOLDING OUT.
THAT'S RIGHT! I'M TIRED OF PUSSYFOOTING AROUND.
THEY WANT A WAR? THEY GOT ONE!
NOW, WHERE WOULD ALIEN INVADERS CONCEAL THEMSELVES?
IN THE COSMOS.
WE'RE ALL IN THE COSMOS.
IT'S A BIG PLACE.
NAH, ACROSS TOWN, THE COSMOS CASINO.
COSMOS

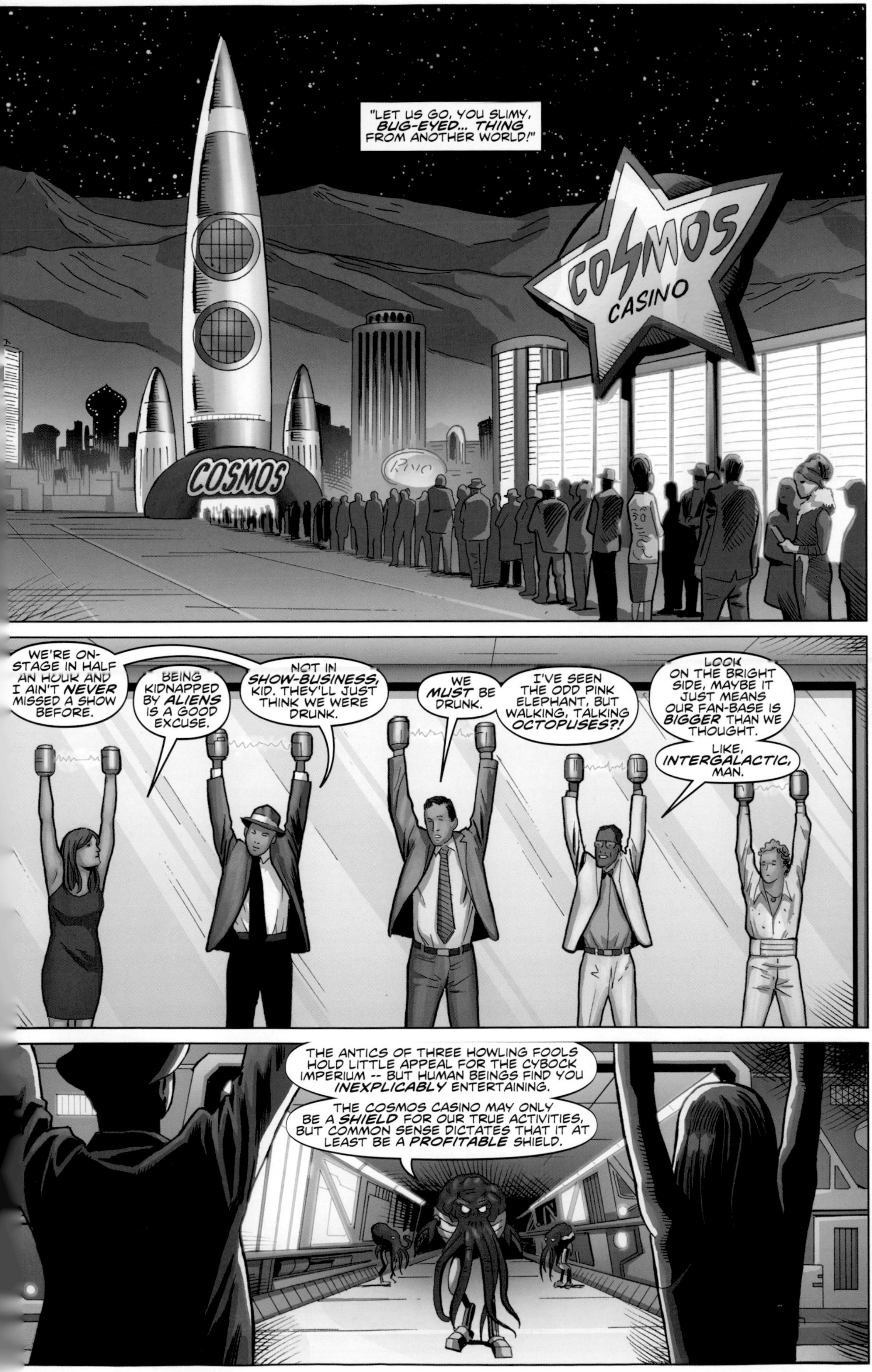
"LET US GO, YOU SLIMY, BUG-EYED... THING FROM ANOTHER WORLD!"
COSMOS CASINO
COSMOS
WE'RE ON-STAGE IN HALF AN HOUR AND I AIN'T NEVER MISSED A SHOW BEFORE.
BEING KIDNAPPED BY ALIENS IS A GOOD EXCUSE.
NOT IN SHOW-BUSINESS, KID. THEY'LL JUST THINK WE WERE DRUNK.
WE MUST BE DRUNK.
I'VE SEEN THE ODD PINK ELEPHANT, BUT WALKING, TALKING OCTOPUSES?!
LOOK ON THE BRIGHT SIDE, MAYBE IT JUST MEANS OUR FAN-BASE IS BIGGER THAN WE THOUGHT.
LIKE, INTERGALACTIC, MAN.
THE ANTICS OF THREE HOWLING FOOLS HOLD LITTLE APPEAL FOR THE CYBOCK IMPERIUM -- BUT HUMAN BEINGS FIND YOU INEXPLICABLY ENTERTAINING.
THE COSMOS CASINO MAY ONLY BE A SHIELD FOR OUR TRUE ACTIVITIES, BUT COMMON SENSE DICTATES THAT IT AT LEAST BE A PROFITABLE SHIELD.

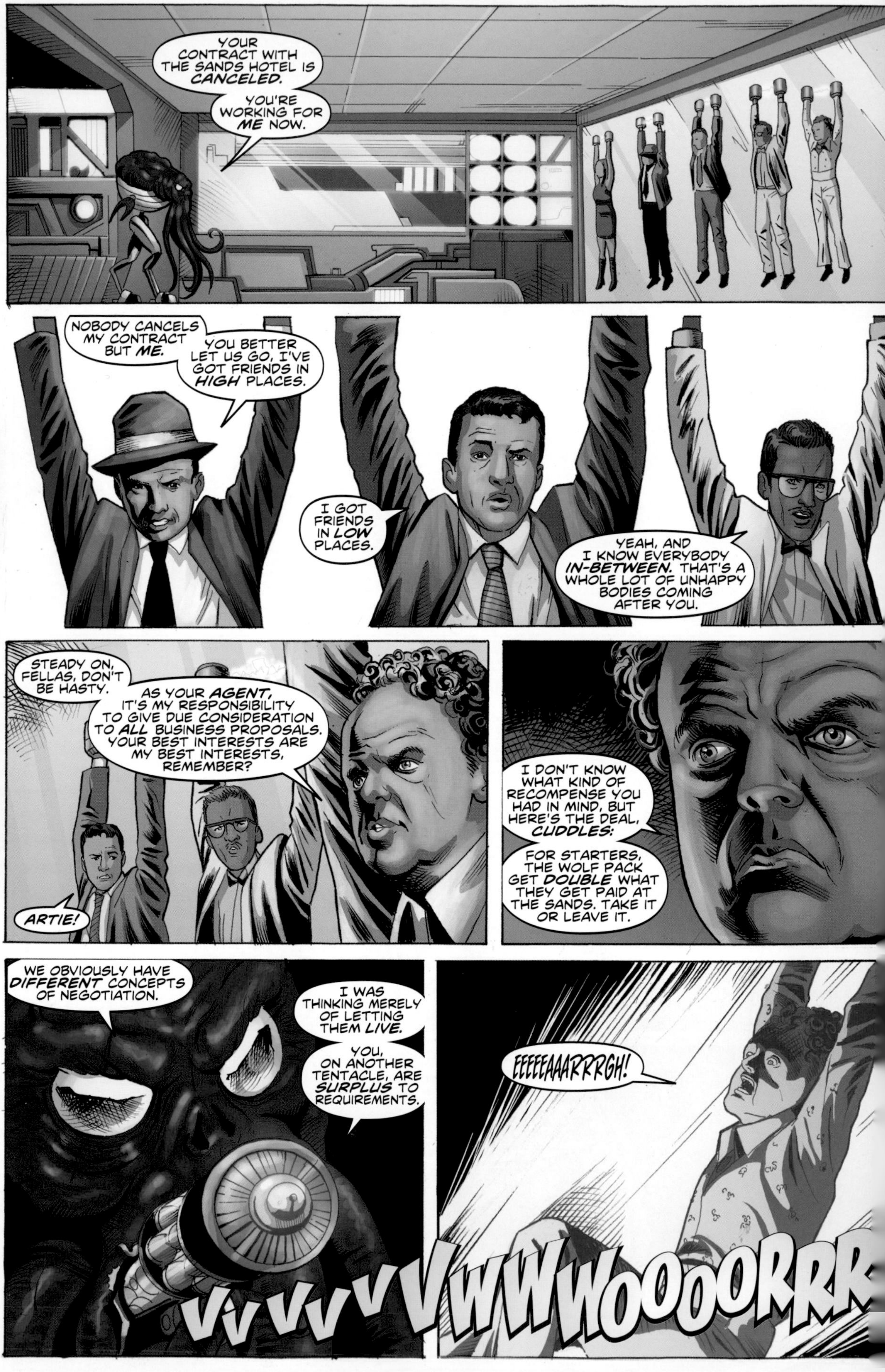
YOUR CONTRACT WITH THE SANDS HOTEL IS CANCELED.
YOU'RE WORKING FOR ME NOW.
NOBODY CANCELS MY CONTRACT BUT ME.
YOU BETTER LET US GO, I'VE GOT FRIENDS IN HIGH PLACES.
I GOT FRIENDS IN LOW PLACES.
YEAH, AND I KNOW EVERYBODY IN-BETWEEN. THAT'S A WHOLE LOT OF UNHAPPY BODIES COMING AFTER YOU.
STEADY ON, FELLAS, DON'T BE HASTY.
AS YOUR AGENT, IT'S MY RESPONSIBILITY TO GIVE DUE CONSIDERATION TO ALL BUSINESS PROPOSALS. YOUR BEST INTERESTS ARE MY BEST INTERESTS, REMEMBER?
ARTIE!
I DON'T KNOW WHAT KIND OF RECOMPENSE YOU HAD IN MIND, BUT HERE'S THE DEAL, CUDDLES:
FOR STARTERS, THE WOLF PACK GET DOUBLE WHAT THEY GET PAID AT THE SANDS. TAKE IT OR LEAVE IT.
WE OBVIOUSLY HAVE DIFFERENT CONCEPTS OF NEGOTIATION.
I WAS THINKING MERELY OF LETTING THEM LIVE.
YOU, ON ANOTHER TENTACLE, ARE SURPLUS TO REQUIREMENTS.
EEEEEAAARRRGH!
VVVVVVWWWWOOOORRR

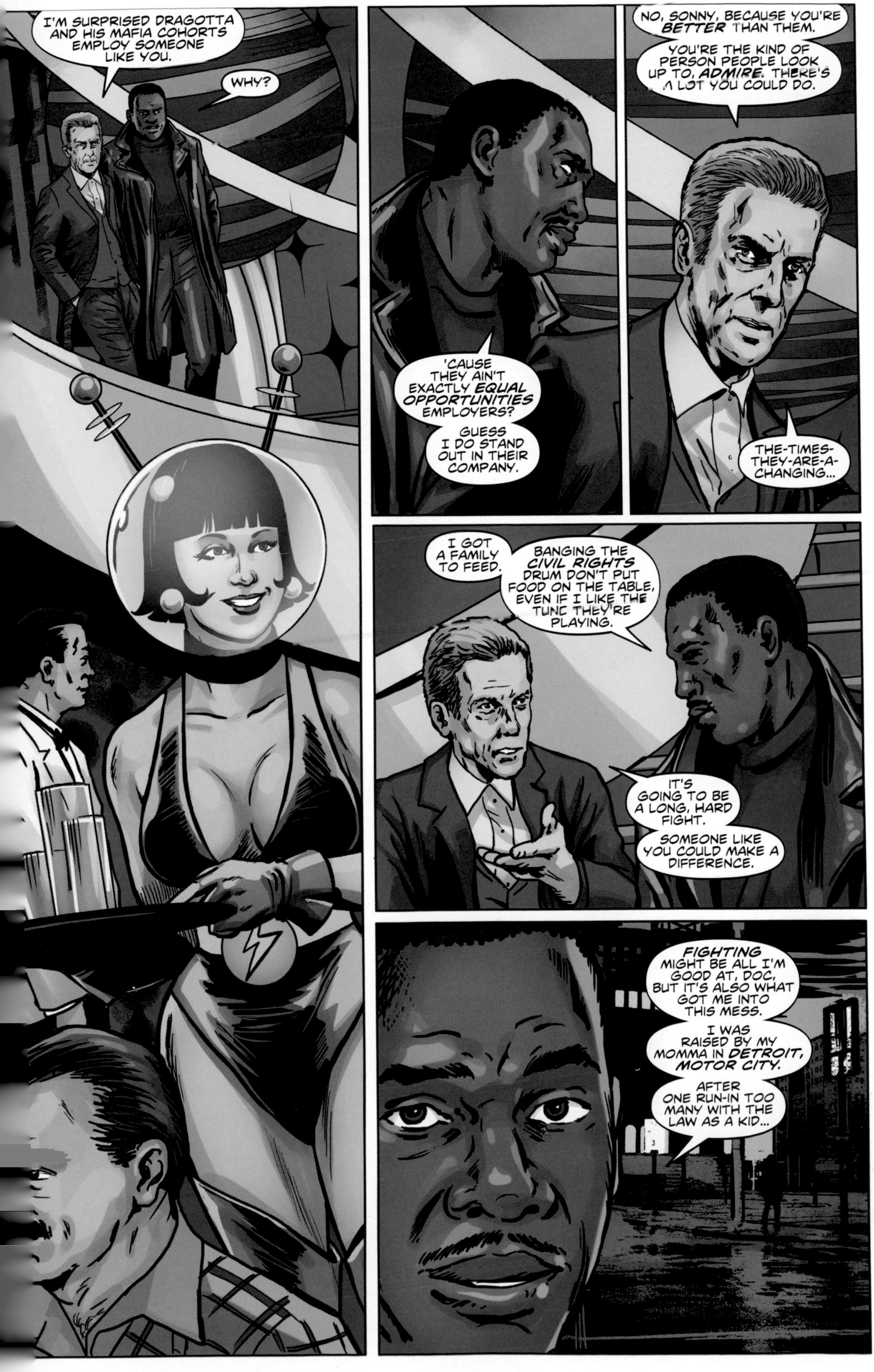
I'M SURPRISED DRAGOTTA AND HIS MAFIA COHORTS EMPLOY SOMEONE LIKE YOU.
WHY?
'CAUSE THEY AIN'T EXACTLY EQUAL OPPORTUNITIES EMPLOYERS?
GUESS I DO STAND OUT IN THEIR COMPANY.
NO, SONNY, BECAUSE YOU'RE BETTER THAN THEM.
YOU'RE THE KIND OF PERSON PEOPLE LOOK UP TO, ADMIRE. THERE'S A LOT YOU COULD DO.
THE-TIMES-THEY-ARE-A-CHANGING...
I GOT A FAMILY TO FEED.
BANGING THE CIVIL RIGHTS DRUM DON'T PUT FOOD ON THE TABLE, EVEN IF I LIKE THE TUNE THEY'RE PLAYING.
IT'S GOING TO BE A LONG, HARD FIGHT.
SOMEONE LIKE YOU COULD MAKE A DIFFERENCE.
FIGHTING MIGHT BE ALL I'M GOOD AT, DOC, BUT IT'S ALSO WHAT GOT ME INTO THIS MESS.
I WAS RAISED BY MY MOMMA IN DETROIT, MOTOR CITY.
AFTER ONE RUN-IN TOO MANY WITH THE LAW AS A KID...

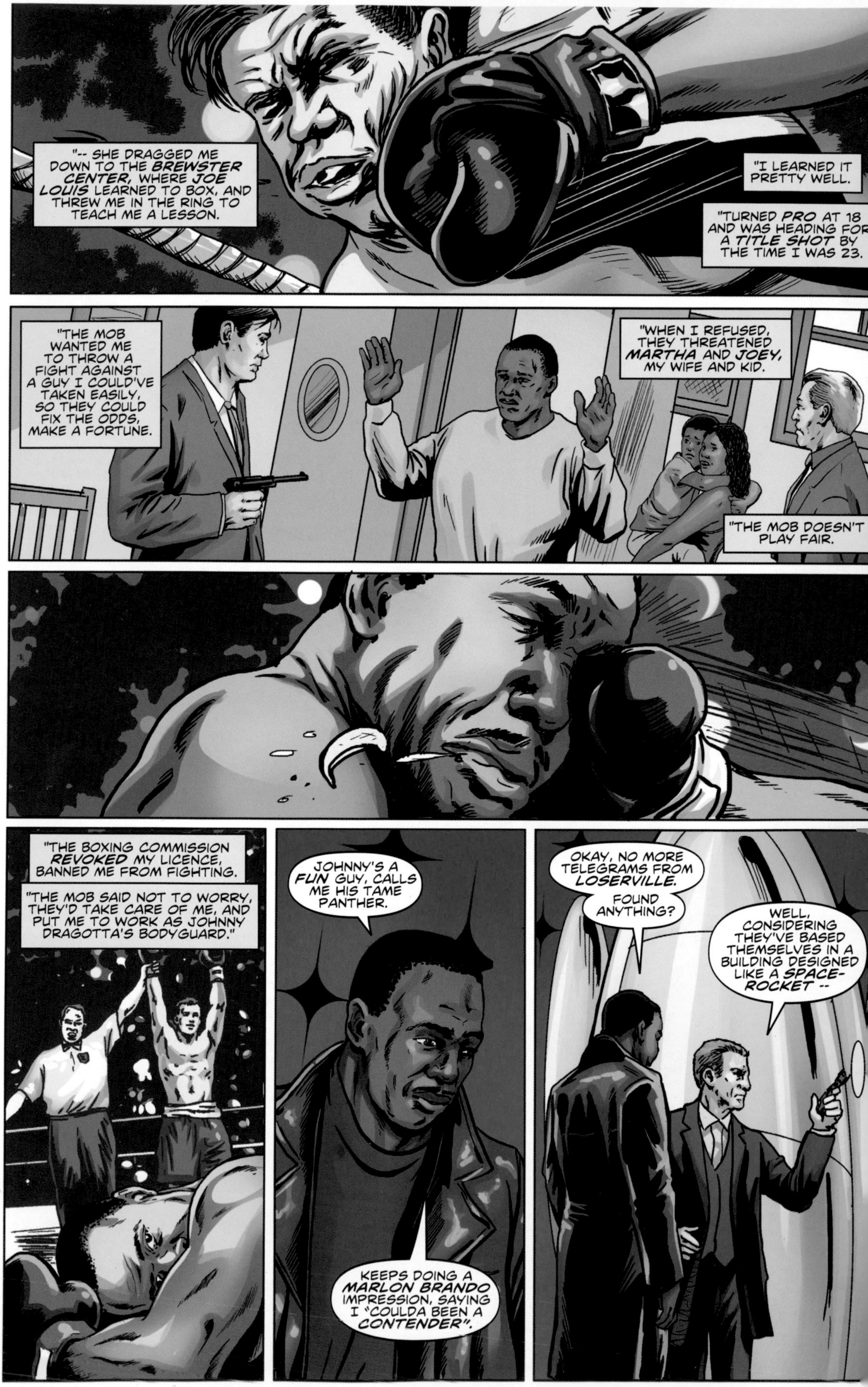
"-- SHE DRAGGED ME DOWN TO THE BREWSTER CENTER, WHERE JOE LOUIS LEARNED TO BOX, AND THREW ME IN THE RING TO TEACH ME A LESSON.
"I LEARNED IT PRETTY WELL.
"TURNED PRO AT 18 AND WAS HEADING FOR A TITLE SHOT BY THE TIME I WAS 23.
"THE MOB WANTED ME TO THROW A FIGHT AGAINST A GUY I COULD'VE TAKEN EASILY, SO THEY COULD FIX THE ODDS, MAKE A FORTUNE.
"WHEN I REFUSED, THEY THREATENED MARTHA AND JOEY, MY WIFE AND KID.
"THE MOB DOESN'T PLAY FAIR.
"THE BOXING COMMISSION REVOKED MY LICENCE, BANNED ME FROM FIGHTING.
"THE MOB SAID NOT TO WORRY, THEY'D TAKE CARE OF ME, AND PUT ME TO WORK AS JOHNNY DRAGOTTA'S BODYGUARD."
JOHNNY'S A FUN GUY, CALLS ME HIS TAME PANTHER.
KEEPS DOING A MARLON BRANDO IMPRESSION, SAYING I "COULDA BEEN A CONTENDER".
OKAY, NO MORE TELEGRAMS FROM LOSERVILLE.
FOUND ANYTHING?
WELL, CONSIDERING THEY'VE BASED THEMSELVES IN A BUILDING DESIGNED LIKE A SPACE-ROCKET --

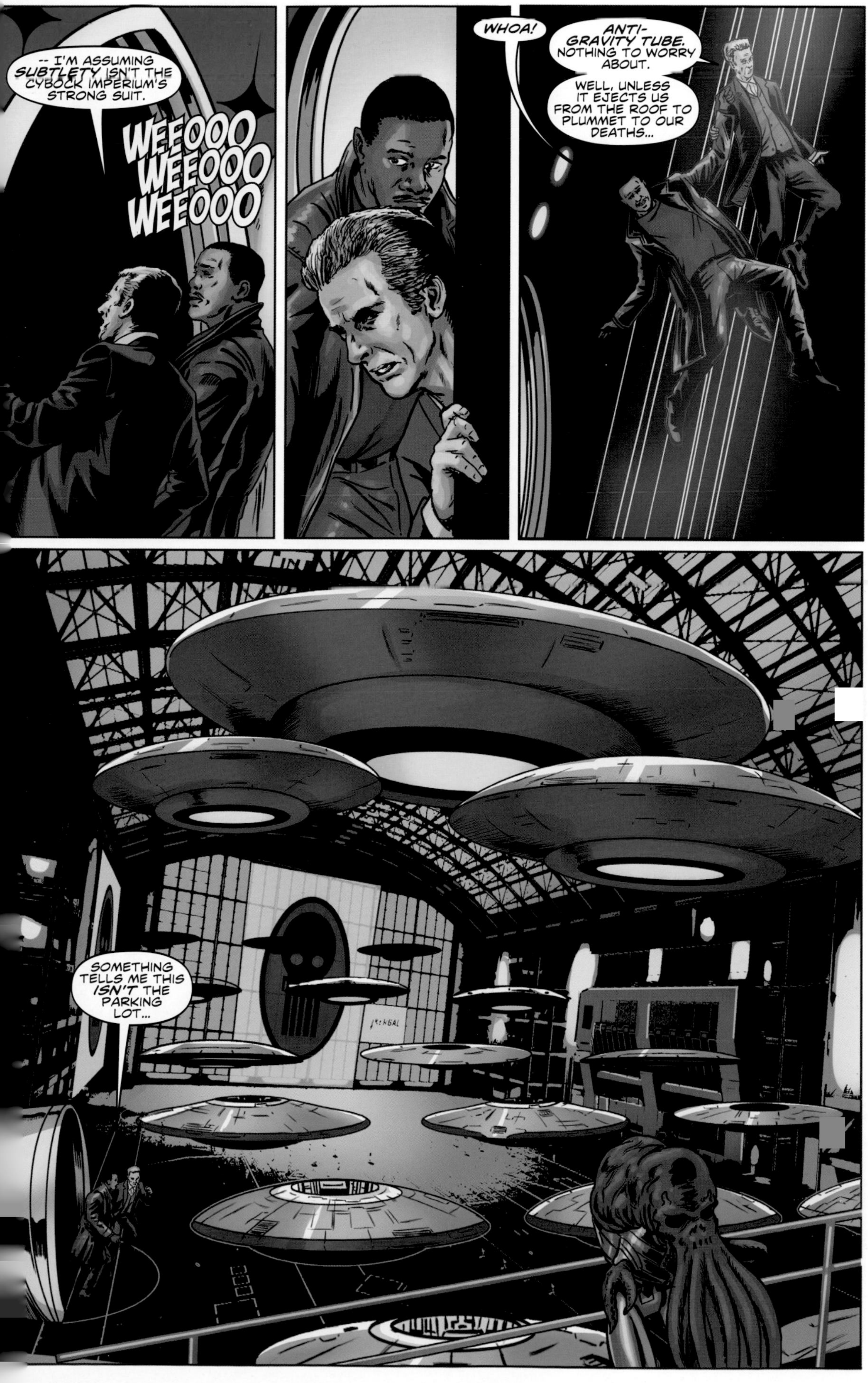
-- I'M ASSUMING SUBTLETY ISN'T THE CYBOCK IMPERIUM'S STRONG SUIT.
WEEOOO WEEOOO WEEOOO
WHOA!
ANTI-GRAVITY TUBE. NOTHING TO WORRY ABOUT.
WELL, UNLESS IT EJECTS US FROM THE ROOF TO PLUMMET TO OUR DEATHS...
SOMETHING TELLS ME THIS ISN'T THE PARKING LOT...

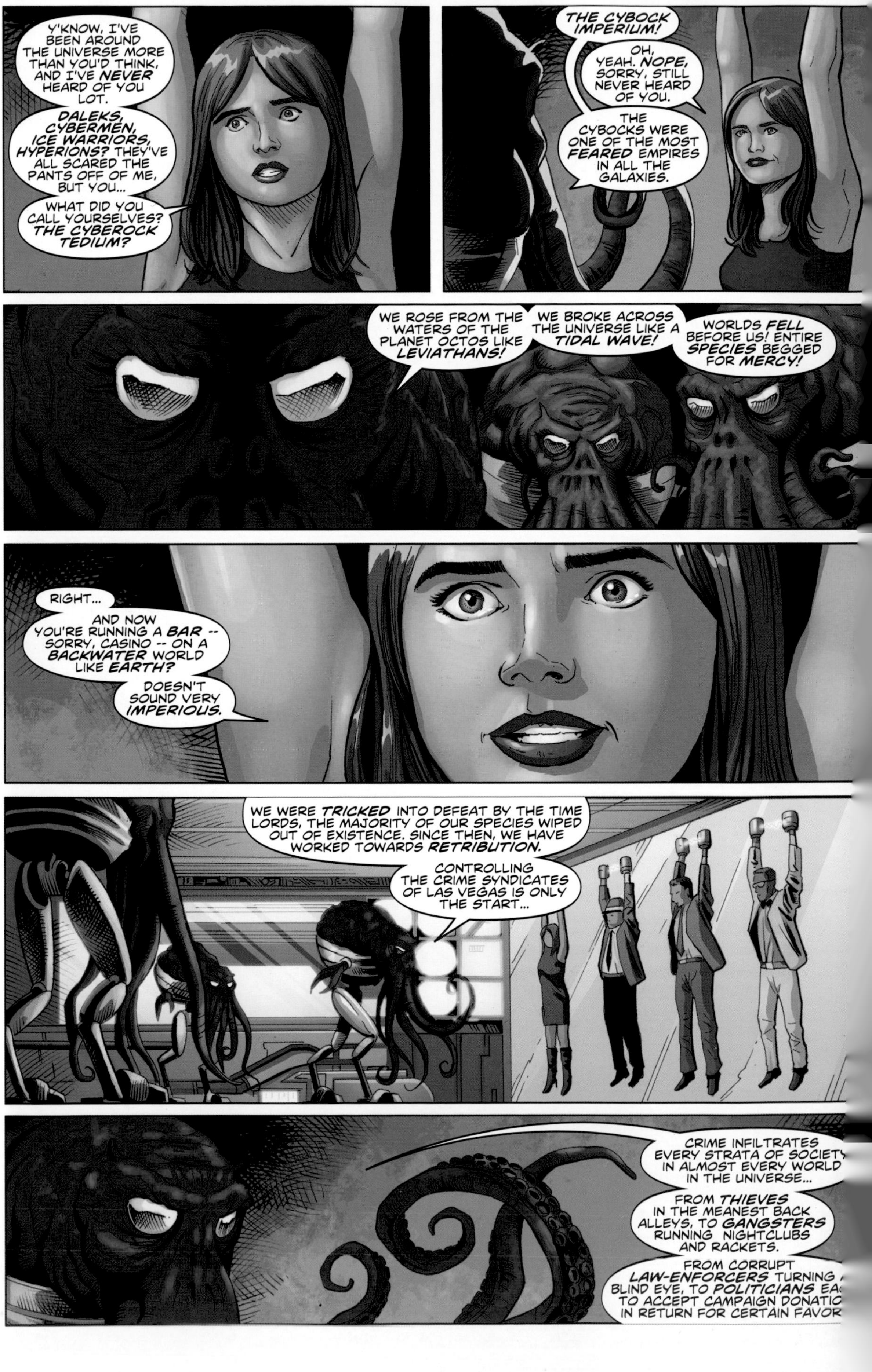
Y'KNOW, I'VE BEEN AROUND THE UNIVERSE MORE THAN YOU'D THINK, AND I'VE NEVER HEARD OF YOU LOT.
DALEKS, CYBERMEN, ICE WARRIORS, HYPERIONS? THEY'VE ALL SCARED THE PANTS OFF OF ME, BUT YOU...
WHAT DID YOU CALL YOURSELVES? THE CYBEROCK TEDIUM?
THE CYBOCK IMPERIUM!
OH, YEAH. NOPE, SORRY, STILL NEVER HEARD OF YOU.
THE CYBOCKS WERE ONE OF THE MOST FEARED EMPIRES IN ALL THE GALAXIES.
WE ROSE FROM THE WATERS OF THE PLANET OCTOS LIKE LEVIATHANS!
WE BROKE ACROSS THE UNIVERSE LIKE A TIDAL WAVE!
WORLDS FELL BEFORE US! ENTIRE SPECIES BEGGED FOR MERCY!
RIGHT...
AND NOW YOU'RE RUNNING A BAR -- SORRY, CASINO -- ON A BACKWATER WORLD LIKE EARTH?
DOESN'T SOUND VERY IMPERIOUS.
WE WERE TRICKED INTO DEFEAT BY THE TIME LORDS, THE MAJORITY OF OUR SPECIES WIPED OUT OF EXISTENCE. SINCE THEN, WE HAVE WORKED TOWARDS RETRIBUTION.
CONTROLLING THE CRIME SYNDICATES OF LAS VEGAS IS ONLY THE START...
CRIME INFILTRATES EVERY STRATA OF SOCIETY IN ALMOST EVERY WORLD IN THE UNIVERSE...
FROM THIEVES IN THE MEANEST BACK ALLEYS, TO GANGSTERS RUNNING NIGHTCLUBS AND RACKETS.
FROM CORRUPT LAW-ENFORCERS TURNING A BLIND EYE, TO POLITICIANS EAG TO ACCEPT CAMPAIGN DONATIO IN RETURN FOR CERTAIN FAVOR

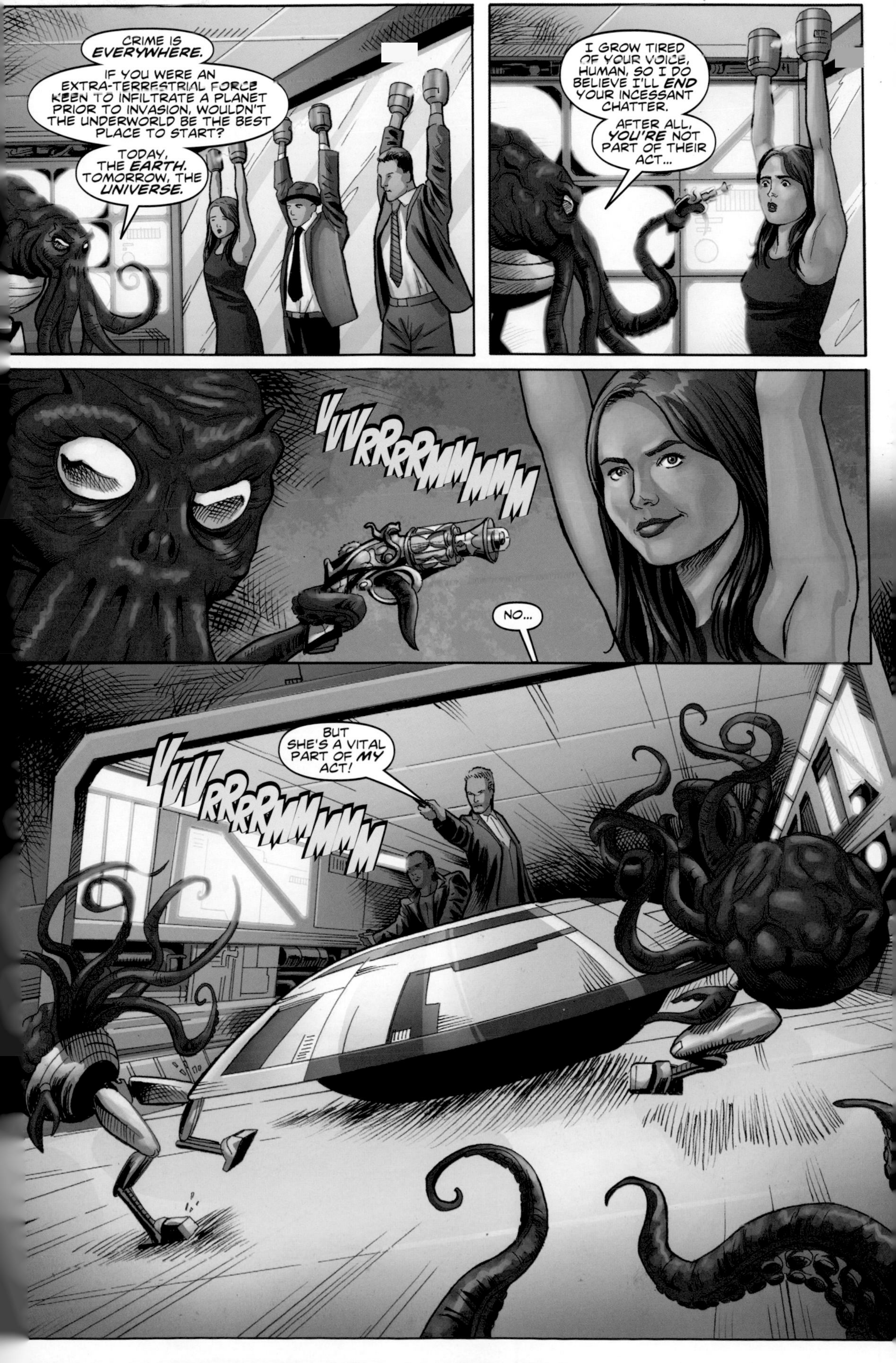
CRIME IS EVERYWHERE.
IF YOU WERE AN EXTRA-TERRESTRIAL FORCE KEEN TO INFILTRATE A PLANET PRIOR TO INVASION, WOULDN'T THE UNDERWORLD BE THE BEST PLACE TO START?
TODAY, THE EARTH. TOMORROW, THE UNIVERSE.
I GROW TIRED OF YOUR VOICE, HUMAN, SO I DO BELIEVE I'LL END YOUR INCESSANT CHATTER.
AFTER ALL, YOU'RE NOT PART OF THEIR ACT...
VVVRRRRMMMMMM
NO...
BUT SHE'S A VITAL PART OF MY ACT!
VVVRRRRMMMMMM

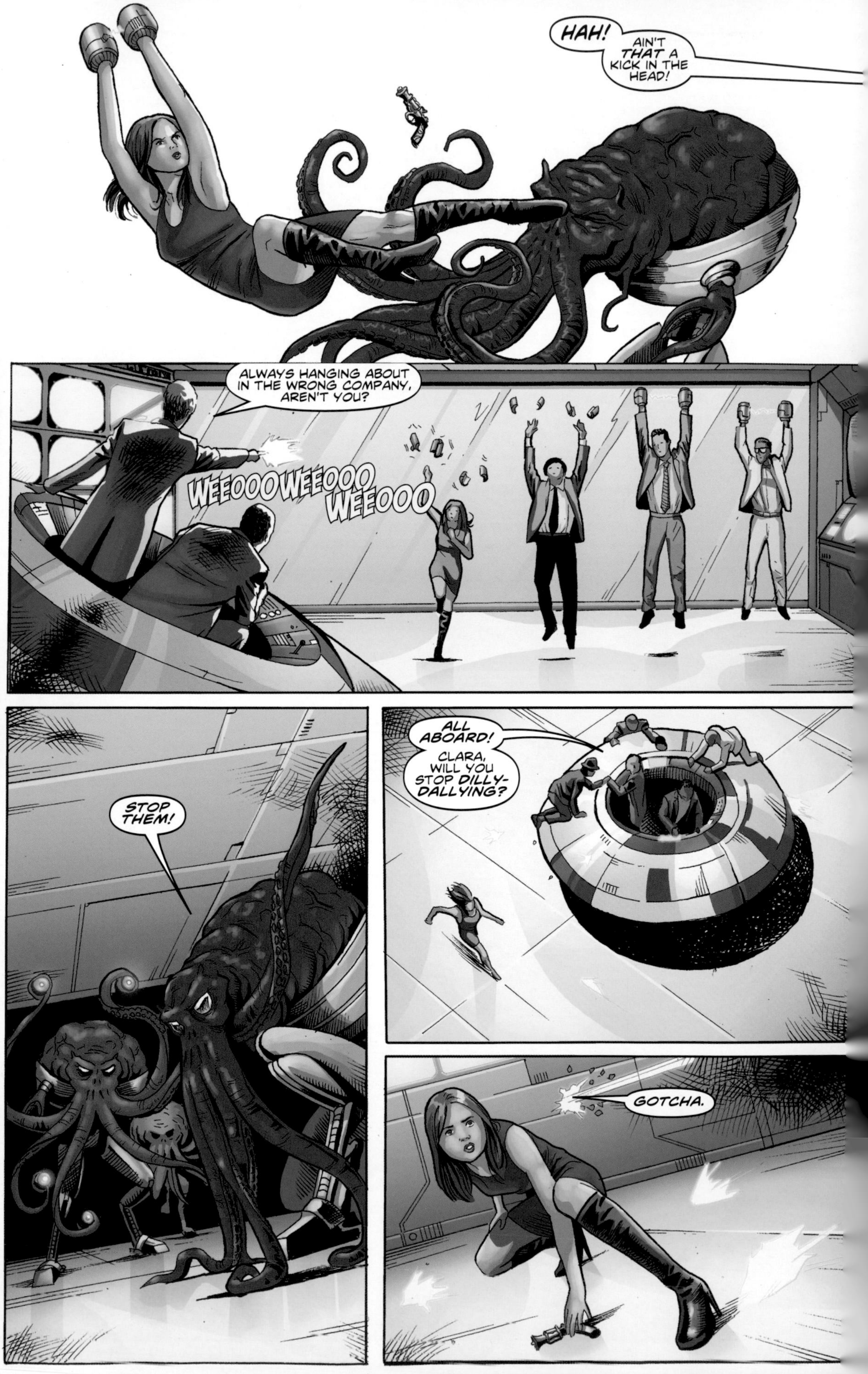
HAH!
AIN'T THAT A KICK IN THE HEAD!
ALWAYS HANGING ABOUT IN THE WRONG COMPANY, AREN'T YOU?
WEEOOO WEEOOO WEEOOO
STOP THEM!
ALL ABOARD!
CLARA, WILL YOU STOP DILLY-DALLYING?
GOTCHA.

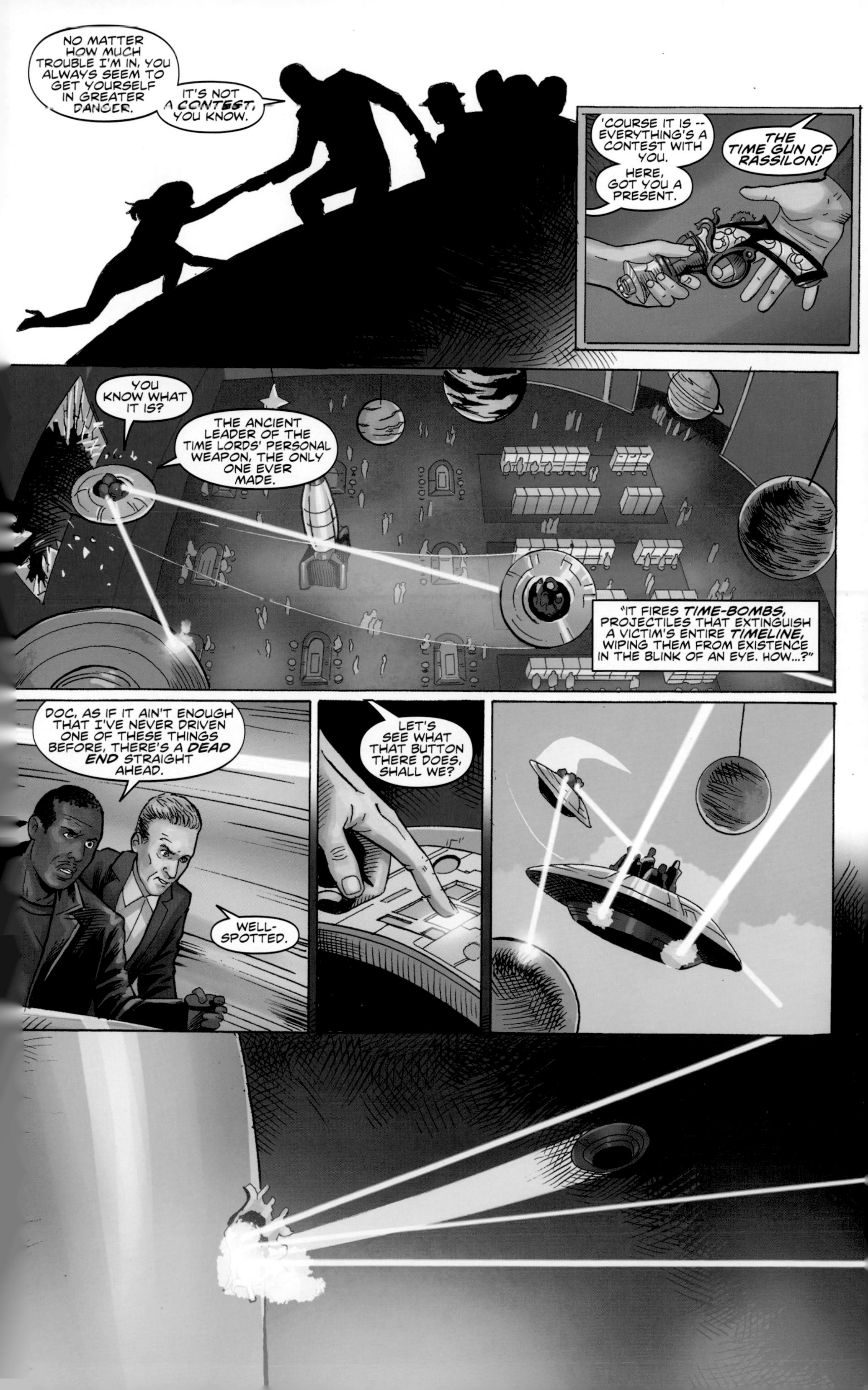
NO MATTER HOW MUCH TROUBLE I'M IN, YOU ALWAYS SEEM TO GET YOURSELF IN GREATER DANGER.
IT'S NOT A CONTEST, YOU KNOW.
'COURSE IT IS -- EVERYTHING'S A CONTEST WITH YOU.
HERE, GOT YOU A PRESENT.
THE TIME GUN OF RASSILON!
YOU KNOW WHAT IT IS?
THE ANCIENT LEADER OF THE TIME LORDS' PERSONAL WEAPON, THE ONLY ONE EVER MADE.
"IT FIRES TIME-BOMBS, PROJECTILES THAT EXTINGUISH A VICTIM'S ENTIRE TIMELINE, WIPING THEM FROM EXISTENCE IN THE BLINK OF AN EYE. HOW...?"
DOC, AS IF IT AIN'T ENOUGH THAT I'VE NEVER DRIVEN ONE OF THESE THINGS BEFORE, THERE'S A DEAD END STRAIGHT AHEAD.
WELL-SPOTTED.
LET'S SEE WHAT THAT BUTTON THERE DOES, SHALL WE?

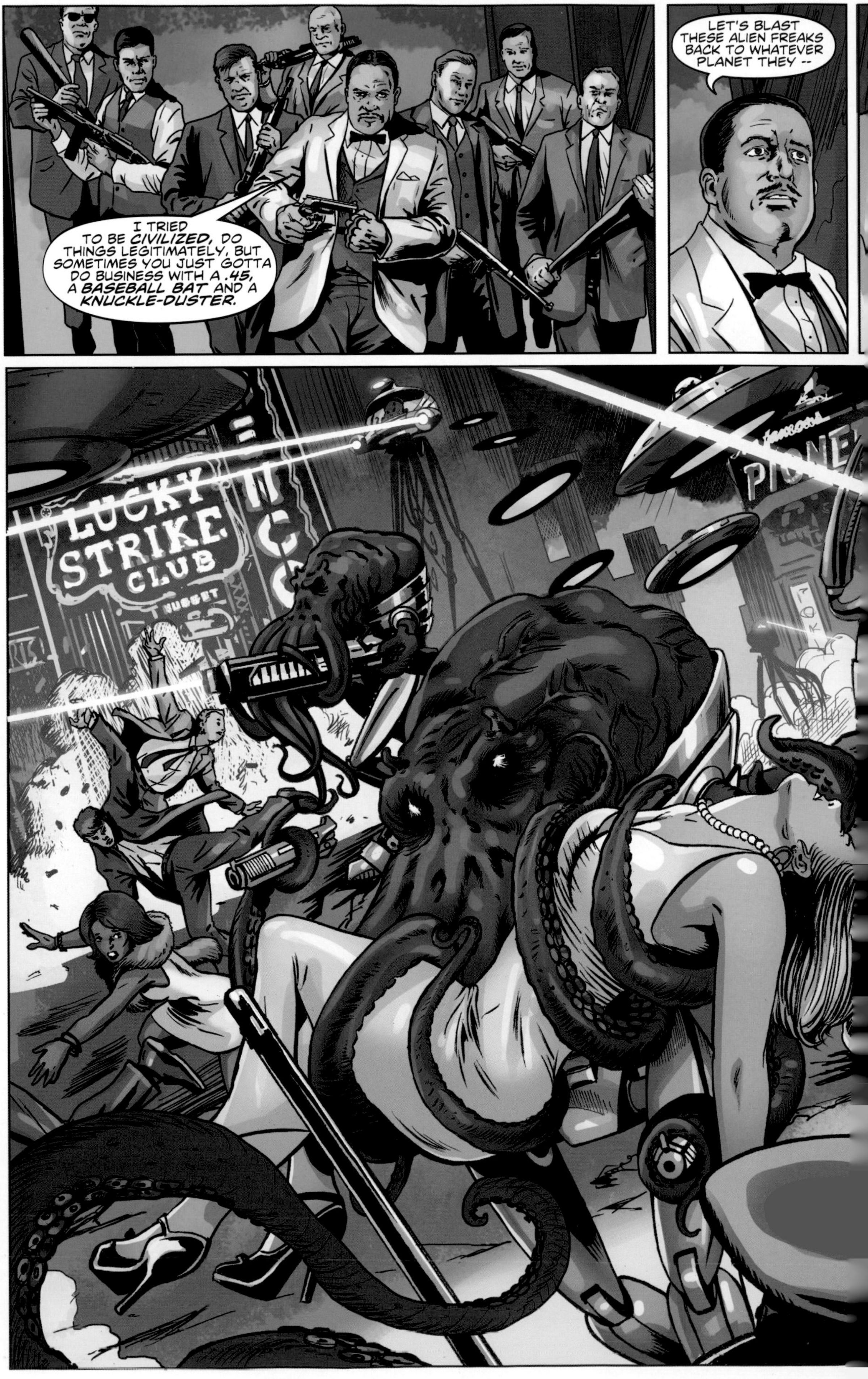
I TRIED TO BE *CIVILIZED,* DO THINGS LEGITIMATELY, BUT SOMETIMES YOU JUST GOTTA DO BUSINESS WITH A *.45,* A *BASEBALL BAT* AND A *KNUCKLE-DUSTER.*
LET'S BLAST THESE ALIEN FREAKS BACK TO WHATEVER PLANET THEY --
LUCKY STRIKE CLUB
NUGGET

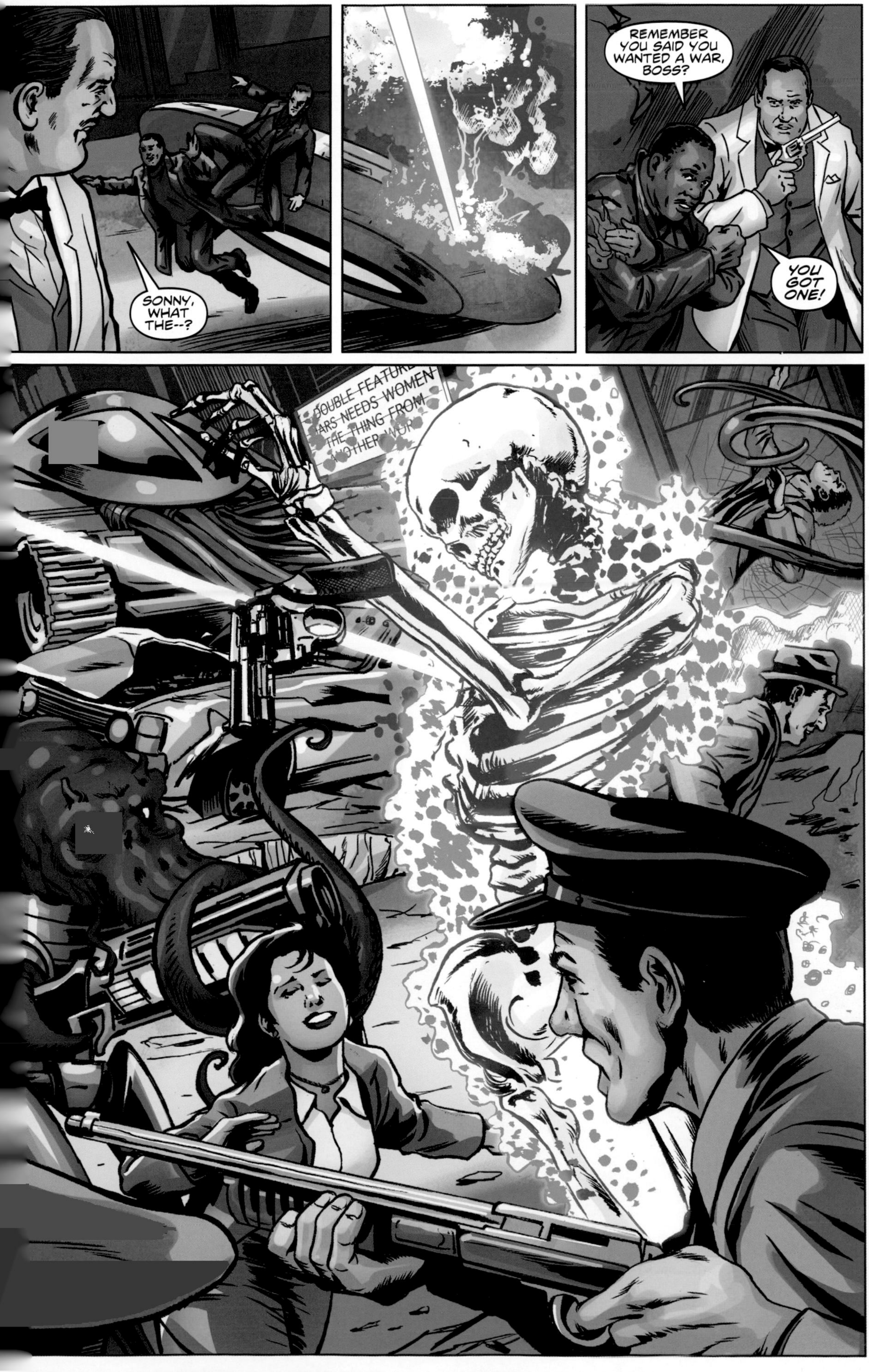
SONNY, WHAT THE--?
REMEMBER YOU SAID YOU WANTED A WAR, BOSS?
YOU GOT ONE!
NEEDS WOMEN
THE THING FROM

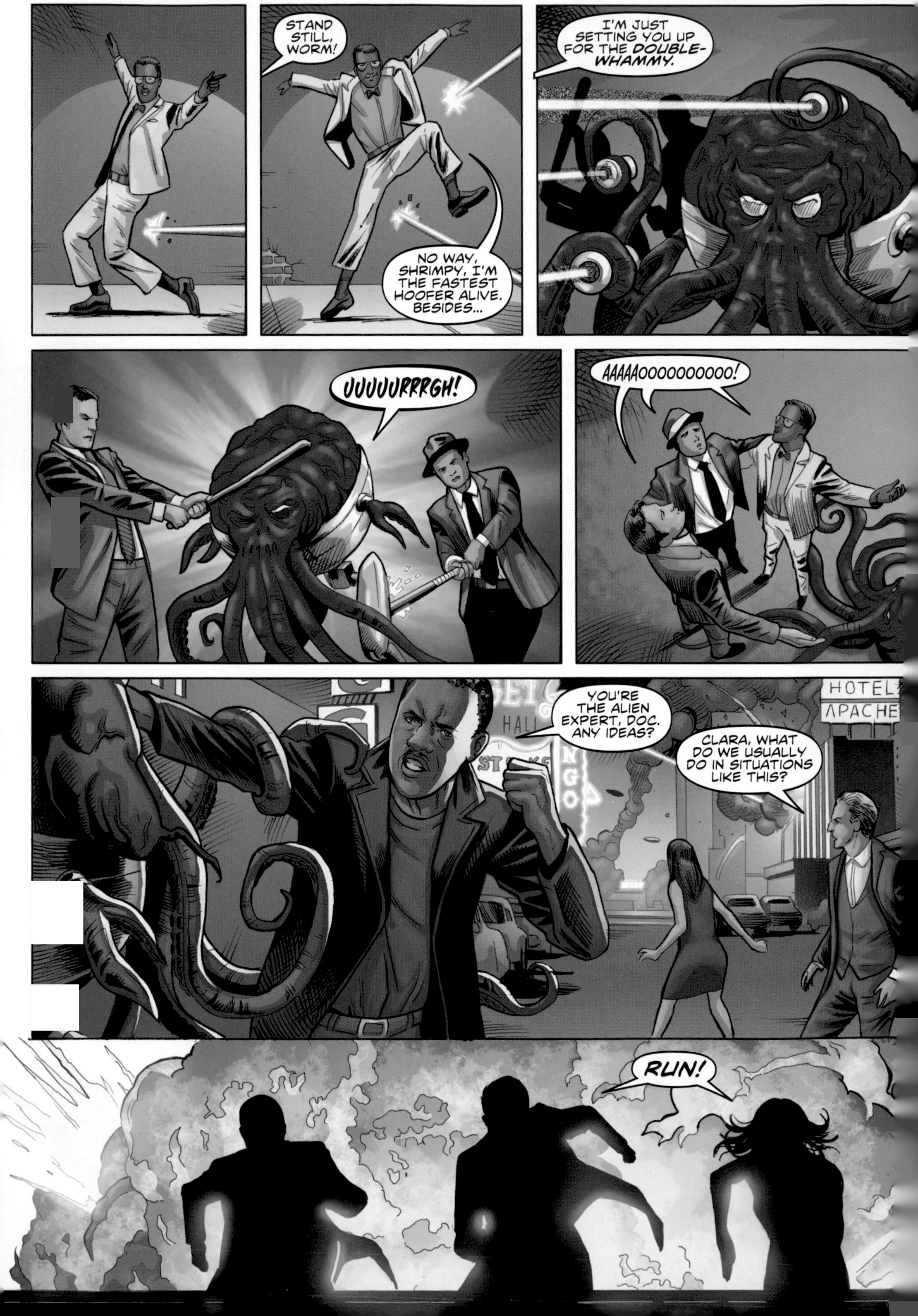
STAND STILL, WORM!
NO WAY, SHRIMPY, I'M THE FASTEST HOOFER ALIVE. BESIDES...
I'M JUST SETTING YOU UP FOR THE DOUBLE-WHAMMY.
UUUUURRRGH!
AAAAAOOOOOOOOOO!
YOU'RE THE ALIEN EXPERT, DOC. ANY IDEAS?
CLARA, WHAT DO WE USUALLY DO IN SITUATIONS LIKE THIS?
HOTEL
APACHE
RUN!

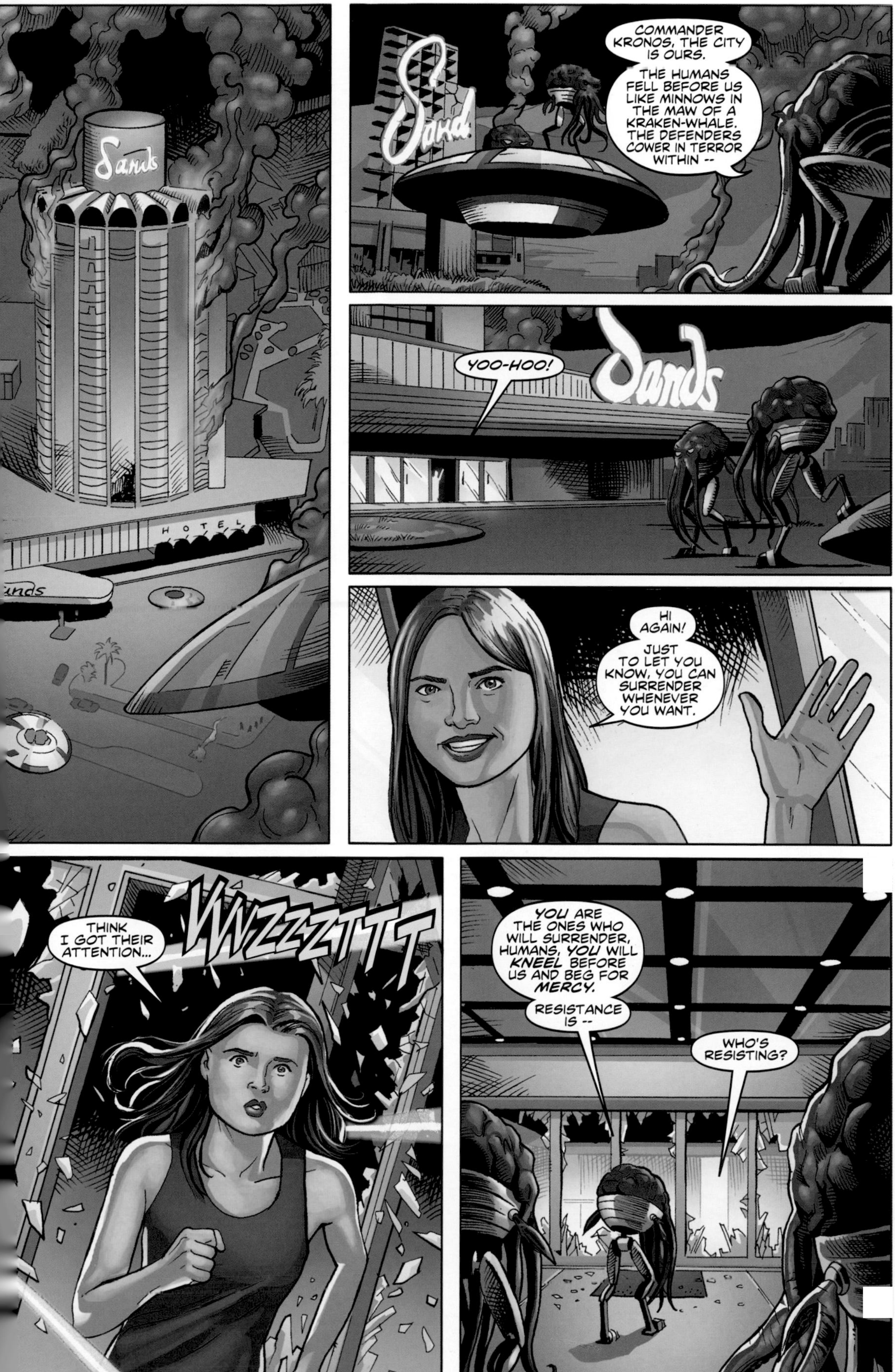
Sands
HOTEL
Sands
Sands
COMMANDER KRONOS, THE CITY IS OURS.
THE HUMANS FELL BEFORE US LIKE MINNOWS IN THE MAW OF A KRAKEN-WHALE. THE DEFENDERS COWER IN TERROR WITHIN --
Sands
YOO-HOO!
HI AGAIN!
JUST TO LET YOU KNOW, YOU CAN SURRENDER WHENEVER YOU WANT.
THINK I GOT THEIR ATTENTION...
VVVZZZZTTTT
YOU ARE THE ONES WHO WILL SURRENDER, HUMANS, *YOU* WILL *KNEEL* BEFORE US AND BEG FOR *MERCY*.
RESISTANCE IS --
WHO'S RESISTING?

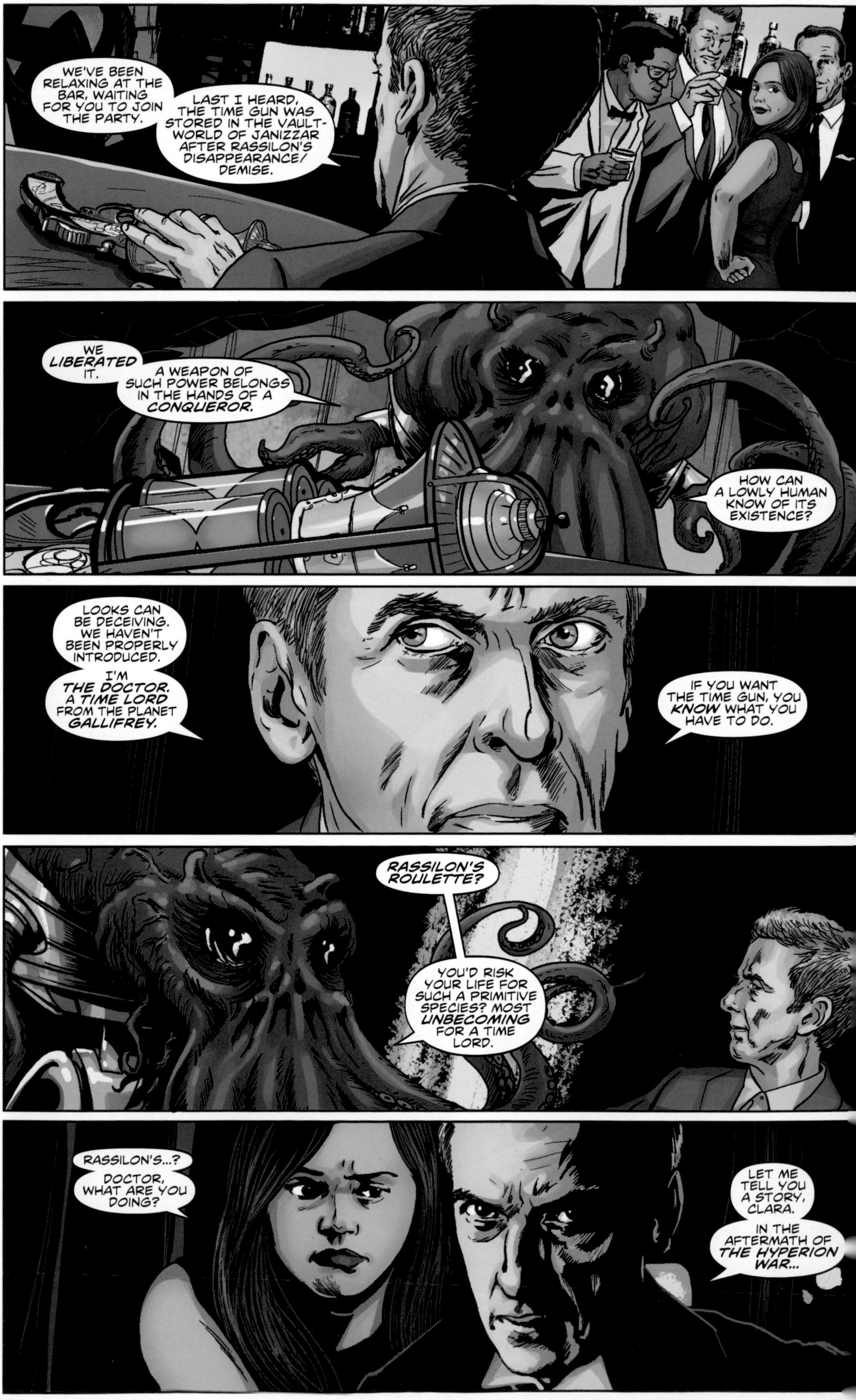
WE'VE BEEN RELAXING AT THE BAR, WAITING FOR YOU TO JOIN THE PARTY.
LAST I HEARD, THE TIME GUN WAS STORED IN THE VAULT-WORLD OF JANIZZAR AFTER RASSILON'S DISAPPEARANCE/ DEMISE.
WE *LIBERATED* IT.
A WEAPON OF SUCH POWER BELONGS IN THE HANDS OF A *CONQUEROR.*
HOW CAN A LOWLY HUMAN KNOW OF ITS EXISTENCE?
LOOKS CAN BE DECEIVING. WE HAVEN'T BEEN PROPERLY INTRODUCED.
I'M *THE DOCTOR.* A *TIME LORD* FROM THE PLANET *GALLIFREY.*
IF YOU WANT THE TIME GUN, YOU *KNOW* WHAT YOU HAVE TO DO.
RASSILON'S ROULETTE?
YOU'D RISK YOUR LIFE FOR SUCH A PRIMITIVE SPECIES? MOST *UNBECOMING* FOR A TIME LORD.
RASSILON'S...? DOCTOR, WHAT ARE YOU DOING?
LET ME TELL YOU A STORY, CLARA.
IN THE AFTERMATH OF *THE HYPERION WAR...*

ONE TIME-TWISTING TALE LATER...

WHAT ARE THE STAKES?

THE PLANET EARTH.

DOCTOR, YOU *CAN'T!*

THINK OF ALL THE PEOPLE, THE WORLDS, THE GALAXIES YOU'VE SAVED.

IF YOUR TIMELINE IS ERADICATED, THEN *NONE* OF THAT WILL HAPPEN. THE UNIVERSE WILL FALL TO THE DALEKS, OR THE CYBERMEN --

AND THE STAKES GET *HIGHER.*

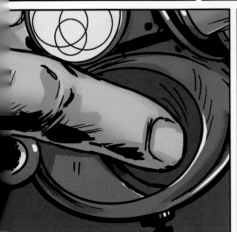

CLICK

YOUR TURN, I BELIEVE.

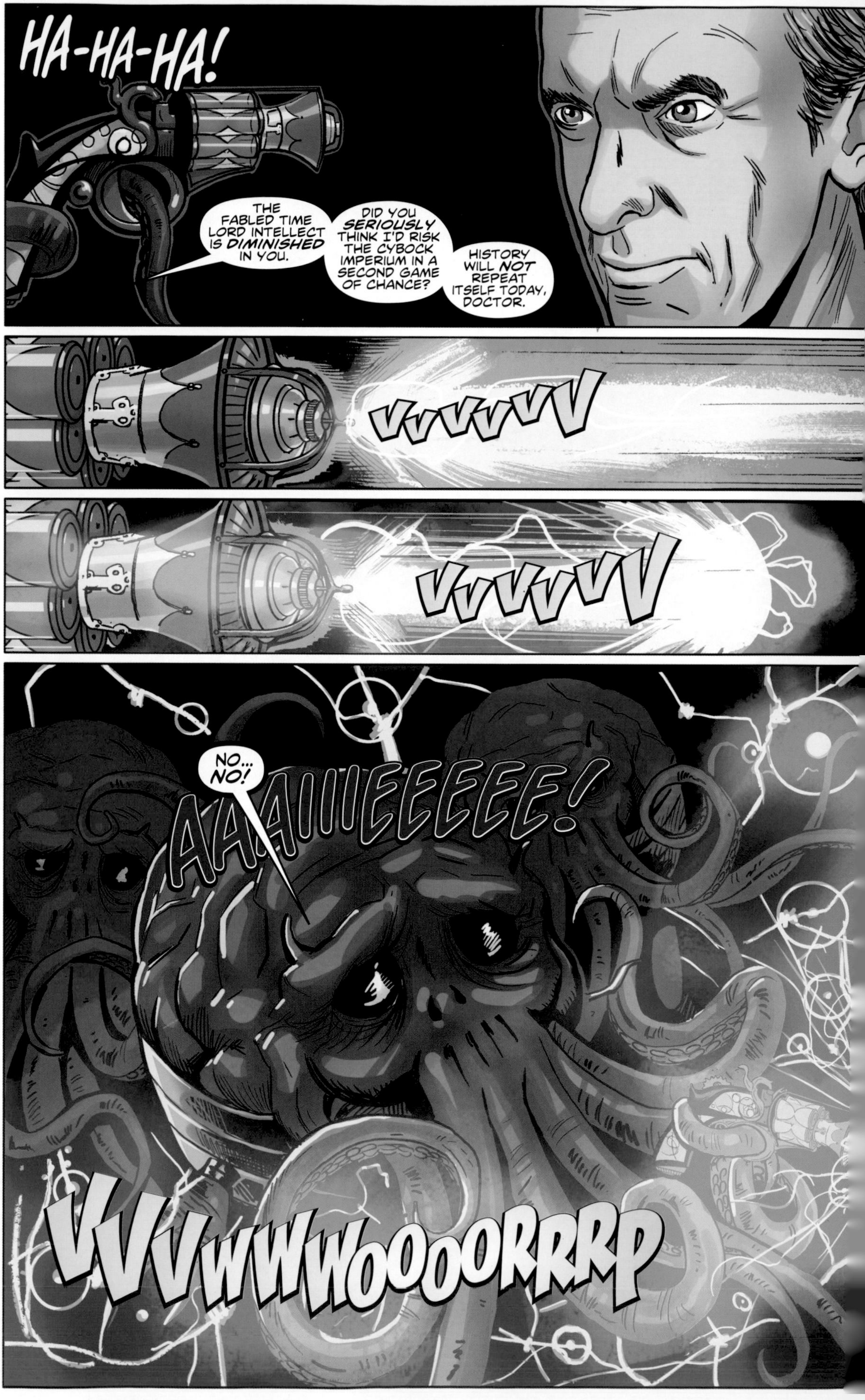
HA-HA-HA!
THE FABLED TIME LORD INTELLECT IS DIMINISHED IN YOU.
DID YOU SERIOUSLY THINK I'D RISK THE CYBOCK IMPERIUM IN A SECOND GAME OF CHANCE?
HISTORY WILL NOT REPEAT ITSELF TODAY, DOCTOR.
VVVVVV
VVVVVV
NO... NO!
AAAIIIEEEEEE!
VVVWWWOOOORRRP

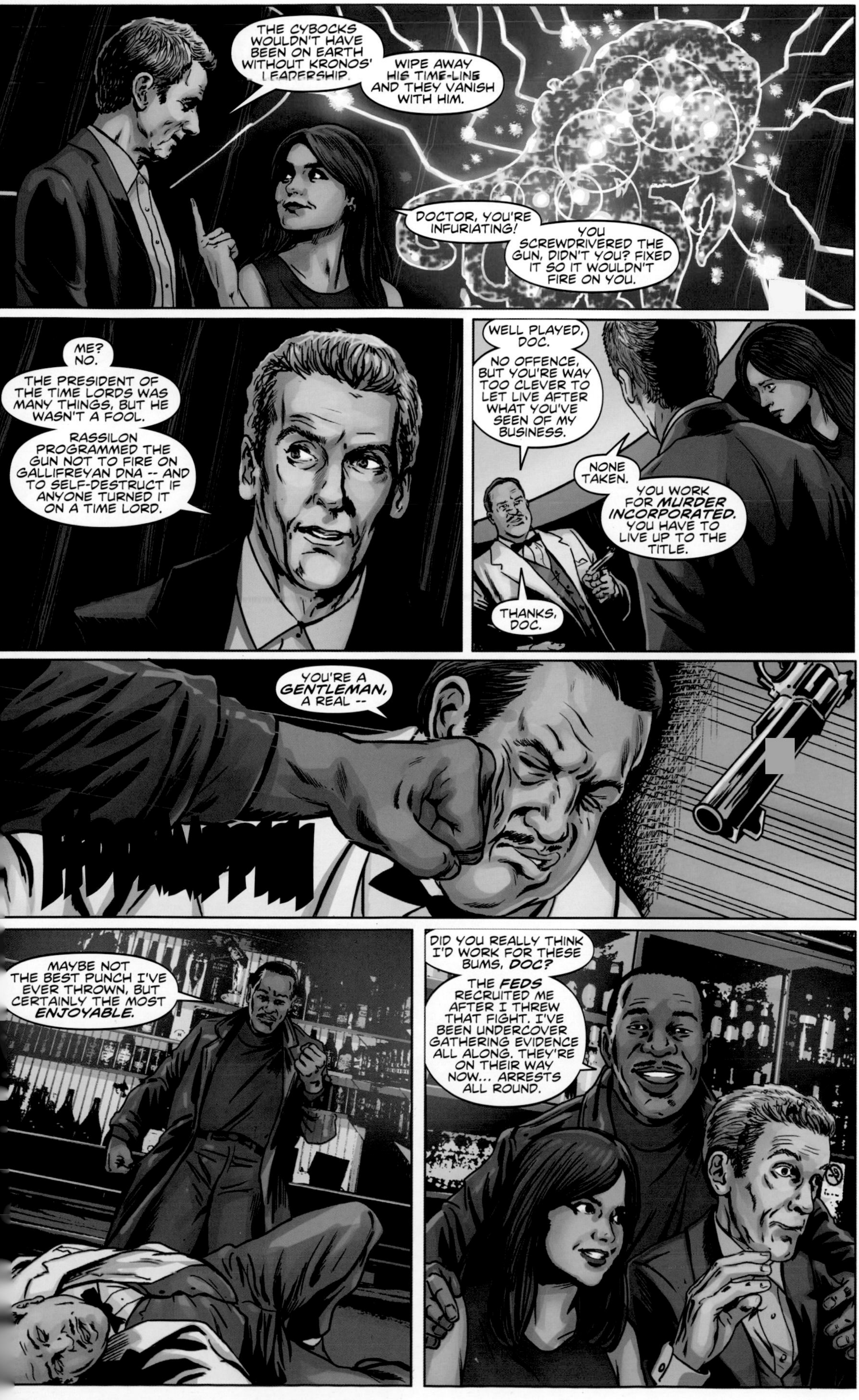
THE CYBOCKS WOULDN'T HAVE BEEN ON EARTH WITHOUT KRONOS' LEADERSHIP.
WIPE AWAY HIS TIME-LINE AND THEY VANISH WITH HIM.
DOCTOR, YOU'RE INFURIATING!
YOU SCREWDRIVERED THE GUN, DIDN'T YOU? FIXED IT SO IT WOULDN'T FIRE ON YOU.
ME? NO.
THE PRESIDENT OF THE TIME LORDS WAS MANY THINGS, BUT HE WASN'T A FOOL.
RASSILON PROGRAMMED THE GUN NOT TO FIRE ON GALLIFREYAN DNA -- AND TO SELF-DESTRUCT IF ANYONE TURNED IT ON A TIME LORD.
WELL PLAYED, DOC.
NO OFFENCE, BUT YOU'RE WAY TOO CLEVER TO LET LIVE AFTER WHAT YOU'VE SEEN OF MY BUSINESS.
NONE TAKEN.
YOU WORK FOR MURDER INCORPORATED. YOU HAVE TO LIVE UP TO THE TITLE.
THANKS, DOC.
YOU'RE A GENTLEMAN, A REAL --
MAYBE NOT THE BEST PUNCH I'VE EVER THROWN, BUT CERTAINLY THE MOST ENJOYABLE.
DID YOU REALLY THINK I'D WORK FOR THESE BUMS, DOC?
THE FEDS RECRUITED ME AFTER I THREW THAT FIGHT. I'VE BEEN UNDERCOVER GATHERING EVIDENCE ALL ALONG. THEY'RE ON THEIR WAY NOW... ARRESTS ALL ROUND.

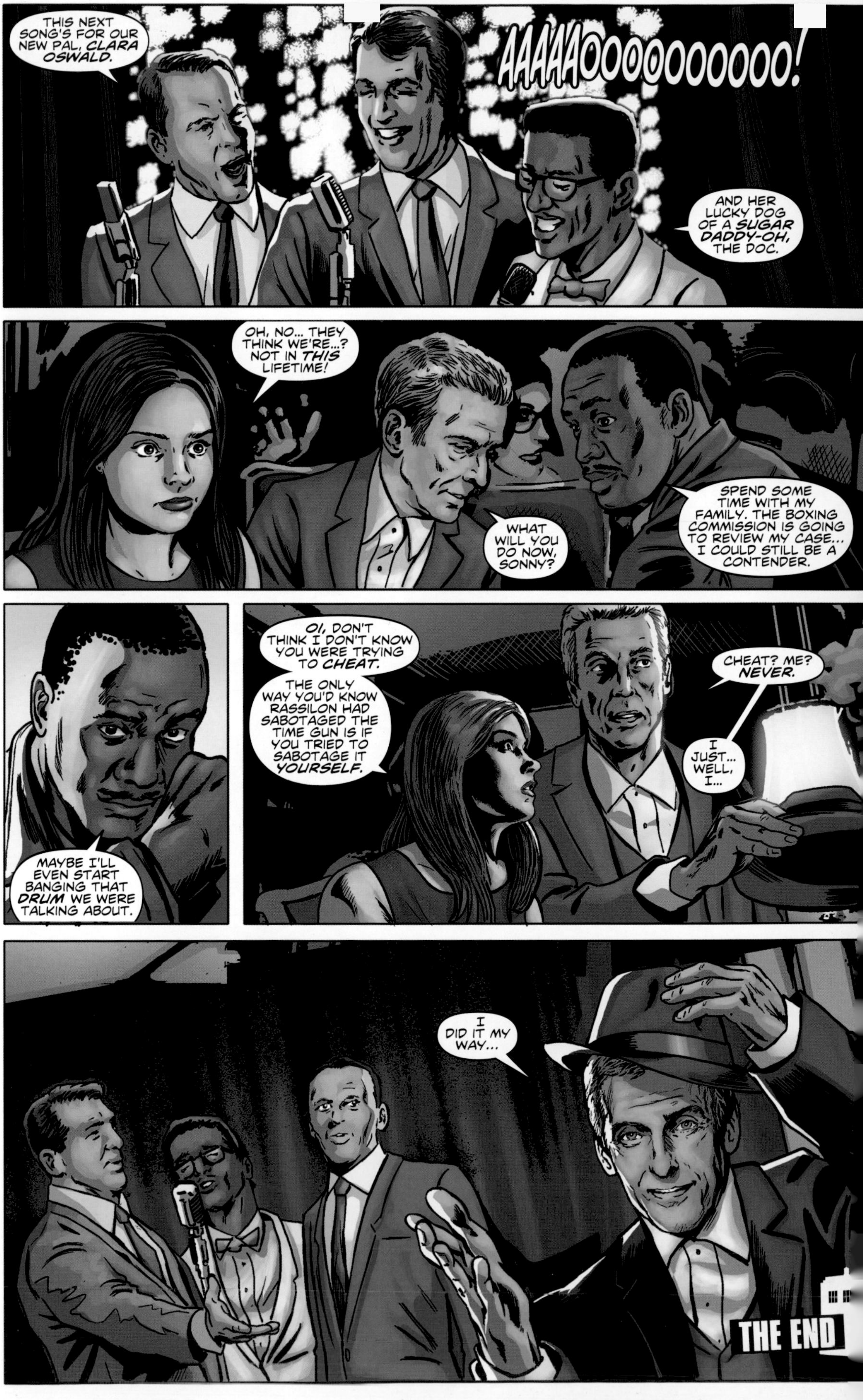
THIS NEXT SONG'S FOR OUR NEW PAL, CLARA OSWALD.
AAAAAOOOOOOOOOO!
AND HER LUCKY DOG OF A SUGAR DADDY-OH, THE DOC.
OH, NO... THEY THINK WE'RE...? NOT IN THIS LIFETIME!
WHAT WILL YOU DO NOW, SONNY?
SPEND SOME TIME WITH MY FAMILY. THE BOXING COMMISSION IS GOING TO REVIEW MY CASE... I COULD STILL BE A CONTENDER.
MAYBE I'LL EVEN START BANGING THAT DRUM WE WERE TALKING ABOUT.
OI, DON'T THINK I DON'T KNOW YOU WERE TRYING TO CHEAT.
THE ONLY WAY YOU'D KNOW RASSILON HAD SABOTAGED THE TIME GUN IS IF YOU TRIED TO SABOTAGE IT YOURSELF.
CHEAT? ME? NEVER.
I JUST... WELL, I...
I DID IT MY WAY...
THE END

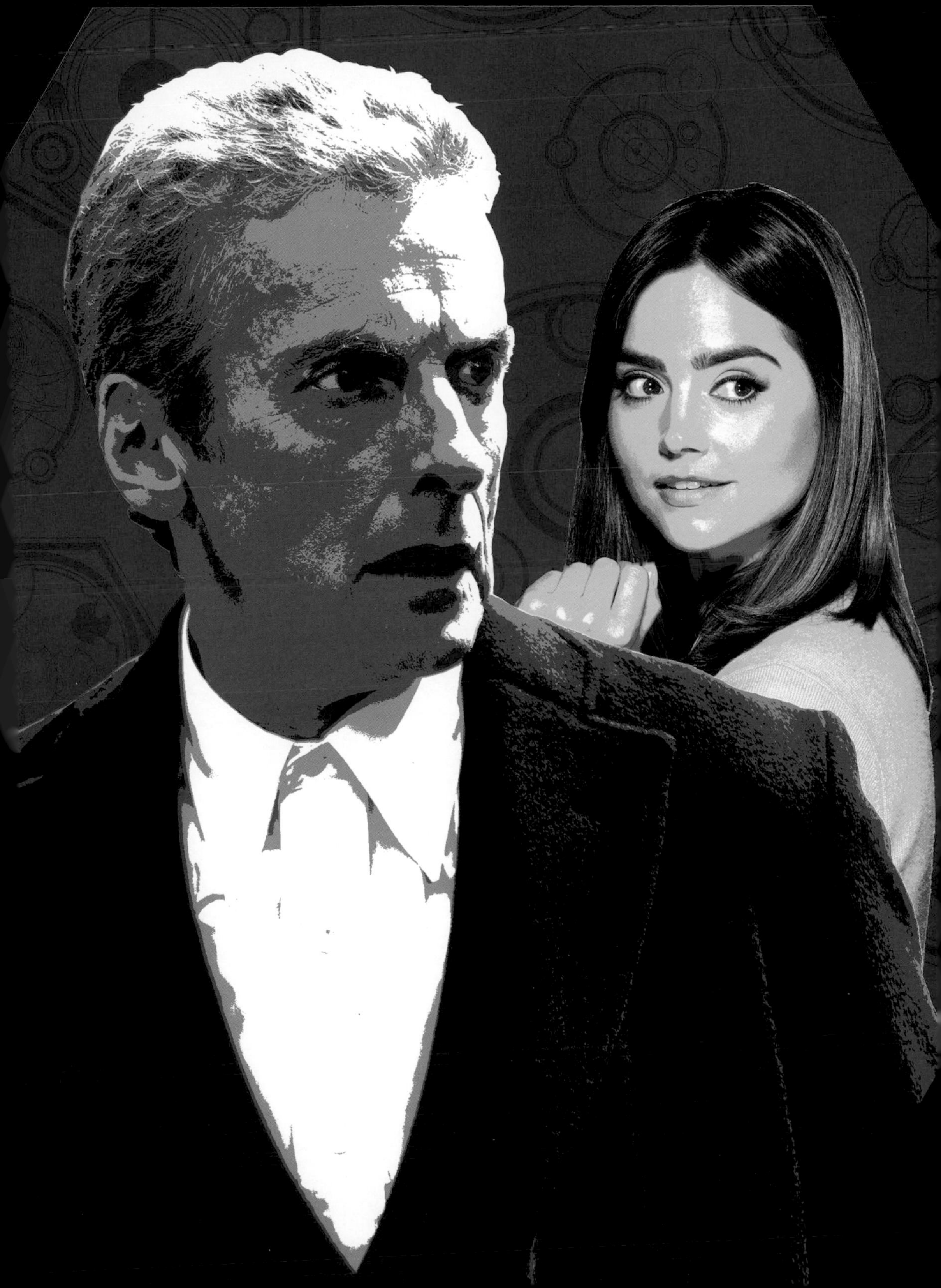

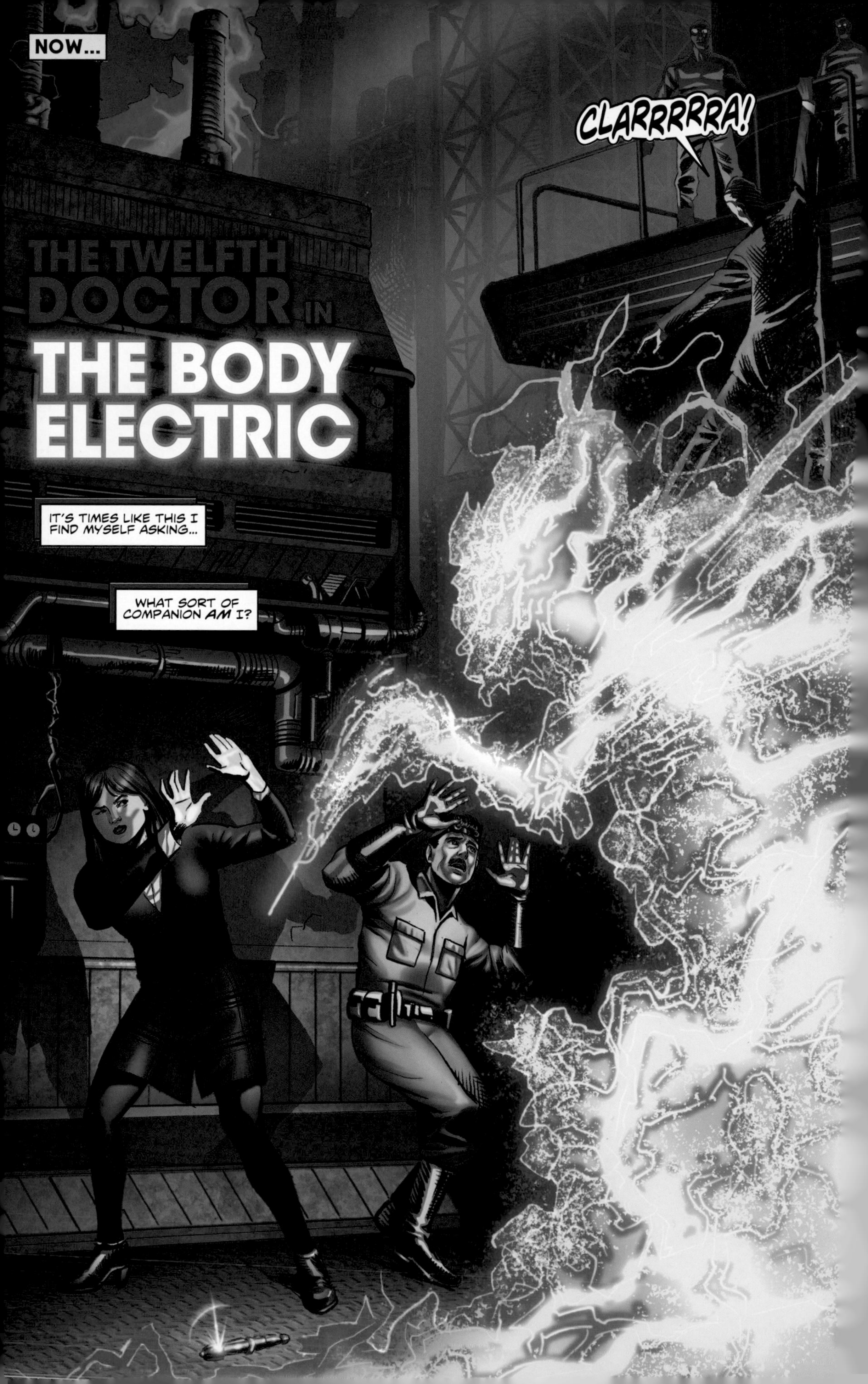
NOW...
CLARRRRRA!
THE TWELFTH DOCTOR IN
THE BODY ELECTRIC
IT'S TIMES LIKE THIS I FIND MYSELF ASKING...
WHAT SORT OF COMPANION AM I?

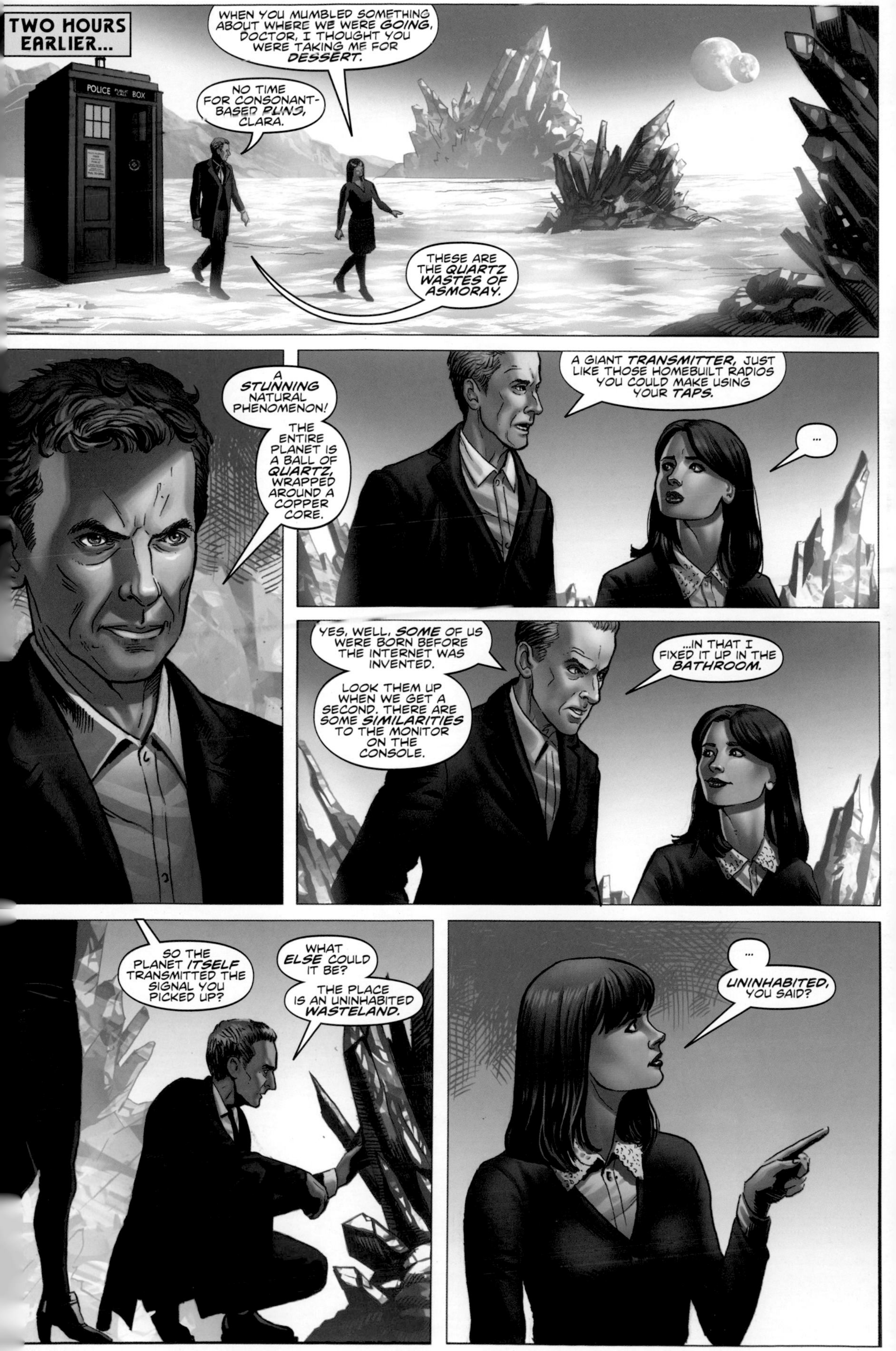
TWO HOURS EARLIER...
WHEN YOU MUMBLED SOMETHING ABOUT WHERE WE WERE GOING, DOCTOR, I THOUGHT YOU WERE TAKING ME FOR DESSERT.
NO TIME FOR CONSONANT-BASED PUNS, CLARA.
POLICE PUBLIC CALL BOX
THESE ARE THE QUARTZ WASTES OF ASMORAY.
A STUNNING NATURAL PHENOMENON!
THE ENTIRE PLANET IS A BALL OF QUARTZ, WRAPPED AROUND A COPPER CORE.
A GIANT TRANSMITTER, JUST LIKE THOSE HOMEBUILT RADIOS YOU COULD MAKE USING YOUR TAPS.
...
YES, WELL, SOME OF US WERE BORN BEFORE THE INTERNET WAS INVENTED.
LOOK THEM UP WHEN WE GET A SECOND. THERE ARE SOME SIMILARITIES TO THE MONITOR ON THE CONSOLE.
...IN THAT I FIXED IT UP IN THE BATHROOM.
SO THE PLANET ITSELF TRANSMITTED THE SIGNAL YOU PICKED UP?
WHAT ELSE COULD IT BE?
THE PLACE IS AN UNINHABITED WASTELAND.
...
UNINHABITED, YOU SAID?

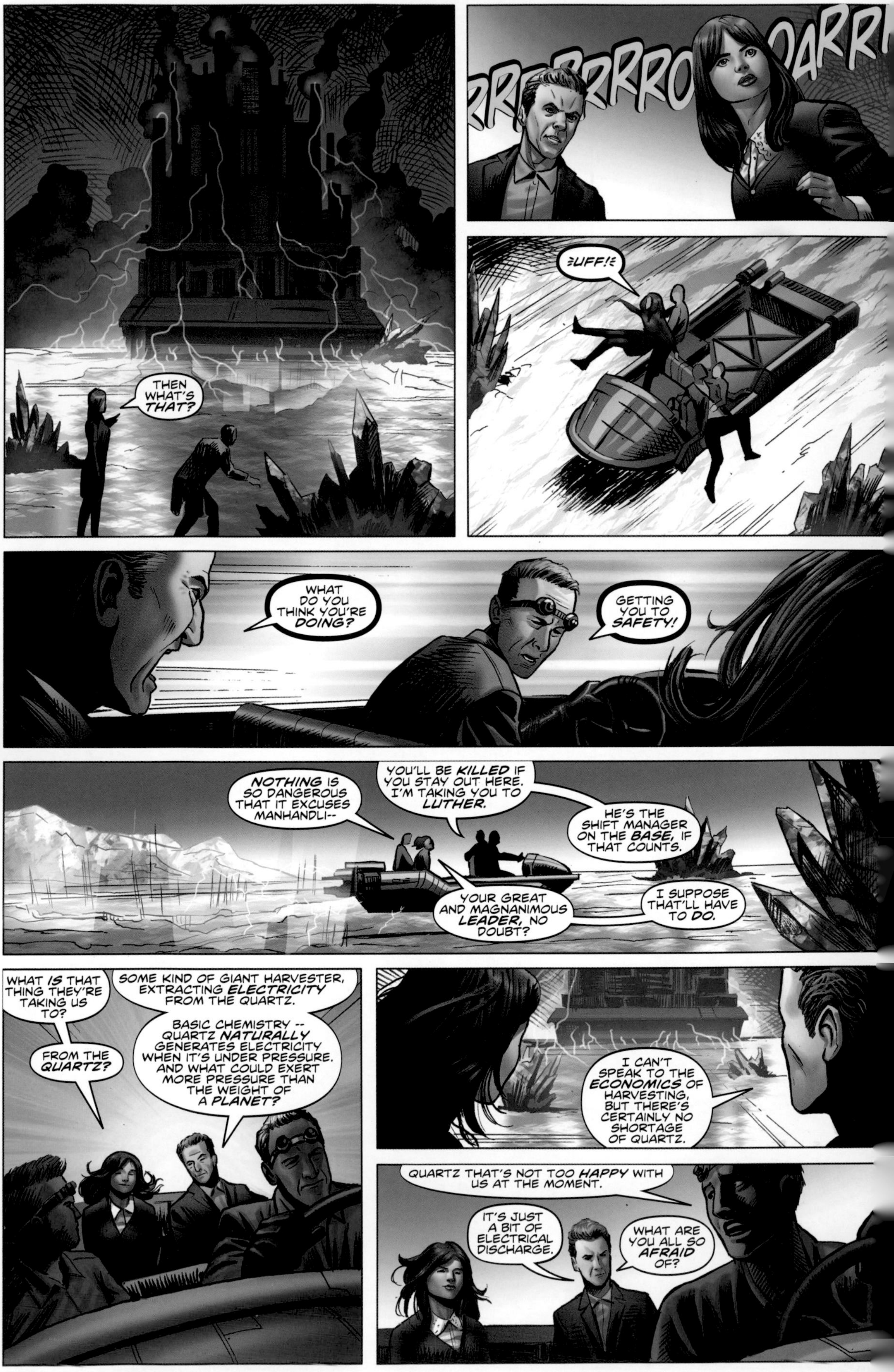
THEN WHAT'S THAT?
RRRRRRRRO
OARR
UFF!
WHAT DO YOU THINK YOU'RE DOING?
GETTING YOU TO SAFETY!
NOTHING IS SO DANGEROUS THAT IT EXCUSES MANHANDLI--
YOU'LL BE KILLED IF YOU STAY OUT HERE. I'M TAKING YOU TO LUTHER.
YOUR GREAT AND MAGNANIMOUS LEADER, NO DOUBT?
HE'S THE SHIFT MANAGER ON THE BASE, IF THAT COUNTS.
I SUPPOSE THAT'LL HAVE TO DO.
WHAT IS THAT THING THEY'RE TAKING US TO?
SOME KIND OF GIANT HARVESTER, EXTRACTING ELECTRICITY FROM THE QUARTZ.
FROM THE QUARTZ?
BASIC CHEMISTRY -- QUARTZ NATURALLY GENERATES ELECTRICITY WHEN IT'S UNDER PRESSURE. AND WHAT COULD EXERT MORE PRESSURE THAN THE WEIGHT OF A PLANET?
I CAN'T SPEAK TO THE ECONOMICS OF HARVESTING, BUT THERE'S CERTAINLY NO SHORTAGE OF QUARTZ.
QUARTZ THAT'S NOT TOO HAPPY WITH US AT THE MOMENT.
IT'S JUST A BIT OF ELECTRICAL DISCHARGE.
WHAT ARE YOU ALL SO AFRAID OF?

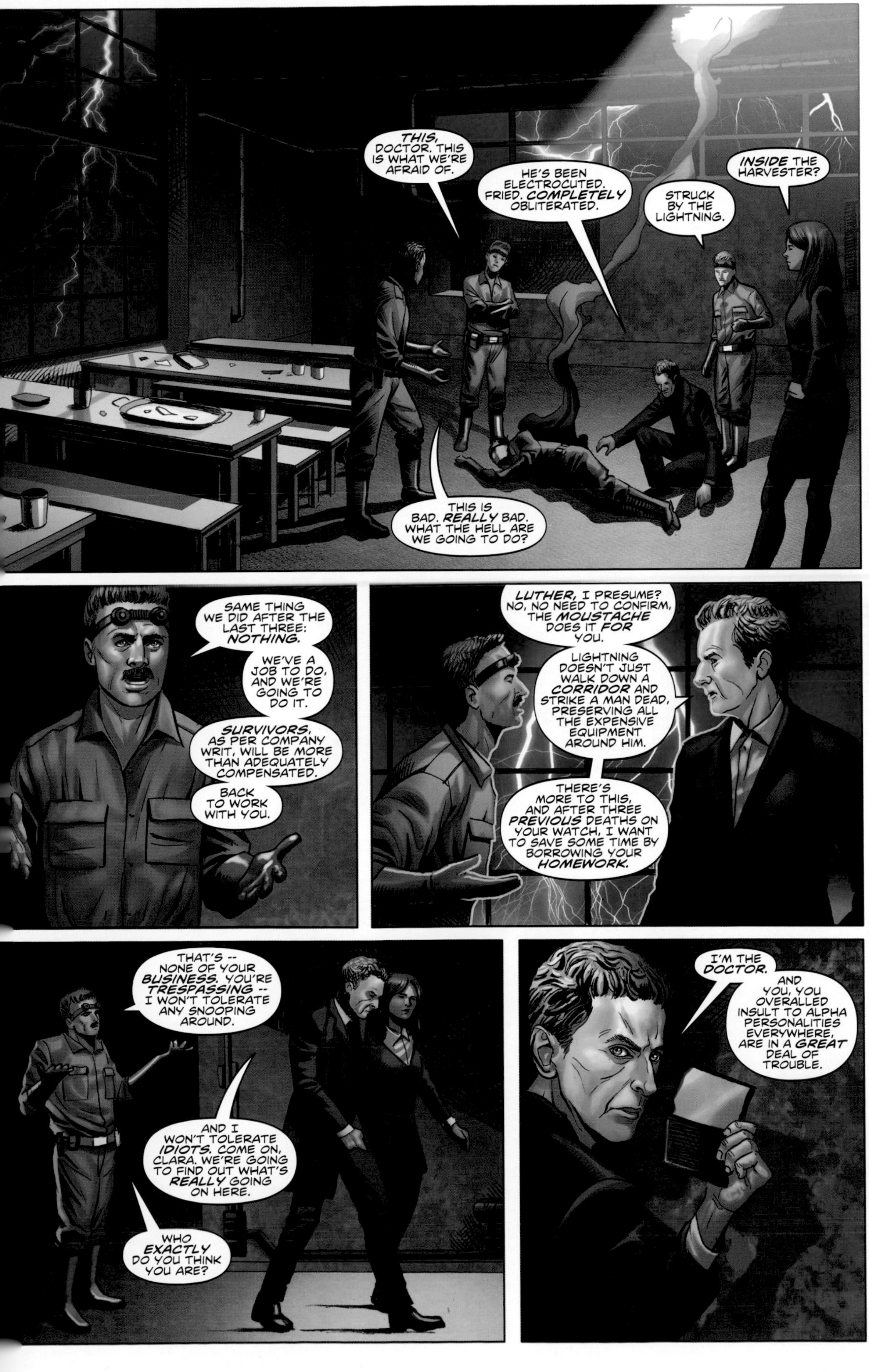
THIS, DOCTOR. THIS IS WHAT WE'RE AFRAID OF.
HE'S BEEN ELECTROCUTED. FRIED. COMPLETELY OBLITERATED.
STRUCK BY THE LIGHTNING.
INSIDE THE HARVESTER?
THIS IS BAD. REALLY BAD. WHAT THE HELL ARE WE GOING TO DO?
SAME THING WE DID AFTER THE LAST THREE: NOTHING.
WE'VE A JOB TO DO, AND WE'RE GOING TO DO IT.
SURVIVORS, AS PER COMPANY WRIT, WILL BE MORE THAN ADEQUATELY COMPENSATED.
BACK TO WORK WITH YOU.
LUTHER, I PRESUME? NO, NO NEED TO CONFIRM, THE MOUSTACHE DOES IT FOR YOU.
LIGHTNING DOESN'T JUST WALK DOWN A CORRIDOR AND STRIKE A MAN DEAD, PRESERVING ALL THE EXPENSIVE EQUIPMENT AROUND HIM.
THERE'S MORE TO THIS, AND AFTER THREE PREVIOUS DEATHS ON YOUR WATCH, I WANT TO SAVE SOME TIME BY BORROWING YOUR HOMEWORK.
THAT'S -- NONE OF YOUR BUSINESS. YOU'RE TRESPASSING -- I WON'T TOLERATE ANY SNOOPING AROUND.
AND I WON'T TOLERATE IDIOTS. COME ON, CLARA. WE'RE GOING TO FIND OUT WHAT'S REALLY GOING ON HERE.
WHO EXACTLY DO YOU THINK YOU ARE?
I'M THE DOCTOR.
AND YOU, YOU OVERALLED INSULT TO ALPHA PERSONALITIES EVERYWHERE, ARE IN A GREAT DEAL OF TROUBLE.

RIGHT THEN. LET'S TAKE A *LOOK* AT YOU, YOU MAGNIFICENT WEB OF SENTIENT ELECTRONS!

NO, NO, *NO!*

GAH! *GONE.* VANISHED INTO THE CIRCUITRY.

RMMMMBBBUUUUUU

DOCTOR?

WHY ATTACK *NOW?* THINK! WHAT'S *CHANGED?* WHAT'S *NEW?*

WHAT DO THEY *WANT?*

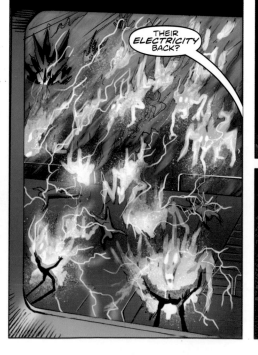

THEIR *ELECTRICITY* BACK?

BRILLIANT, CLARA! THAT'S *IT!* THEY LIVE *IN* THE ELECTRICITY, SO THEY'RE BEING *TRAPPED* -- LIKE DOLPHINS CAUGHT IN TUNA NETS!

THEY'RE BEING SUCKED INTO THE STORAGE BATTERIES?

EXACTLY! THE HARVESTER CAN'T TELL THE DIFFERENCE.

THEY'RE ONLY ATTACKING BECAUSE THEY'RE *BEING* ATTACKED.

COME ON, IT'S TIME I PUT THIS RIGHT.

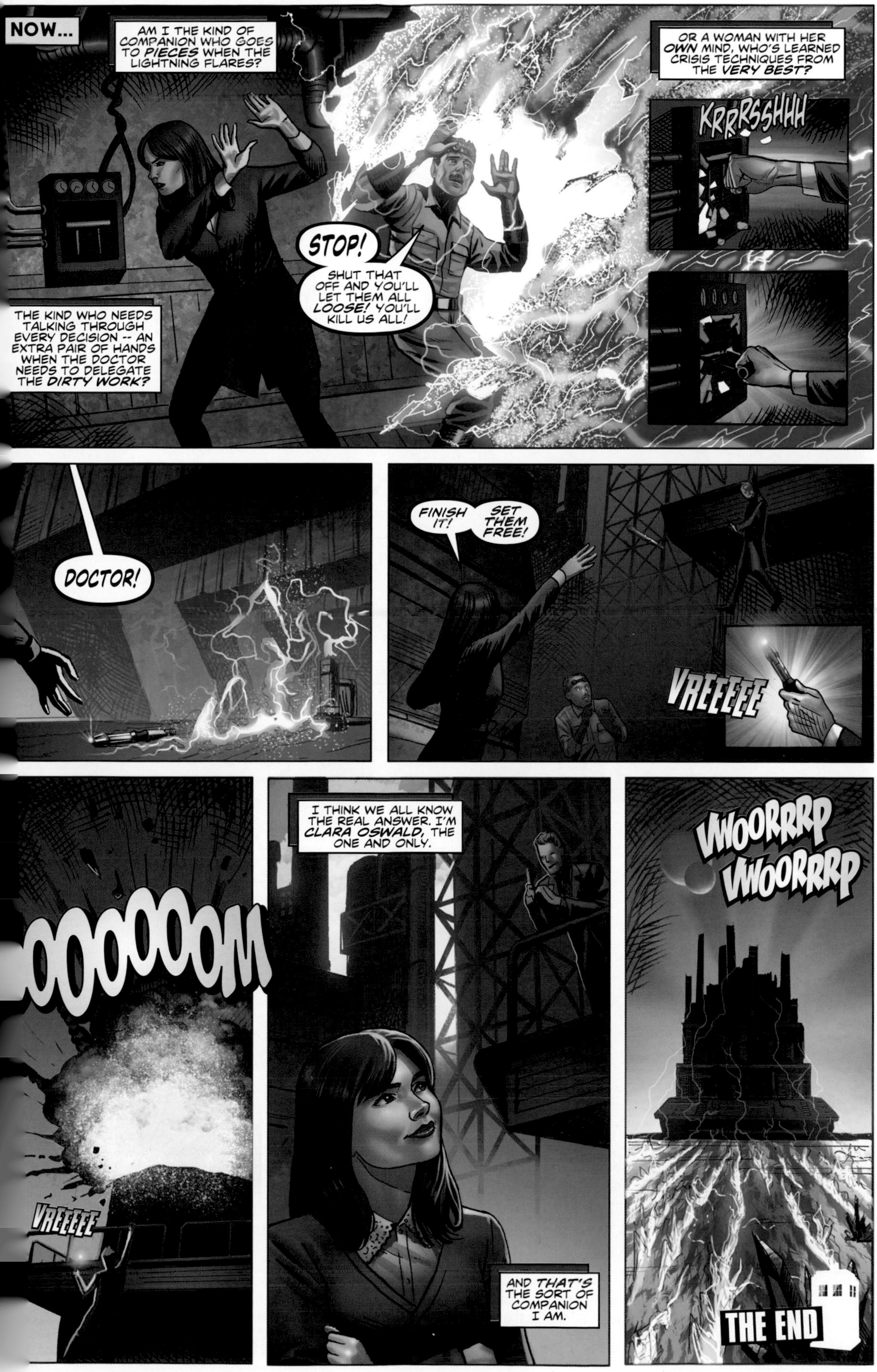
NOW...
AM I THE KIND OF COMPANION WHO GOES TO PIECES WHEN THE LIGHTNING FLARES?
THE KIND WHO NEEDS TALKING THROUGH EVERY DECISION -- AN EXTRA PAIR OF HANDS WHEN THE DOCTOR NEEDS TO DELEGATE THE DIRTY WORK?
STOP!
SHUT THAT OFF AND YOU'LL LET THEM ALL LOOSE! YOU'LL KILL US ALL!
OR A WOMAN WITH HER OWN MIND, WHO'S LEARNED CRISIS TECHNIQUES FROM THE VERY BEST?
KRRRSSHHH
DOCTOR!
FINISH IT!
SET THEM FREE!
VREEEEE
OOOOOOM
VREEEEE
I THINK WE ALL KNOW THE REAL ANSWER. I'M CLARA OSWALD, THE ONE AND ONLY.
AND THAT'S THE SORT OF COMPANION I AM.
VWOORRRP
VWOORRRP
THE END

THE TRIUMPHANT FIRST COLLECTIONS!
AVAILABLE NOW!

DOCTOR WHO: THE TWELFTH DOCTOR VOL. 1: TERRORFORMER

COLLECTS DOCTOR WHO: THE TWELFTH DOCTOR ISSUES #1-5

ON SALE NOW $19.99 / $22.95 CAN

ISBN: 9781782761778

DOCTOR WHO: THE TENTH DOCTOR VOL. 1: REVOLUTIONS OF TERROR

ISBN: 9781782761730
ON SALE NOW - $19.99 / $22.95 CAN

DOCTOR WHO: THE ELEVENTH DOCTOR VOL. 1: AFTER LIFE

ISBN: 9781782761747
ON SALE NOW - $19.99 / $22.95 CAN

COMING SOON - THE ADVENTURE CONTINUES!

BBC NEW ADVENTURES WITH THE TWELFTH DOCTOR
DOCTOR WHO
ROBBIE MORRISON
BRIAN WILLIAMSON
HI-FI
TITAN

DOCTOR WHO: THE TWELFTH DOCTOR VOL. 2: FRACTURES

COLLECTS DOCTOR WHO: THE TWELFTH DOCTOR ISSUES #6-10

ON SALE NOW $19.99 / $25.99 CAN

ISBN: 9781782763017

DOCTOR WHO: THE TENTH DOCTOR VOL. 2: THE WEEPING ANGELS OF MONS

BBC NEW ADVENTURES WITH THE TENTH DOCTOR
DOCTOR WHO
THE WEEPING ANGELS OF MONS
ROBBIE MORRISON • DANIEL INDRO • ELENA CASAGRANDE
HI-FI • ARIANNA FLOREAN

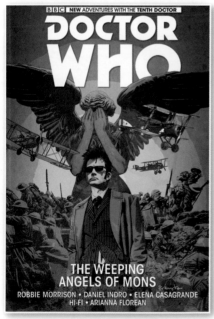

ISBN: 9781782761754

ON SALE NOW - $19.99 / $25.99 CAN

DOCTOR WHO: THE ELEVENTH DOCTOR VOL. 2: SERVE YOU

BBC NEW ADVENTURES WITH THE ELEVENTH DOCTOR
DOCTOR WHO
SERVE YOU
AL EWING • ROB WILLIAMS • SIMON FRASER • BOO COOK • WARREN PLEECE
GARY CALDWELL • HI-FI

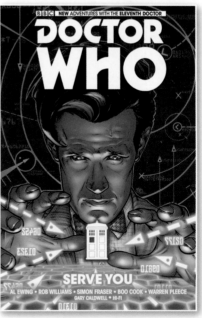

ISBN: 9781782761

ON SALE NOW - $19.99 / $25.99 CAN

AVAILABLE IN ALL GOOD COMIC STORES, BOOK STORES, AND DIGITAL PROVIDERS!

BBC

BIOGRAPHIES

Robbie Morrison is a Scottish comics writer living in England, who has written popular titles such as *Drowntown*, *Spider-Man*, and *The Authority*. He is perhaps best known for his work at 2000 AD, where he co-created the Eagle Award-winning series *Nikolai Dante*, with artist Simon Fraser, and *Shimura*, with Frank Quitely, along with stints on *Judge Dredd*.

Brian Willamson is a London-based comics, book and storyboard artist who has drawn *Torchwood*, *Primeval*, *Spider-Man* and many more - as well as comic book biographies of Michael Jackson (*Neverland*) and The Ramones (*Gabba Gabba Hey!*).

Mariano Laclaustra is a fast-rising talent with a background in the Fine Arts. A freelance artist based in Argentina, he has worked with publishers across Europe and the United States, including for *Dark Horse Presents*. In between drawing and coloring comics, he teaches oil painting.

Hi-Fi Colour Design was founded in 1998 by Brian and Kristy Miller and provides digital color for comic books, toys, video games, and animation, and tutorials on color through masterdigitalcolor.com.